THROUGH a TRAIL of TEARS

Words of Praise for *Through a Trail of Tears: A Black Family's Story of Generational Wealth*

"*Through a Trail of Tears: A Black Family's Story of Generational Wealth* is a work in social history—bottoms-up history. Gloria Petgrave Scoggins's family story is also a history of America's evolving systems of racial oppression. The story begins with her family's enslavement by the Five 'Civilized' Tribes in Oklahoma and ends with her mother's tenacious fight against systemic racism in the Bay Area housing market to become a wealthy property owner and civic leader. Family histories can yield interesting stories about families. And when combined with research and compelling analysis can also yield important understandings of a people and of a nation. This is what Scoggins accomplishes in this captivating book."

—Robert C. Smith, Emeritus Professor of Political Science at San Francisco State University, author of *From the Bayou to the Bay: Autobiography of a Black Liberation Scholar*

"This profound story of a family's move from challenging circumstances toward university education and achievement is for all learners to appreciate! *Through a Trail of Tears: A Black Family's Story of Generational Wealth* is a 'must' for any middle or high school English and social studies curriculum. The reader learns of the importance of the Historically Black College and University in the family's rise as they go from being 'allowed' to own land to real estate prominence. There are topics for good classroom discussion that allow learners to connect their firsthand experiences to the family's journey through three generations."

—James M. Mitchell, Professor of Teacher Education at Cal State University, East Bay, and Director, Online Single Subject Credential Program

"*Through a Trail of Tears* offers the reader a chance to follow the heroine's journey through the lens of the unique relationship that only Black Americans have with this country. As a History and English teacher, I rarely come across a literary work that encapsulates the story of who this country is. This written history is all that an educator could hope for. *Through a Trail of Tears* is broken into forty-six 'Game Changer' chapters that tell the captivating story of one family while capturing the history of a nation. Through its pages it affirms that the American dream was not given but was acquired through the constant push and pull of hope, desire, decisions, consequences, and navigating the ever-changing landscape of a country whose very essence is one of oppression and opposition. This book encourages the reader to face the fabric of tragedy and success that was forcefully woven into the genealogy of every Black American."

—Jamela Smith-Folds, Mother and Educator,
West Contra Costa Unified School District School Board Trustee
Hercules, California

"Redlining policies, which began in this country more than eighty years ago, bolstered prosperity for some but increased disparities in homeownership, wealth, and health for others. Leaders like Ermestine Martin did everything they could to break through these restrictive policies and build communities where all people can thrive.

Mrs. Martin worked to achieve equity in housing for her community, and now her daughter and granddaughters are following in her footsteps to prevent gentrification and displacement in this same community. This is their story, and we, the readers, are invited to the 'kitchen table' to hear the tales."

—James A. Becker, President and CEO,
Richmond Community Foundation
Richmond, California

"*Through a Trail of Tears* is a heartwarming tribute to a life well lived. The affection and reverence of a daughter for her mother is profoundly captured in this living history, which reflects the saga that so many black immigrants experienced in the Richmond / Bay Area region over the past century. Scoggins powerfully and skillfully portrays the essence of a self-made, self-directed Black woman in a pre-civil rights America. This work gives us a glimpse into the legacy of strength and tenacity that so many of our mothers and ancestors instilled."

—Dr. Stefanie Phillips, Associated Professor
University of Southern California

THROUGH a TRAIL of TEARS

A BLACK FAMILY'S STORY OF GENERATIONAL WEALTH

EPM
LIVING PRESS

GLORIA PETGRAVE SCOGGINS

EPM Living Press
P O Box 5190; Hercules, California 94547
EPMLivingPress.net

Through a Trail of Tears: A Black Family's Story of Generational Wealth / Gloria Petgrave Scoggins
979-8-9856930-0-3 paperback
979-8-9856930-1-0 ebook
979-8-9856930-2-7 hardcover
Library of Congress Control Number: 2022901778

Front cover photograph: The Williams family house, Checotah, Oklahoma, circa 2021
Back cover photograph: The back of the Williams family house, Checotah, Oklahoma, circa 2021

Publisher's Cataloging-in-Publication data

Names: Scoggins, Gloria Petgrave, author.

Title: Through a trail of tears : a black family's story of generational wealth / Gloria Petgrave Scoggins.

Description: Includes bibliographical references and index. | Hercules, CA: EPM Living Press, 2022.

Identifiers: LCCN: 2022901778 | ISBN: 979-8-9856930-2-7 (hardcover) | 979-8-9856930-0-3 (paperback) | 979-8-9856930-1-0 (ebook)

Subjects: LCSH Martin, Ermestine. | African Americans--Oklahoma--History. | African Americans--Housing--Oklahoma. | Blacks--Oklahoma--Relations with Indians. | Oklahoma--Race relations. | African Americans--West (U.S.)--Social life and customs--19th century. | African Americans--West (U.S.)--Social life and customs--20th century. | African Americans--West (U.S.)--Social life and customs--21st century. | BISAC BIOGRAPHY & AUTOBIOGRAPHY / Cultural, Ethnic & Regional / African American & Black | HISTORY / African American & Black

Classification: LCC E185.93.O4 .S36 2022 | DDC 976.6/00496073--dc23

This book is affectionately dedicated to my mother, Ermestine Martin.

Although at the time of this writing, she is in the final stages of Alzheimer's and doesn't know who I am, her loving spirit, advice, and faith surround me.

They have everywhere manifested a great desire to become land-owners, a desire in the highest degree laudable and hopeful for their future civilization. Next to a proper religious and intellectual training, the one thing needful to the freedmen is land and a home.

—Report of Brevet Major General O. O. Howard,
Commissioner Bureau of Refugees,
Freedmen, and Abandoned Lands,
to the Secretary of War, October 20, 1869

ACKNOWLEDGMENTS

First and foremost, I am greatly indebted to my parents and my grandparents. Their unconditional love and wisdom are the catalyst behind this story.

I would like to acknowledge, with gratitude, the support and love of my family: my husband, Al; my daughters, Kim and Fallon; my son, Roman; and my cousins, Larry and Richard.

I am grateful to Lee Arthur and Laura Johnson and Scottie Smith for encouragement, academic support, and friendship.

I would like to acknowledge my love and deep appreciation for the Alpha Nu Omega, Omega Upsilon Omega, and Xi Gamma Omega Chapters of Alpha Kappa Alpha Sorority, Incorporated. We are following the paths of our Founders, service to all mankind.

I would also like to acknowledge:

Linda Jay, copyeditor, for showing confidence in my work and becoming the driving force to help create this book. Her introduction to the Bay Area Independent Publishers Association provided the resources and increased confidence that I could and would accomplish my goal.

Patricia Heinicke, book developer, for her unwavering support and guidance toward the book's fullest potential.

Melissa Stein, copyeditor, for expanding my mind about how to share the story clearly and vividly with a smooth flow.

Paula Dragosh, proofreader

Ruth Schwartz, project management and cover concept

Lorna Johnson, text pages design and layout

Black Cat Studio, digital scans for reproduction

CONTENTS

PREFACE

Throughout the United States and, indeed, the world, we are inundated with print, online, and televised media about the plight of Black families and communities and their quest for universal freedom. The fight for Black freedom and dignity has its roots in the race riots of Tulsa, Oklahoma; the Timothy James McVeigh bombing; and the many other atrocities that have been, and continue to be, leveled against Blacks, Native Americans, and other citizens of color in the United States.

There is a biblical phrase: "There but for the grace of God go I." This phrase was emblazoned on my mind by my parents and grandparents. I was fortunate to be surrounded by a loving family who taught me the important things in life. I am now aware of the advantages our family received because my grandmother, as a citizen of Creek Nation, received her entitlement of forty acres of land on May 23, 1905.

The entitlement of land in Checotah, Oklahoma, that the Commission to the Five Civilized Tribes granted to my grandmother, Tressie Williams, allowed her daughter Ermestine to create her own little oasis on the family farm. Working beside her parents, brother, and sister, surrounded by acres of their own land, she lived a comfortable farmer's lifestyle and acquired a strong work ethic.

While the Williamses were respected, thriving farmers who lived in harmony with their White neighbors, they were fully aware of the intense racism that had long penetrated all aspects of life in the South for people of color, especially Black people. After World War II, Ermestine's parents joined the Black migration from the South, moving to Richmond, California, in search of a better life. But they soon learned that they would face racism no matter where they lived. Housing discrimination practices presented their biggest challenge to re-creating the life they left behind in Oklahoma.

My grandfather, Roy Williams, was sixty-one when I was born in 1949, and I was lucky enough to become his fishing buddy. He knew the best fishing spots in Richmond, and he was a great storyteller. Storytelling was his way of teaching lessons. He would fish for hours, smoking his Lucky Strikes and reminiscing about his childhood growing up in Indian Territory and his experiences farming in Oklahoma. I remember his colorful visual snapshots of his experiences as a farmer in Oklahoma. As a little girl, I would follow him and listen to his stories, spellbound, while he was tending his vegetable and rose gardens or caring for the many rabbits he raised in his backyard.

Puffing away on his cigarette, he would say to me, "It's one thing to own land, but it's quite another to know how to work the land."

Grandfather knew not only how to work his land but also how to hold on to his land, and he instilled that knowledge in his children, hoping it would be passed on to future generations.

My mother, Ermestine Martin, also told stories of past experiences to share wisdom, build a bridge of knowledge, and expand her listeners' understanding of the world. Hearing her stories helped me understand her parents' struggles to ensure that the economic success of Creek Freedmen was transmitted to future generations. When she arrived in Richmond, she was young, vibrant, and determined to write her own script while facing the destructive behaviors of a racist society. Her idealism was shattered by the inequity surrounding her, which lit a fire of distrust and anger. She refused to be intimidated or looked down on, and did not go along with unfair treatment to get along with anyone. Soon she was a real estate broker, fighting redlining, structural racism, and other unfair practices against Blacks who were attempting to find a decent place to live.

Before her diagnosis of Alzheimer's disease in 2015, my mother had built a sizable fortune for her family while constantly supporting her community through educational advocacy and preaching about the need to acquire and hold on to property as a means of self-determination for both present and future generations. Alzheimer's is the final game changer for her, as she lost the ability to reason and can no longer navigate day-to-day living without help.

She is still a talker, though! I often listen to conversations she has with herself; Mother still believes she is going to work every day, talking to folks about real estate. Those battles she encountered years ago are still fresh in her mind. And the anger in her stories is unfiltered. The prevalence of discrimination in mortgage lending and the race-based system of justice still loom large in those stories. It is my wish that these pages will reveal to you her vibrant, unquenchable spirit of love for her community as well as the anger and pain that accompany it.

• • •

A few words about the book itself: "Game Changers" are those life experiences that effect changes in our way of thinking, way of doing, way of acting, way of responding, way of deciding, way of inspiring. I have crafted my mother's story into a series of Game Changers that transformed how she thought about the world—those that seemed to have the greatest impact on her, and on me as well.

The facts presented in this book are as close as I can come to the truth. Any mistakes in this regard are mine alone. I've changed a few names for privacy and have attempted to contact other people mentioned to get their permission to include them.

Many of the stories in this book were told and retold by my maternal grandparents, my mother and her siblings, and other relatives at family gatherings, sometimes with laughter and sometimes with sadness. Some were difficult to bring up. Some were told as cautionary tales, some as celebrations. But there was always a focus on the land and the importance of owning property—and holding on to it.

After he was released from Veterans Hospital, my father—Isaac Petgrave—and I spent a lot of time in the kitchen—he in his wheelchair, cooking and cleaning and just talking. So his voice is present here, too. And my cousins—Larry, Yvonne, and Clarice—were like siblings to me, and as an only child, I loved to be around them. We often would talk about events in our lives, especially things that got us into trouble. Their voices are here, too. Together we will tell you stories that may be painfully like your own as well as stories that may be new to you. The words spoken by these voices are not exact, but the feelings and messages expressed in their words are crystal clear. Thank you for listening.

Gloria Scoggins

Creek Freedmen testifying before the Commission of the Five Civilized Tribes

*The Williams family house,
Checotah, Oklahoma, circa 2021*

PART ONE: OKLAHOMA

Members of the Creek Nation, circa 1877

2--Tressie Malvern.

Mary Malvin, witness.

By the Commission.

Q When was she born? A She will be six years old the 13th, I think, of this coming July--that will be '98.
Q Can you read and write? A Yes, sir.
Q Do you know the nature of an oath? A No, sir; I don't know it xxxx in----
Q In what? A In full.
Q Do you know that a person who takes an oath before a person authorized to administer oaths, and then testifies falsely is liable to imprisonment in the United States penitentiary? (Mxxxxxxxxxx)xxxxxxxxx
A Why that is one reason I didn't want to bother with it after there was such-------
Q Can you swear positively that Tressie Malvern was three years old last past March? A Yes, sir.
Q Are you sure she wasn't born in March, 1902? A I didn't have no children in 1902. Let me see---------
Q Do you keep the dates of the birth of your children in a book or on a paper or anything of that kind? A No, sir; I never had but one and it got burnt up, and I never put it down any more, and that was this one (Indicating Luanna), and my house got burnt up and I lost the date of it.
Q What is the name of Tressie's father? A John Malvern.

John Malvern, being duly sworn, testified as follows.

By the Commission:
Q What is your name? A John Malvern.
Q What is your age? A I think I am about twenty-eight this coming July.
Q What is your post office address? A Checotah.
Q Have you filed on your allotment? A Yes, sir.
Q Are you a citizen of the Creek Nation? A Yes, sir.
Q Are you the husband of Mary Malvern? A Yes, sir.
Q Did she have a child by the name of Tressie? A Yes, sir.
Q Is that your child? A Yes, sir.
Q Can you read and write? A Well mighty little. I can write my name though, and can read writing.
Q Who does the writing for your family? A Why my wife does the most of it.
Q Do you know when Tressie was born? A Why I think I know.
Q What is your best recollection? A Why I think it was along about March 25th, 1901, that is the best I can remember.
Q How many crops have you raised since Tressie was born? A I think it is two, if I haint mistaken.
Q Is that counting this year? A No, sir; I think it is two besides this one.
Q Can Tressie talk? A Yes, sir; she can talk a little.
Q How long has she been talking? A Oh she has been jabbering now for about a year, I reckon, trying to talk.
Q How many teeth has she? A She has got them all.
Q How many words can she say? A Why I don't know, she can call me and mamma to give her some water and bring her candy, ask me when I am going to town.

Mary Malvin, recalled, testified as follows:

By the Commission.
Q Were there any other children in this neighborhood born about the time Tressie was born? A Yes, sir.
Q Whose child? A I know Sarah has one.
Q Sarah who? A Sarah Martin.
Q Any others? A I am just thinking now---I know there were children

Testimony of Mary Malvern before the Commission of the Five Civilized Tribes, June 23, 1904

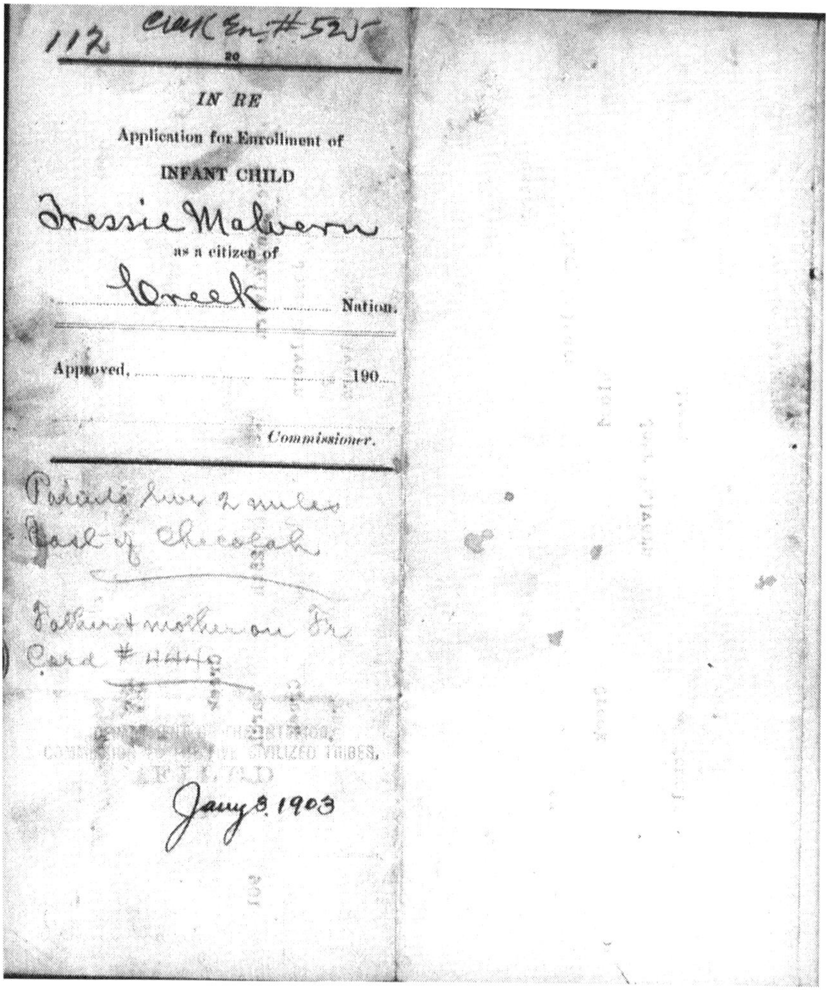
112 Creek En. #521
20
IN RE
Application for Enrollment of
INFANT CHILD
Tressie Malvern
as a citizen of
Creek Nation.
Approved, ... 190..
.... Commissioner.
Parents live 2 miles East of Checotah
Father + mother on Cr Card # 4440
DEPARTMENT OF THE INTERIOR,
COMMISSION TO THE FIVE CIVILIZED TRIBES,
FILED
Jany 3. 1903

Application for Enrollment of Tressie Malvern, Creek Nation, January 3, 1903

GAME CHANGER 1

FORTY ACRES AND A MULE

In 1836, when the Muscogee Creek were forced from their ancestral land in Alabama and sent to Indian Territory, some of them brought along the people they had enslaved. Other enslaved families were forced onto cramped boats and shipped down the Alabama River to Indian Territory. Somewhere in the chaos were my ancestors, who were held as slaves by tribal members. In this way Black slave history and Native American history were knitted together, sadly united and severely connected. The Five Civilized Tribes would remain committed to slavery, and in their new homes they immediately rebuilt racialized Black codes, exploited slave labor, fought slave rebellions, and sided with the Confederacy in the Civil War.

All Indigenous American cultures had systems of privilege and stature, and among the Five Civilized Tribes, slave ownership was a status symbol. Forced copulation and intermarriage between Native Americans and African slaves were common among these tribes. In the Civilized Tribes, in an economy driven by cotton, wealthy slave owners believed they were superior to Blacks and oppressed the Blacks they owned.

The particular history of my ancestors' struggles and the hardships they encountered during this time, whether enduring the Trail of Tears or surviving on overcrowded boats to Indian Territory, is uncertain. Whatever they faced is lost and buried in Paradise Cemetery, within a stone's throw of the property still owned by our family, which my mother always referred to as the "Forty Acres and a Mule property," even though it was actually 160 acres by the time it got to my grandmother. I can only imagine their suffering and the fear embedded in their souls as they were forcibly deported to unknown territory. I fervently hope that their slave owners provided them shoes, proper clothing, food, and a doctor's care for health issues as minimal compensation for their labor.

This kind of erasure is not unusual among descendants of people enslaved by Native Americans. Although Black presence on the Trail of Tears is a historical fact, the tears our ancestors shed out of sight of the slave masters are not part of the history that most people know about the Five Civilized Tribes. It's also not common knowledge that after the war, the United States negotiated a new treaty with the Creek Nation requiring the tribes to emancipate their slaves and to grant them Creek citizenship, making them eligible for voting rights and a share of annuities and land settlements. Upon emancipation some Creek Freedmen decided to stay in the Creek Nation in Indian Territory.

Near the turn of the century, Congress passed the Dawes Allotment Act, which broke up tribal landholdings to allot communal land to individuals, allowing them to acquire property. This included the descendants of Creek Freedmen. To receive their land allotments and rights as tribal members, people were required to present evidence of their ancestry to the four-man Commission of the Five Civilized Tribes, more commonly called the Dawes Commission. Led by Senator Henry Dawes of

Massachusetts, the commission registered tribal members into categories, distinguishing between "Creek by Blood"; "Creek Freedmen"—anyone with visible physical traits suggesting African ancestry, regardless of their proportion of Creek ancestry; and "Intermarried Whites."[1] The commission sometimes classified members of the same family into different groups.

In other words, my ancestors had to prove who they were in order to receive the land and the rights they deserved for their labor and the hardship their families endured as slaves.

• • •

My grandmother, Tressie Malvern, was born in 1901 in Checotah, Indian Territory. In 1904, her mortally ill mother, twenty-nine-year-old Mary Malvern, appeared under oath before the Commission to the Five Civilized Tribes. Mary and her husband, John Malvern, had already filed with the commission to add their older daughter, Luanna, to the Dawes Rolls. Now it was Tressie's turn.

Feeding my historical imagination with the transcripts of my ancestors' testimony before the Dawes Commission, along with family stories I have heard and generations of pictures seen, I envision my great-grandmother's experience before the commission in 1904. I imagine that Mary's traits mirror those I know in my grandmother Tressie—both are mild, gentle souls, God-fearing women who always have a Bible within reach. I imagine that Mary seldom smiles, for her front teeth have a gap, and perhaps she has other reasons as well. I watch as Mary prepares carefully for the journey she will take from her home in the town of Canadian, Oklahoma, to the commissioners' office in Muskogee, Indian Territory, with her husband and two young daughters by her side.

It is June 23, 1904. Mary is ill, has been ill for a long time, and her body rages in pain as she listens to her young daughters, Tressie and Luanna, babbling and playing with each other. She tries to quiet her mind. I am pretty sure Mary had to testify before the commissioners for her older daughter Luanna. Ever since she heard about the commission and its purpose, she has been filled with anxiety about testifying before these four White men from Washington. She has hardly ever even seen a White man, much less spoken with one, not to mention four, and stories from neighbors and family who have already been questioned by the commission do little to calm her mind.

Mary wears her Sunday-best clothes, a long trumpet skirt brushing the floor, a full-sleeved, ruffled, stiff-collared blouse a few sizes larger than her sickly frame. For the occasion, she adds a broad-brimmed hat, trimmed with masses of feathers protecting her frail face from the sun. Pointed-toe shoes irritate the bunions passed on through the generations. Now, fully dressed, Mary comes into better view: a short, big-boned, twenty-nine-year-old lady, fragile and weak and mustering up sheer determination to ensure her daughter's pursuit of happiness and freedom. Her husband, John, provides physical and emotional support throughout the ordeal. Together the family journeys to Muskogee in a mule-drawn wagon, with food packed for the thirty-mile trip. They travel at slow speed, stopping periodically to let the mule rest and eat.

The next scene I see is in the small building in Muskogee where the commission meets. The entire family, tired from the long journey and still dressed in their best clothes, must sit for hours on hard chairs in the back of the room, an uncomfortable and intimidating atmosphere. They watch other families they know testifying in front of these men, dealing with offensive and despairing expressions and words that challenged their truth, yet determined to acquire property wealth for their children. Mary and John take inspiration from their fellow Freedmen, intent on demanding compensation for the inhumane conditions their great-grandparents labored under.

Now Mary, with Tressie on her lap, testifies under oath: She is a citizen of the Creek Nation who can read and write, living in the town of Canadian. Repeatedly asked by the commission when her daughter was born, her response is always the same, March 25, 1901.

The commission asks, "Why is it you have waited so long to appear and give testimony in this case? Why didn't you come in to the Commission and bring your witnesses and present your evidence?"

Mary responds, "Well, last year I was sick all the time until late along in the spring. I haven't been well, I said in [*sic*] about, I guess, about three months."

After yet more questions about Tressie's age and birthdate, the commission asks, "Do you know that a person who takes an oath before a person authorized to administer oaths, and then testifies falsely, is liable to impressment in the United States penitentiary?"

At this point my great-grandmother is probably as angry as a wet hen; the feathers on her hat are probably standing straight up. But she keeps her composure and replies, "Why, that is one reason I didn't want to bother with it after there was such . . ."

The commission interrupts her, "Can you swear positively that Tressie Malvern was three years old last past March?"

"Yes, sir."

"Are you sure she wasn't born in March 1902?"

Now I am sure she is getting more and more agitated as she responds, "I didn't have no children in 1902." After a few more questions, she is dismissed.

I visualize her slowly rise and walk cautiously to the back of the room, conscious of the people watching, keeping her eyes on John's face. Her husband has risen from his seat, and he helps her sit down before going to the commissioner's table to testify.

• • •

I remember my grandmother saying her father always wore a scarf. So, in my mind I envision a man short in stature, composed and straightforward, wearing clothes neat but somewhat tattered and worn, shoes scuffed with age. And his signature scarf tied around his neck.

This man, twenty-eight-year-old John Malvern, is sworn in to testify. A citizen of the Creek Freedmen "by blood," he testifies that he can read and write "mighty little," explaining, "I can write my name and can read writing." He states that his wife does most of the writing for the family.

When the commission asks, "Do you know when Tressie was born?" he replies, "Why, I think I know."

"What is your best recollection?"

"Why I think it was along about March 25, 1901, that is the best I can remember."

The commission continues asking questions about Tressie, such as how many teeth has she? Can she talk? How many words can she say?

Her father responds, "Yes, sir; she can talk a little. Oh, she has been jabbering now for about a year, I reckon, trying to talk. She has got all her teeth. I don't know how many words she can say. She can call me and mamma to give her some water and bring her candy, ask me when I am going to town."

Then Mary is called to testify again: Were there any other children in this neighborhood born about the same time as Tressie? Which child was born first? What were their names? Again, one of the commissioners asks, "How do you know Tressie was born on the twenty-fifth of March, 1901? What is it you go by?"

She gives a mother's answer: "Why because I didn't have any [children] in 1902, because Tressie nursed all up—because I was nursing her in 1902."

Again, the commissioner asks, "How do you know Tressie was born in March and not in some other month of 1901?"

"Why I know it was in the month of March, but just what note to give you, I couldn't produce any."

"When you didn't set it down in a book, I want to know how you remember it?"

At this point I envision my grandmother's frustration growing and her tone of voice changing. "Well, I am telling you now, I am giving it to you just as near as I can possibly remember."

At this point, the commission ends her testimony and swears in fifty-two-year-old Tena Manuel, a citizen of the Creek Nation, who testifies that she was the midwife when Tressie was born. She can't remember when Tressie was born and replies, "I was the midwife. I never keeps account of that."

"Do you keep a record of your services in a book?"

"No, sir; because I can't read nor write, and I never keeps no account of it, because I can't." When asked how old Tressie is, she replies, "Why Mister, I couldn't tell you, because I couldn't tell exactly how old Tressie is . . . I never bothers to keep the time of the month, and I never knows nothing about that."

• • •

Less than three months later, on November 20, 1904, Mary Malvern passed while staying at her mother's house in Boynton, leaving her two young daughters in the care of their father and paternal grandmother in Checotah.

Grandmother Tressie never talked about her mother's death. Perhaps she was too young to remember that trip to Muskogee when her parents testified before the commission. Perhaps she was too young to remember her twenty-nine-year-old mother's passing three months later. I suspect cancer caused the death of my great-grandmother and great-aunt as well as many of my other ancestors, as three generations later, cancer continues to run rampant through the bodies of family members.

On December 9, 1904, John Malvern received a letter requesting him to return for further testimony, also requiring two more witnesses who knew Tressie's date of birth to appear before the commission at its office in Muskogee.

Traveling to that time in my historical imagination, I am sure John is still in the throes of deep emotion at the recent death of his wife. But his strength prevails, and he wills himself not to show vulnerability in front of the commission. Nor will he exhibit weakness under attack from the commission's challenge of what he knows to be true. Instead, he envisions what could be for Tressie, his daughter. Standing on the strength of his beliefs, unintimidated by the commission's demands, facing harsh and brutal winter weather, once again he makes the trip to Muskogee, this time with his brother and neighbor, who are to be interrogated about the birth of his daughter.

During a Supplemental Testimony on January 4, 1905, with attorneys for the Creek Nation and the applicants present, Carrie Magill, twenty-three years old, testifies that she lives two miles from John and Mary Malvern and is not related to them. She testifies that she saw Tressie about the next day after she was born. When asked when Tressie was born, Carrie responds, "March 25, 1901."

"How old is Tressie Malvern now?"

"I just don't know how old she is."

"Well, you say she was born on the twenty-fifth of March; this coming March, how old will she be?"

Carrie begins counting and responds, "She will be five years old."

"How long was the mother of Tressie sick after the birth of child?"

"Well, I don't know, it seems to me that she was sick, well just all the time sick until her death."

Next, thirty-eight-year-old Robert Malvern, Tressie's uncle, comes forward to testify before the commission. He states that Tressie was with her mother at the time of her death and that her sister, Luanna, had also died.[2] Robert testifies that he lives a quarter of a mile from his brother, John, and their mother, and he was present at Tressie's birth. He explains that he had encouraged his brother to follow through with the application for Tressie after Mary died in November.

I see these family members, neighbors, and a midwife testifying before the commission to validate the birth of Tressie with unwavering support. The image of the Malvern brothers testifying before the commission is that of physically strong men in their thirties, hardworking farmers producing crops, carrying out their duties as providers, as husbands and fathers. The historical weight and emotional burdens of enslavement and war, economic instability, and racism did not prevent Mary and these men from speaking to the commissioners.

Among their memories danced the stories, shared by parents and grandparents, aunts and uncles, tracking their struggles as slaves to the powerful Creeks, and seeing the Creeks resist and then succumb to the Trail of Tears, banished to Indian Territory. Stories of the Creek Freedmen's emancipation—after which they remained poor and underprivileged, still treated as inferior and uneducable. The Creek Freedmen arrived to testify under oath for their entitlement to land, seeking justice from the tribe, holding America accountable to the great words of the founding fathers: "We hold these truths to be self-evident, that all men are created equal." Demanding to be seen.

Perhaps family stories of the powerlessness their father and grandfather felt through life lit the fire and created the energy for the Malverns to stand in front of the commission instead of giving in to intimidation and fear. My great-grandfather didn't succumb when his wife and older daughter passed. He prevailed in his goal to ensure prosperity through property wealth for his young daughter.

* * *

On March 15, 1905, the Department of the Interior, Commission of the Five Civilized Tribes, sent notification of its decision on the application for the enrollment of Tressie Malvern as a Creek Freedman: "It is, therefore, the opinion of the Commission that said Tressie Malvern should be enrolled as a Creek Freedman, in accordance with the provisions of the act of Congress, June 30, 1902 (32 State., 500), and it is so ordered."

On June 5, 1905, Rutherford & Cravens, Attorneys, sent notification: "You are hereby advised that the name of Tressie Malvern is contained in the partial list of Creek Freedmen, approved by the Secretary of the Interior May 23, 1905, and that application for a selection of land in the Creek Nation may now be made at the office of the Commission in Muskogee, Indian Territory."

Oh, happy day! Four-year-old, dark-skinned Tressie was a landowner with the opportunity for prosperity, self-determination, and economic growth.

My daughter Fallon and her grandmother Ermestine, visiting the Checotah property in 2000

Baldie Williams taking a peek at the Checotah outhouse, circa 1970s. At the time of this picture she was married, last name Strickland.

GAME CHANGER 2

KEEPING THE LAND

In 2019, my cousin Larry and I flew to Checotah with our spouses to visit Grandmother's acres of land, conduct some research at the county offices, meet with real estate agents, and reflect on our parents' youth. We went on historic field trips to points of interest our parents talked about so often, which included the Paradise Cemetery.

Walking through the cemetery was a ritual of remembrance. The headstone of my grandmother's sister, Luanna, stood tall among many that had crumbled throughout the years. Their epitaphs, etchings, and engravings made every memorial unique and special. All showed signs of deterioration in a cemetery where the grass was well kept, reminding me that their memory and life should be forever cherished. We were following the shadows of our ancestors' lives and searching for the light for their descendants.

Grandmother Tressie's house still stood intact—you'll see it on the front of this book. Her place was now surrounded by old homes from early in the twentieth century, but across the road sat modern, ranch-style homes with three-car garages and lots that stretched behind them for acres. I saw tractors and other farm equipment; clearly they were raising chickens and cows, much like my great-grandparents did. Seeing these modern homes on this beloved landscape that had once been owned by Creek Freedmen brought to mind the stories about my family's determination to hold on to their property.

• • •

After her mother's death, Tressie lived in Rentiesville, an all-Black town, with her father and paternal grandmother. She joined a Baptist church and attended local schools. Within a few years, her father remarried.

Tressie wasn't a pretty child, but she had a beautiful smile and a heart of gold. A loner, she isolated herself in her studies, and her desire for higher education led her to the Kansas Industrial Educational Institute in Topeka. Then Tressie taught school for several years. She was very involved in church and extremely confident in herself. And at this point, Tressie met her man.

My grandfather, Roy Williams, was born in 1888 in Checotah. He received his schooling and religious training at the Paradise, Oklahoma, community schools and church. He and his first wife had three children before he entered military service in 1917. Roy served in the Army as a cook during World War I, and he received an honorable discharge. He returned to Checotah to find that his wife had given birth to a new baby by another man—a man who was now living in Roy's house! He then moved in with his mother, Rose, but remained a constant in his children's lives.

On August 9, 1923, at age thirty-five, Roy married twenty-two-year-old Tressie Malvern and began living on her property. They had three children: one son, Leodry (lovingly always called "Son"), and two daughters, Ermestine and Leothia ("Baldie"). Everything they ate was either grown, produced, or raised on their farm. They earned money by selling their homegrown produce and other products made from working the land, such as cream, butter, molasses cookies, sweet potato pies, and root beer served in mason jars. On the property was a pond that the family called the "big hole." Friends and family loved to fish there.

The family raised cotton, corn, wheat, oats, garden vegetables, fruit, farm animals, and cattle. They owned their own tractors and farm equipment, which most farmers didn't have. Occasionally, Ermestine's parents would hire help for setting up the land or planting crops. But the family did most of the work, and the children worked beside their parents doing farm chores.

Roy and Tressie were compelled to work hard and taught their children to do the same. They shared their own talents with the children as well. For instance, Roy taught them the art of storytelling. Tressie taught them to worship God and give Him all the praise; she carried her Bible with her like we carry our cell phones. She frequently said to her children, "God and God alone will get us through this."

Growing up, the children played outside with White children who lived on nearby farms, but they never visited one another's homes. Reflecting on her childhood, my mother would always say, "We got along with White folks, and they got along with us."

Yet not all was well on that front. Few Blacks were able to hold on to their given allotments of property or pay mortgages on land they had purchased. Land owned by Blacks was often swindled away by Whites. My grandparents told how family members and friends had their land taken by manipulating and conniving cheats. In time, more and more Blacks were unable to pay their bills and abandoned their farms, then headed to California.

My grandparents and my mother always talked about a relative who was conned out of his property. He sold most of his land to a White man for a brown-and-white horse and a beautiful saddle. The horse died shortly after he signed the contract, so then he had no use for the saddle. My mother would go on and on about how foolish this man was. She was proud of her mother for staying strong and holding on to her land, despite many attempts by White men to steal her birthright. This is the land Mother loved and referred to as "our Forty Acres and a Mule"—acres of land she never considered selling, or living on again.

• • •

My mother and her siblings attended Paradise School, an all-Black school. Because the family owned land, Roy had the money to buy a secondhand school bus from some White folks. At the age of seventeen, Son would leave early in the morning to drive the school bus, picking up Black children along the way, and he would drop them off at home after school, too. Occasionally, Roy and Son would drive the bus to Eufaula, the county seat of McIntosh County, to pick up school supplies and food to take to Paradise School.

Son was valedictorian of his class, a very smart, straight-A student. My mother always felt that he never had to put much effort into studying to make good grades. Each day when he returned home from school, he would complete his farm chores and then do his homework.

Ermestine would do her morning chores before driving the family car to school with Baldie by her side. She was proud that she was the only student driving a family car to school and that her brother was responsible enough to transport children in a school bus. At the age of twelve, Ermestine was already driving equipment like trucks and tractors around the farm.

As the youngest child, Baldie was not required to do as many chores as her siblings. Throughout the years, my mother would share stories of Baldie hiding underneath the porch or in other out-of-sight places to avoid her responsibilities. My grandmother had purchased a piano and encouraged her daughters to learn how to play, so Baldie played the piano while everyone else was working. Ermestine resented that Baldie kept getting special treatment.

However, my mother still brags about how she stood up for her baby sister when other children were being mean to her. Ermestine didn't hesitate to fight anyone for mistreating Baldie. In turn, Baldie would also retaliate with force and fire if she believed her older sister was being treated wrongly. They did have sibling rivalry conflicts through the years, but they loved each other. No doubt about it, if you messed with one, you were messing with the other.

Baldie and Son were very social, "people-persons" like their dad, and they enjoyed being around friends. Ermestine, like her mother, was more of an introvert, content to be alone and always busy doing something. Each was unique, but they shared a family bond and love that superseded all differences and conflicts.

• • •

Roy owned property in Boley, one of the wealthiest, and definitely the largest and best known, of all Black towns in the Creek Nation, Indian Territory. It was Grandfather's favorite place to visit. Boley was established as an independent township in 1903, and its residents were Blacks and Creek Freedmen, many of whom Grandfather knew well. Grandfather believed the Creek Freedmen's allotments of land provided the foundation for this first town comprising people with Black and Native American ancestry. He spoke with pride about Boley; he was proud of his family's and his friends' contributions to the town's success.

Booker T. Washington, founder of the National Negro Business League, called Boley "the youngest, the most enterprising, and in many ways the most interesting of the negro towns in the United States . . . [T]he majority of these negro settlers have come here with the definite intention of getting a home and building up a community where they can, as they say, be 'free' . . . Boley, like the other negro towns that have sprung up in other parts of the country, represents a dawning race consciousness, a wholesome desire to do something to make the race respected; something which shall demonstrate the right of the negro, not merely as an individual, but as a race, to have a worthy and permanent place in the civilization that the American people are creating."[3]

My grandparents purchased land in Boley before migrating to California. Grandfather's frequent trips back to Oklahoma to see his children from his first marriage always included visiting Boley. During the late 1960s, most of his family and friends were living in other urban areas, but Boley still remained home to them and to many other descendants of the town's original settlers. As for my grandfather, Boley was always a special place to him. It was his San Francisco, his New York, his space to reconnect with his past.[4] The vacant land he purchased still remains in the family estate. His one-time dream of building a family home in Boley was slowly forgotten. He was determined to become a homeowner in the Golden State.

• • •

My grandparents were comfortable on their farm, got along well with their White neighbors, and had established themselves in their community. They made a decent living without being bothered or harassed. But they had heard the horror stories about violence against Blacks and Black communities. The Tulsa Race Massacre in 1921 permanently changed their view of the world and created fear of what lay outside their farm, fear of the power that White people held.

Then, in the early 1930s, severe drought gripped the Great Plains. The impact of the Dust Bowl was felt all over the United States. After the dust storm called "Black Sunday" in April 1935, more and more dust storms forced Checotah farmers to migrate north or west. Many years of crop failure followed. Times were hard, and the Williams family struggled to earn enough money to survive.

Some family members and friends had already abandoned their farms to avoid poverty and look for a better life; Whites then quickly homesteaded the forsaken property. Tressie's cousin, Gladys Jordan, a teacher, had migrated to Richmond, California, in 1943. Stories of Gladys's upward mobility in California became the inspiration for my grandparents' eventual decision to migrate to Richmond.

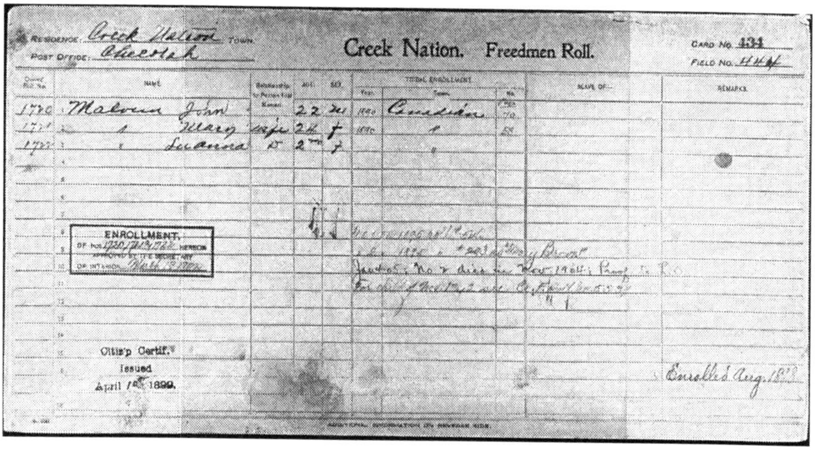

Residence: Creek Nation Town

Post Office: Checotah

Creek Nation. Freedmen Roll.

Card No. 434

Field No. 444

Roll No.	Name	Relationship	Age	Sex	Tribal Enrollment Year	Town	No.	Slave of—	Remarks
1720	Malvern John		22	m	1890	Canadian			
1721	" Mary	wife	24	f	1890	"			
1722	" Susanna	D	2mo	f		"			

ENROLLMENT.
of Nos. 1720, 1721, 1722 hereon
approved by the Secretary
of Interior Mar 1 1902

Citiz'p Certif.
Issued
April 1st 1899.

Enrolled Aug. 18

Tressie, the last Malvern to receive a land allotment as a Creek Freedmen

Ermestine Williams's last year at Langston University

Baldie Williams before leaving Checotah

GAME CHANGER 3

LANGSTON UNIVERSITY

Family migration stories passed down from that time paint a vivid picture, with each storyteller adding an individual perspective, some with laughter and some at least hinting at the uncertainty and fears that came with leaving one's beloved home. Mother always shared with pride one story in particular: her departure from Langston University. She boasted of her bravery in sneaking out of the dorm and expressed her regret at not graduating from college. This is my interpretation of her story.

In 1945, Son was serving in the Army and Baldie was a high school student. My mother had just graduated from high school. She enrolled at Langston University in Langston, Oklahoma, and was living in the dorms when my grandparents—Tressie and Roy—decided to migrate to Richmond, California, because the challenge of working the farm had become too daunting. They had heard that better opportunities were available for Blacks out West.

What living in Richmond would be like was uncertain; they might have to return to Oklahoma. So they didn't sell. Instead, my grandparents worked out an agreement to pay a cousin to look after their farm and tend the land. Then they sold some of their farm equipment, packed their personal belongings into their 1940 Chevy, and began the long journey west. Their first stop was Langston University, to let Ermestine know they were moving to California.

Ermestine was so surprised the day her family arrived at her dorm to say good-bye. Her father shared the challenges they were having on the farm, and he displayed confidence that this was best for the family. Her mother seemed hesitant and fearful, and Baldie was upset about leaving her friends. Ermestine could tell that her parents had been thinking about making the move for a while.

Ermestine had heard a lot of good things about California from her classmates at Langston, and she wanted to go along. "Come on, help me pack; I am going with you," she said to Baldie.

But her father said firmly, "Ermestine, you need to study and graduate from Langston. Get knowledge into your brain, because that's the only thing the White man can't take from you!"

She was disheartened at his words, his firm tone. Her mother remained silent, avoiding eye contact.

Ermestine knew that was the end of the conversation. Baldie then captured everyone's attention by asking, "Why do we have to go? I don't want to leave my friends!" With tears streaming down her cheeks, she screamed, "Why can Ermestine stay, yet I have to go? I don't want to go to California!"

Ermestine was curious about Richmond. Her parents didn't seem to know much about it other than that cousin Gladys was there and doing fine. Her father shared that he had been in communication with a couple of his friends who had migrated there the previous year, and that he was going to connect with them upon arrival. Just before the sun started to go down, the family left to stay the night at a place called Miss Mary's rooming house. They had plans to get some rest and have their car tuned up for the journey to California. Ermestine walked her family to the car, kissed them good-bye and, with tears in her eyes, watched them drive off. She returned to her dorm, feeling sad and upset that they were going to California without her.

Later that night, Ermestine packed her belongings and snuck out of the dorm. She didn't know who Miss Mary was, or where her rooming house was. But in the darkness, carrying her suitcase, she made her way to the bus terminal, frightened but determined to find her family. She started asking random folks, did they know a Miss Mary? "I do, Miss," said one of the men working there, and after some discussion he agreed to take her to Miss Mary's house after he got off work.

It was late at night by the time the man clocked out and took Ermestine to his car. She was scared and felt uncomfortable in a strange man's car, headed to what might be the wrong Miss Mary and who knows what else, and even if she did find Miss Mary's rooming house, she worried how her father would greet her.

Finally, they arrived at a little house. Ermestine was relieved to see her parents' car parked in the driveway and hopped out of the man's car, grabbing her belongings. She knocked on the door.

It seemed a very long time before a light finally came on in the house. A short woman dressed in her bedclothes, with a scarf around her head and with no front teeth, opened the door and said, "May I help you?"

Ermestine dreaded how her parents might react to seeing her there. Baldie was the first family member to appear. She ran into the room and asked, "What are you doing here?" Their parents then rushed into the living room. Before they could say anything, my mother cried out that she wanted to go to California, too. She could help drive, get a job, and go to college there. Most of all, she wanted to be with her family. My grandparents listened closely as she expressed why it was so important for her to go with them.

Her father picked up her suitcase and said, "Well, come on, Sister. It's been a long day, and tomorrow we have a long journey ahead of us. So, let's get some sleep."

Everyone followed him into the bedroom. That was the first time Ermestine could recall sleeping with her parents and sister in the same room. But it would not be the last time.

As Ermestine snuggled next to Baldie on a cot in this unfamiliar house, Baldie yelled out, "Get your feet off me!"

Their mother simply said, "Thank God we are all together, and now let's go to sleep."

But Ermestine couldn't go to sleep, and she just lay there, thinking how she had found her way to Miss Mary's rooming house mysteriously, by sheer luck and chance.

Ermestine had left some of her belongings in the dorm, and she wondered if she would be able to get them. She was in the midst of planning to become a member of Alpha Kappa Alpha, Incorporated—an organization she desired to belong to—and the reality of leaving Langston University was truly bittersweet. What was her dorm mother going to do when she found out that Ermestine had slipped out of the dorm, unbeknownst to anyone? Now, she was on her way to California, a state she had heard and read so much about! The excitement had her fired up. Lying on the cot next to her sister, Ermestine was thinking sometimes happy, sometimes worried thoughts about what tomorrow would bring.

When Ermestine woke up, her parents were already out of the bedroom.

In the kitchen, their mother and Miss Mary were talking and eating breakfast.

"Your father has already left to get the car checked out, so sit down and have some breakfast."

While Ermestine was eating Spam, rice, toast with apple butter, and applesauce, Miss Mary asked my mother how she liked attending Langston. Baldie came into the kitchen, listened for a moment while putting shredded wheat and milk in her bowl, and said, "Yeah, and Dad told you that's where you needed to stay. I don't know why you want to go to California anyway." Baldie started dominating the conversation, reciting all the reasons she didn't want to leave Checotah.

Miss Mary responded with words of encouragement: "Baldie, you are going to be just fine!"

After breakfast, Miss Mary and Tressie read the Bible and prayed. Baldie kept pouting and objecting to the move, and Ermestine was content to sit quietly, just happy to be going to California. Miss Mary's house seemed to be a gathering place for neighbors; Roy was outside talking to a few curious men who had stopped by. She heard him tell a group of younger men that some of his friends had migrated to Richmond and found work at the shipyards. One of the men responded with, "You are pretty old to start over."

Noticing that Ermestine was staring out of the window, Roy smiled, showing the noticeable large gap between his front teeth, and responded, "You know, everyone who is successful must have dreamed of something. I'm thinking about my children and grandchildren. We're not selling our land in Checotah. I do love the land where my wife and I were brought up. We will never let our hold on this land go. Our grandfathers paid for that land with their lives and suffered much hardship."

At that moment, Ermestine realized that her father was getting old and, at fifty-seven, appeared more fragile than the men he was talking with. He repeated several times why the family was moving out West, as if trying to convince himself that the move was for the betterment of his family. He ended all these conversations with, "And of all the got-dang bad luck, Mother Nature has not been good to us."

After lunch the family began their journey. First, they returned to Langston University and retrieved the rest of Ermestine's personal belongings, explaining to the dorm mother that she was accompanying them out West.

Along the way to California, Ermestine drove the car; her father seemed to appreciate her helping out that way, since her mother and Baldie didn't know how to drive. The family spent hours on the trip sharing memories, good and bad experiences, laughing and talking.

With tears in her eyes, Tressie said, "You girls are lucky you have a mother and a father. My mother died when I was a baby. I don't remember her. Growing up, I always felt like a motherless child."

Ermestine glanced back and saw Baldie wiping tears from her face. There was silence for a few minutes, and then her mother continued.

"Ermestine, you are just like my sister, Luanna. You know she passed when she was a young girl. Luanna would not back off from a challenging situation. Nope, she was headstrong and determined to do what she wanted to do."

Ermestine was beaming with pride after hearing her mother compare her to Luanna. Smiling, she turned and looked at her sister.

Baldie hollered, "What are you looking at me for?" Then she stuck her tongue out and started to search through her snack bag.

Tressie noticed Baldie's actions and firmly said, "You two are sisters, so be happy you have each other. After Luanna passed, I had a hole in my heart. She was my big sister, my best friend, and I still miss her."

No one spoke for a while, reflecting on their mother's words. Everyone but Baldie was very excited about the possibilities that might lie ahead in California. Ermestine's mind was on getting to Richmond, enrolling in college, becoming a member of Alpha Kappa Alpha Sorority, and discovering a new life.

The well on Checotah property, built by Roy

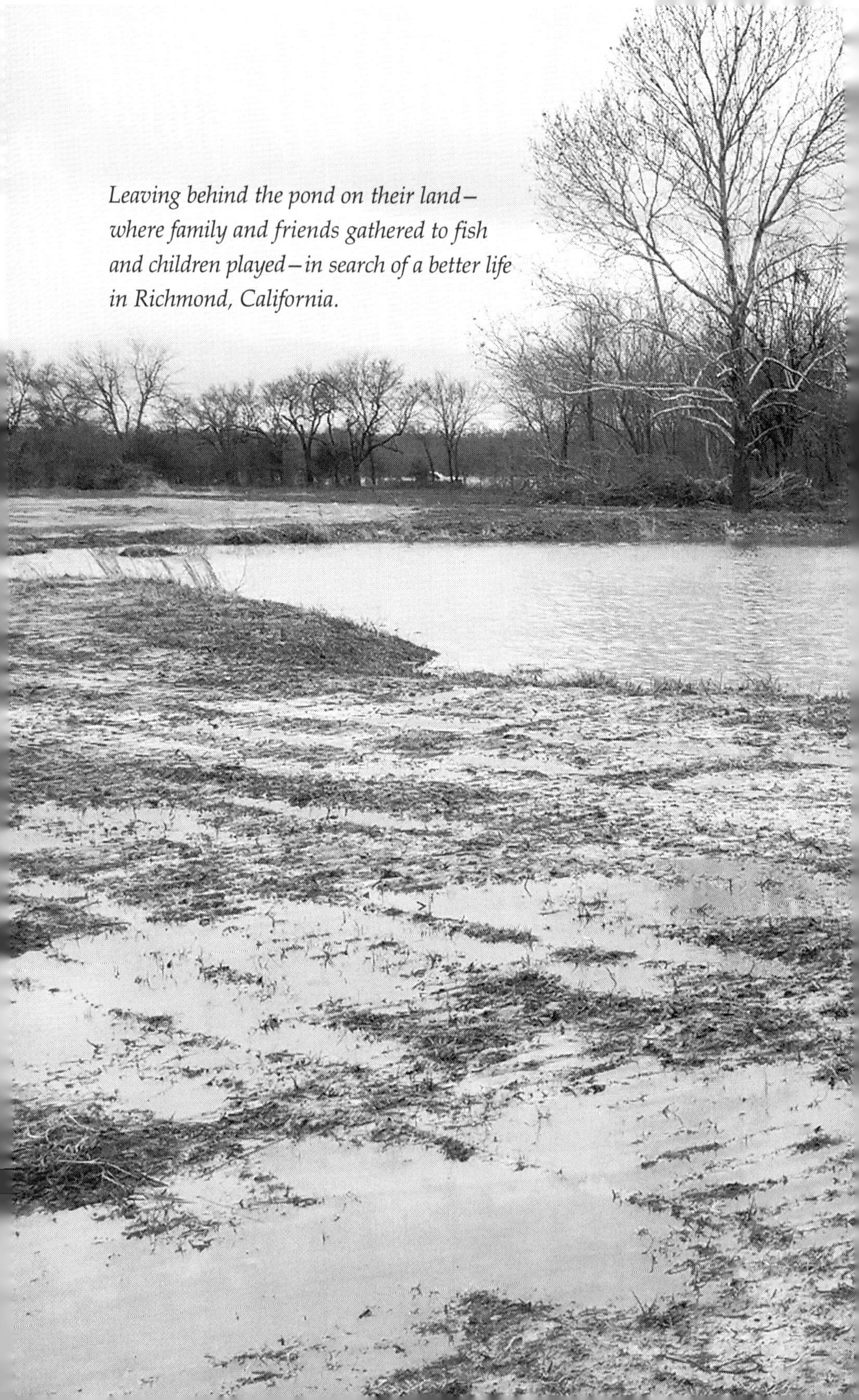

Leaving behind the pond on their land—where family and friends gathered to fish and children played—in search of a better life in Richmond, California.

PART TWO: GETTING SETTLED

Cousin Gladys and John Jordan were doing fine in California, circa 1940

GAME CHANGER 4

NATIVE AMERICAN CAFÉ

One experience from the family's trip out West that left a vivid imprint on my mother's memory was a stop at a small Native American store with a café. As they entered the store, the sisters stopped to look at the beautiful Native American jewelry. My mother told Baldie she had saved some money from working in the beauty shop and could buy her something she liked. Roy continued to walk through the store, headed to the café in the back. The girls spent about thirty minutes in the store, each selecting one piece of jewelry and buying snacks to eat in the car.

After purchasing their merchandise, the sisters walked into the café and saw their father eating at the counter. As they walked toward him, the man working behind the counter shouted, "No, you can't come in here."

Roy, who could be mistaken for being Native American, turned to see who the man was talking to. Tressie, walking in behind her two daughters, immediately stopped, turned around, and left the café.

My mother remembered making eye contact with her father as she paused, not knowing if she should follow her mother or continue to where her father was seated. She remembered hearing the café worker say in a louder voice and a harsh tone, "I said, you don't belong here, so go on! Leave, get out!"

Baldie was already following Tressie toward the door. My mother heard Baldie's new charm bracelet chiming and saddle shoes clicking as she rushed toward Tressie. She saw Baldie's plaid skirt swing back and forth. Her father's face was expressionless, his eyes averted, looking down at his food. Finally the moment broke, and my mother turned and quickly followed her mother and sister out the door.

They returned to the car and sat there for about twenty minutes. Baldie kept asking, "Why did that man tell us to leave?"

Her mother's response was "I don't know, and it doesn't really matter. We do have food."

Baldie was persistent, trying to figure out what had just happened. When Roy returned to the car, Baldie asked her father, "Why did that man tell us to get out? Why did you get to eat there?"

Mother told me she never forgot her father's answer, "That's just the way of the world."

Baldie said, "Well, I don't like it, and that's why I want to go back to Checotah. How come we couldn't eat with you? I wanted some chicken and potatoes."

Looking straight ahead, Roy repeated, "I already told you, Baldie; it's the way of the world."

Roy then started the car, and the family resumed their road trip. For a long time, there was little conversation. My mother looked at the Oh Henry! candy bars she had bought for her father, his favorite candy. He was focused on driving and was unusually quiet. His glasses sat high on his cheekbones, and pronounced strips of silver shimmered throughout his straight black hair. Maybe he was thinking about what happened in the café. She was upset at him for staying in the café until he finished eating.

She left the Oh Henry! in her bag, pulled out some M&M's, and listened to Baldie complain.

Finally, Mother told Baldie, "Be quiet and eat your snacks." For a long time, the only sound Mother heard was the clicking sound of Baldie's charm bracelet and a smacking noise while she ate crackers and cheese.

Mother was now even more fearful and apprehensive about what else they would encounter on their journey. This was one of those moments that was never discussed again by the sisters in front of their parents, but never forgotten, either. It was a Game Changer etched forever in Mother's brain.

The Williams siblings, together again in California
(Ermestine, unknown man, Son, Baldie)

GAME CHANGER 5

ARRIVAL IN RICHMOND

When they arrived in their new town, my grandfather connected with friends from Checotah and Boley, Oklahoma, and then rented a one-bedroom, jerry-built house on Sixth Street in unincorporated North Richmond, a predominantly Black community with Black-owned family businesses, stores, churches, schools, cafés, and nightclubs. Blacks living in North Richmond were hardworking people, some of whom were trying to save a down payment to purchase a home in a more desirable location. North Richmond had a history of being a flood plain, and a series of floods continually destroyed property. It was common to see people walking down the middle of the street to avoid water pools or mud.

Housing was limited, and my mother met Blacks who were living in barns, tents, or shacks. Working families had to live with relatives or squeeze into small apartments. In the 1950s, some Blacks were living in makeshift homes they had built on parcels they purchased in North Richmond; they were unable to get a bank loan to do proper construction. Societal barriers prevented opportunities even for those with means who were employed and seeking homeownership.

Roy quickly joined a union and got a job cleaning up the shipyard. With the war over, the shipyard jobs were mainly gone, and many of Roy's friends had already gone back to Oklahoma. Tressie began to express regrets about leaving their farm, but Roy took a strong stance and was confident that he could make it in California. Mother admired her father for having the courage to migrate to Richmond.

Throughout my childhood, Mother often talked about living in North Richmond and the initial reality of living in a predominantly Black community. She had left a farm surrounded by White neighbors living in relative harmony. North Richmond had a reputation of being a crime-ridden, poverty-stricken area. In North Richmond there were Black-owned businesses and hardworking Blacks, but the area had a reputation of being a crime-ridden, poverty-stricken area. Mother felt that this was because the living conditions were defined and restricted, giving Blacks little voice and limited choices.

She came to believe that North Richmond's reputation promoted racial segregation. Mother believed there was an alarming difference between North Richmond and the rest of Richmond in how resources and police services were provided. The area did not seem to be a high priority among either the White men running the City of Richmond or the county officials. There were in fact distinct income gaps between Black and White households. Throughout the years, Mother often said, "Some people like and want to remain in segregated communities. The City of Richmond cannot neglect Black communities through systematic racism."

Baldie enrolled at Richmond High School and soon made some friends within the community. She adapted to Richmond and bounced back to her happy, people-person self.

My mother found several jobs in San Francisco. She would catch the bus there, and as this new routine sunk in, she began to feel that her daily commute gave her a different perspective on what life could be like in California. She loved the exciting new atmosphere and energy surrounding her.

The job she enjoyed most was working as a nanny for a rich family in a gorgeous house on a hill with a view of the city. This was her first experience of being around wealthy people. Mrs. Timberlake had a cook, and Mother served dinner to the family in the evenings. They all got dressed up for dinner; the older children and the adults came to the table, but not the Timberlake's infant. Mother's primary job was to take care of that infant. She also enrolled in classes at a beauty school in San Francisco.

With her first paycheck, she bought her parents and sister new dress-up clothes for a trip to San Francisco's North Beach. She laughed afterward about how their dress attire was totally wrong for the occasion, but she wanted her family to see what was beyond the boundaries of North Richmond. She remembered Baldie having so much fun in North Beach, but she kept asking, "Why did I have to wear Sunday clothes, when other teenagers are dressed casually?" They spent the entire day in San Francisco, riding the bus, discovering a brand-new city and an environment so different from what they knew.

Within six months of moving to North Richmond, the family was able to rent an apartment in one of the housing projects available to Blacks. The Canal Projects, located near the shipyard and the railroad tracks, was a blessing in my grandmother's view. In a city where housing for Blacks was limited, Black working families who could afford to pay rent often chose to live in the projects.

* * *

Meanwhile, Son had received a Purple Heart from the Army, and after he was released from service, he followed his family to California. Son quickly found a job working in San Francisco at S&W, a company well known for producing canned food to sell to homes both within and beyond the Bay Area. Everyone in the family saw him as intelligent, hardworking, and energetic. But after his military service, his mother expressed concerns about him becoming an alcoholic. He was drinking more and more frequently.

Once again, the family was back together, all living in the same home. But this time they were in California, and instead of everyone helping out with chores and farmwork, they were renting and working different jobs while Tressie took care of the house. Grandmother Tressie also became an active and devoted member of North Richmond Missionary Baptist Church, the oldest Black church in Contra Costa County. Eventually, she and several of her church friends started doing seasonal work at the Filice and Perrelli cannery in Richmond, not far from her home.

The Williams family bought only the necessities and began saving money. Son was eventually able to purchase a new car, and my mother continued to buy clothes for her family and plan special outings to San Francisco. Baldie soon graduated from high school. It seemed they were on their way to finding their California dream.

Tressie and Roy Williams

American Standard factory, where Isaac Petgrave worked. On one side of the street is the building that produced sinks and toilets; the building onthe other side of the street built bathtubs. In the distance are the railroad tracks police used to block one entrance into and out of North Richmond. This photo was taken in 2021.

GAME CHANGER 6

THE KIST ICE CREAM SHACK

Shortly after obtaining a family apartment in the Canal Projects, my grandfather Roy thought he could make a better living by opening a store in the neighborhood. He rented a small shack in the middle of the Canal Projects from a White lady named Thelma. He quit his job cleaning up at the shipyard and opened the Kist Shack, which drew customers from all the housing units in the Canal District.

My grandmother didn't like the idea of Roy quitting his job, but soon the store was a thriving business. He sold household goods, candy bars, soda, and vegetables, but the shop was best-known in the neighborhood for selling ice cream. Mother recalled leaving the beauty school to work in the store with her parents. She said the ice cream was so hard to scoop out, her fingers began to bend and hurt, and she worried they would become deformed.

Eventually, Mother recognized that the contract her dad had signed with Thelma was a rotten deal. Thelma charged him rent, but she also wanted 50 percent of the store's sales profits, although Roy's family did all the work. Roy had started out with his own money and purchased all the merchandise they were going to sell. Through his efforts, the business was growing and becoming profitable. Thelma had nothing to do with that.

My mother noticed a building for sale in the neighborhood and encouraged Roy to buy the property and build his own store. She took her father to Martinez, the Contra Costa County seat, to find out who owned the property, hoping to contact the owners.

Her father then told Thelma what his daughter was encouraging him to do. Thelma told him that was a bad idea, because the owners were Japanese people and were coming back to claim their land. Japanese American families had flourished in Richmond in the early 1900s; they bought property, built homes, and opened businesses there until war with Japan broke out. Suddenly considered "enemy aliens," they were forced into guarded concentration camps in 1942.

After the camps closed in 1946, some Japanese Americans never returned to the West Coast. Those who did return had to rebuild their lives, which had been dramatically changed by the concentration camp experience. Non-Japanese businesses and residents had moved into sections of Richmond that were previously occupied by Japanese Americans. This was all happening at the time my grandfather was thinking about buying a little piece of property for his store. Believing the landlord's story, he decided against moving forward with plans to purchase the building.

Thelma then swooped in and purchased that very property, opening a store that eventually put the Kist shop out of business. Soon thereafter, Thelma hired Grandfather to work for her! He didn't stay long, however; he finally realized that Thelma had bamboozled him.

My mother always felt that Thelma had deliberately deceived her father in order to stop him from pursuing this new opportunity. "It's just another White person taking advantage of a Black man's lack of knowledge," she told her father. She was disheartened and upset at her father for believing and trusting the White woman.

She felt that he lacked confidence in her, refusing to take a risk based on what she had researched and discovered. My mother recognized early on that to achieve economic growth, one had to compete, directly or indirectly, with unscrupulous people.

One of her father's favorite sayings was "Don't take any wooden nickels." In her mind, however, that was exactly what he had done. In time, she learned that before her arrival in Richmond, many new immigrants had endured discriminatory practices, including restrictive covenants in housing that affected where they lived, shopped, and dined.

Not long after Thelma swindled him, Roy began working in construction. He got a job in El Cerrito with Nora Davis, who was building elaborate homes all around the Sunset View Cemetery. He continued to work with her for many years. She was a landscape architect and, under her supervision, Roy did all the landscaping for the expensive homes in El Cerrito. With the utmost respect for land, he had found a job doing what he loved—taking care of land.

* * *

When my family arrived in California, Blacks were not the only communities in the state facing discrimination and teetering on the edge of hope, either unable to purchase or hold on to land or living within imposed boundaries. Californians from many backgrounds, with many accents, dialects, and languages, were fighting policies and racial injustice to create change for their own flesh and blood, determined to foster a nurturing environment and more inclusive opportunities for their children, sometimes in an atmosphere of public threat.

When Mother first came to Richmond, she was not aware of the history and struggles of other racial and ethnic groups in California. Cut from similar but different cloth, neighbors gradually learned about one another, sharing stories and histories of their struggles to survive and prosper. Like quilt patches sewn together, California's ethnic groups worked to thrive in a world of chaos, sometimes with mismatched and diverted values, but always focused on a singular goal: bettering their families' lives. After becoming a real estate agent, Mother would begin to see manifestations of discriminatory practices toward other groups in California, more subtle than those toward Blacks, but still very much in existence.

Mother knew just about where all Black families lived in Richmond and El Cerrito. If she knew their names, she knew their struggles from the past and the desire to find the best education possible for their children. That was her business and knowledge base for pushing forward.

Strategies in her planning occurred on the spot. She always wore gloves to important business meetings, removing them finger by finger while composing her thoughts and response. Removing the gloves, her unique technique for thinking before speaking in business meetings, worked well for her. Outside the walls of financial institutions, City of Richmond offices, or business-related agencies, she was quick witted with responses. She had a process of removing her gloves and preparing a response to a person waiting quietly while watching her remove the gloves one finger at a time in deep thought.

For mother wearing gloves had a dual purpose: of style and thinking time before responding, with deliberate words to increase their understanding of the situation from her perspective. Her delivery was smooth but strong while putting her gloves on to leave. Her last words were, "Come on Glo," and "No Sir, it doesn't appear that I can do what you're asking." Then she walked away, leaving a strong message for them to think about.

Lillian Ellison in her early twenties

Isaac Petgrave, 1945

GAME CHANGER 7

"OKIE"

After arriving in Richmond, my mother worked several jobs. At the Post Office, Mother met Betty. They would ride to work together every day and soon became good friends. In 1947 they planned to meet at Woolworth's and have lunch, and Betty brought a friend with her, Lillian Ellison. After Betty introduced my mother and Lillian, they all had lunch and chitchatted.

Mother's first impression of Lillian was that she was extremely attractive—with beautiful thick, long hair—as well as different from her friends and neighbors in North Richmond. During lunch, she inquired about Lillian's life: where was she born, what did her father do, where did she live, did she have a boyfriend, did she work? Mother listened attentively and learned that Lillian was married to Lawrence (Birt) Ellison and she had one brother, Isaac Petgrave.

After responding to all of Mother's questions, Lillian ended with, "And what about you?" After Mother answered, Lillian said with a smile, "Oh, so you are an Okie."

At that point, Mother was ready to get up and go, so she soon said her good-byes.

In May of that year, Betty decided to throw my mother a twenty-first birthday dinner party at her house. Mother was surprised that her new friend wanted to celebrate her birthday, and she appreciated their friendship even more. She gave Betty the names of eight people to invite.

Mother arrived at Betty's place before the invited guests. The apartment was tastefully decorated, and the aroma of food wafted from the kitchen. Betty had prepared fried chicken, catfish, potato salad, and a green salad. A beautiful birthday cake sat on the counter, with candles already in place. Astonished, Mother became tearful to see all the thoughtful work Betty had done.

The guests began to arrive with gifts for Mother. Betty looked outside and saw Lillian's brother. She asked, "Do you mind if Lillian's brother comes to dinner? I see him outside."

Mother said, "No, I don't mind."

So the last person to arrive was Isaac Petgrave. He didn't come with a gift for Mother, but he handed Betty a beautiful bouquet of flowers. Betty placed them near the cake and began setting out the food.

During dinner, people were chatting with one another, and music played in the background. Mother noticed that Isaac was quieter than everyone else, yet engaged in many conversations. Very soft-spoken, he had a suave and regal manner about him. He seemed to be very popular and to know a lot of folks in Richmond.

A few weeks later, Betty asked Mother if she would be interested in attending a Billy Eckstine concert at the Fillmore Theater. The day of the concert, Mother arrived at Betty's house. While she was waiting for Betty to get ready, Isaac appeared at the door. She thought it strange that Betty had not told her he was joining them. They talked, and he inquired a bit about her life.

Outside, Betty quickly hopped into Isaac's new Plymouth and slid into the middle seat. Then Mother got in, Isaac closed the door, and they were on their way. Mother had never been to a concert before, and she was very excited to see Billy Eckstine. She had heard horror stories about Blacks stepping outside racially biased social codes, though, and didn't know what to expect.

They had a wonderful time, and after the concert, they walked back to the car, talking about the music and the crowd. Isaac unlocked the passenger door and again, Betty eagerly slid into the middle seat. Mother was moving to get in after her when Isaac said, "Betty, I would like for Ermestine to sit in the middle." Silently, Betty eased out, and Mother scooted in.

There was complete silence until Isaac turned on the radio. They drove for a while, listening to music. Betty, who my mother described as physically resembling the singer Etta James, was usually talking and laughing about something. Right now, she was strangely quiet.

When they returned to Betty's house, she got out of the car, saying she was tired but had enjoyed the concert. Mother's response was, "Okay, I'm going home, too. It's been a long day, so see you on Monday." She got into her car.

As Betty walked up the stairs to her apartment, Isaac walked up to Mother's car and asked if she would like to have dinner. She responded, "No, not tonight, thanks, because it's getting late."

Isaac then asked her, "Well, can I at least have your phone number?"

Mother later said that as she drove home and reflected about the night, she began to look at Isaac from a different viewpoint; she liked what she saw. That was the beginning of their courtship.

Mother never broadcast to Betty that she was talking to Isaac more and more on the telephone or that they had started going out to dinner. She told me that she never really knew how Betty had felt about Isaac asking her to sit in the middle seat. Shortly after the concert, Betty was no longer working with her in Benicia, and their friendship ended. But what irritated my mother most was that Lillian and Betty remained friends after she and my father were married. Throughout my parents' marriage, Mother would often lash out in anger at my father, saying that Betty was the cause of what she perceived to be a challenging sister-in-law relationship with Lillian.

* * *

John Spark Petgrave, Isaac and Lillian's father, was a carpenter at Santa Fe Railroads. Born in Jamaica, West Indies, in 1873, Grandfather John had a British flair about him. His voice, tone, accent, and style of dress were noticeably different from most Blacks. When he purchased his home in Richmond in 1920, there were few Blacks living there, and no preexisting racial patterns imposing segregation. This changed when an influx of Black migrants began settling in Richmond during World War II.

John wanted his children to have American citizenship, and he brought his wife to Richmond for their births. Soon after each birth, his wife and children returned to Jamaica to be close to family members. Sadly, his wife passed in Kingston at a young age, and he held her memories close to his heart. He never remarried, seldom spoke about her, and Isaac had few memories of his mother because he was so young when she died.

In the late 1920s, John sent for Isaac and Lillian to come to Richmond by boat; Isaac was six years old at the time. Isaac completed his education through the Richmond Unified School District. He was drafted into the Army and served in the US Mounted Cavalry in remote areas of the United States, later maintaining airstrips overseas during World War II. After receiving an honorable discharge, he was employed in 1945 as a machinist with American Standard, which produced innovative bath and kitchen products.

After serving in World War II, my father acquired a military style of dressing. He wore a uniform to work and, once he returned home, would quickly change into more comfortable clothes. He liked casual button-down shirts, sweaters, shirt jackets, and loafer-type shoes. He wasn't the type of guy to dress for success, but, modeling his father's style, he did have a tweed sports jacket, a hat, and one suit he wore on special occasions. Dad reminded me of Harry Belafonte in his appearance and personal style. I could see how my mother fell for him the night of the concert that began their life together.

Hoffman Homeowners District Association,
Ermestine standing, fourth from the right

Isaac and Ermestine elope to Reno, Nevada

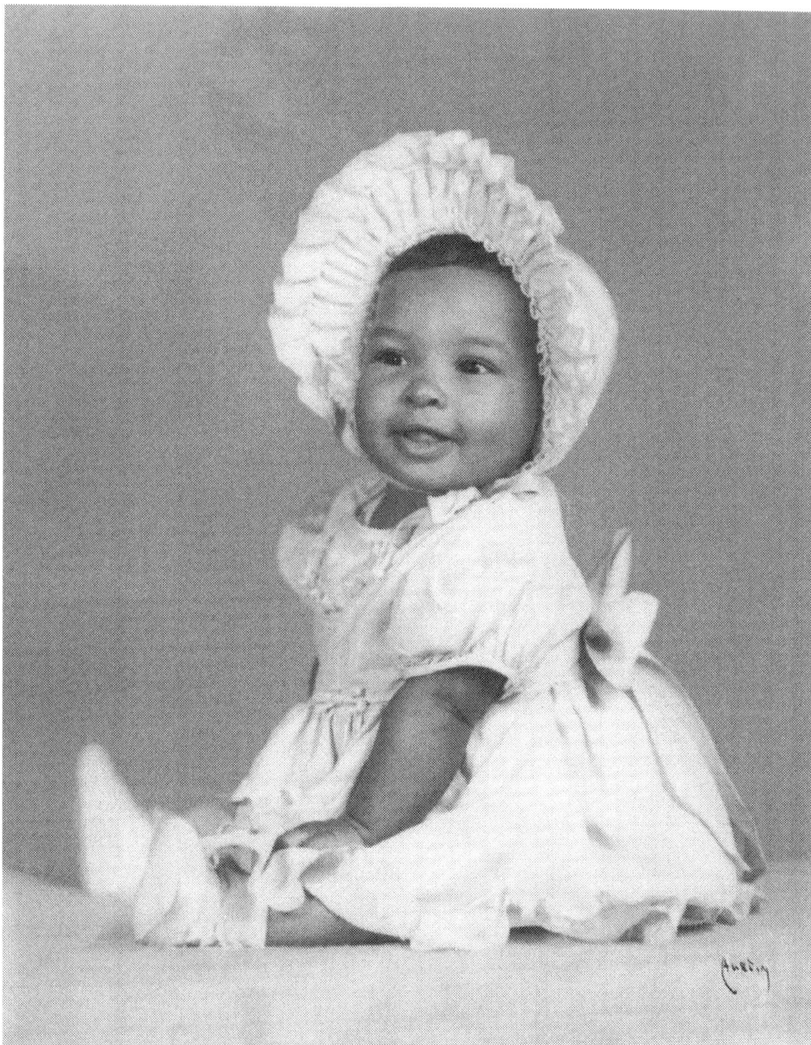

Gloria, 1950

GAME CHANGER 8

NEW FAMILY BONDS

During my parents' courtship, Mother's dream was to have a corner house with a white picket fence. One day my father picked her up after work, drove to a house that was for sale around the corner from his sister's house and a few blocks away from his father's house, and told her that his father had loaned him the down payment. She wondered why he had not applied for a veterans' government-guaranteed mortgage, but Dad had heard that Blacks' applications were being rejected. He told Mother, "Just be happy that my father has the money to loan us."

• • •

My grandfather, John Petgrave, and his children were among the first Black families to live in Richmond. Most of the Blacks who migrated to Richmond to work in the shipyards during World War II lived in jerry-built structures on Cutting Boulevard, in the projects, or in North Richmond. But John owned enough land at his Hoffman Boulevard property to provide his family with their own fruits and vegetables. Farm animals and livestock also supplied a source of food that he shared among family and friends.

John's daughter, Lillian, married in 1942. Her oldest son Richard was born in 1945, and in 1949 she purchased a home at Twenty-Third and Hoffman. She and her family were the first Blacks to move to her block. In 1948, my parents married and moved into their own dream house on Twenty-Second Street. They were the lucky ones. Most Blacks continued to struggle to move out of the projects or North Richmond.

The Twenty-Second Street house had three bedrooms and a formal dining area adjacent to the living room. We used one of the bedrooms as a family room. As far back as I can remember, we had yellow pet canaries always chirping and waking us up in the morning.

Like Lillian's family, my parents were the first Blacks to move to the block. Because my father's sister and father lived close by, my mother assumed that he felt it was a safe neighborhood. Still, the neighborhood was predominantly White.

One morning, when Mother looked out the kitchen window, she saw that someone had put a cross in the front yard. She was very surprised to see her husband's reaction to the cross when he returned home from work. He simply removed it and told her not to worry. She assumed he had heard about incidents like this in Richmond, but she never understood why it didn't seem to bother him. Memories of her father sitting at the counter eating in the Native American Café and the cross placed in her yard lingered in her mind forever.

• • •

When I was born in 1949, it was not in Richmond, but in San Francisco. Family members did not understand why Mother was determined to give birth in San Francisco. That made no sense, when local hospitals were closer to home. But she was strong-minded; she wanted San Francisco on her baby's birth certificate.

Isaac thought it was ridiculous to drive to San Francisco while she was in labor, and he told her it was an unwise idea.

Her response was "All you have to do is drive, and let me deal with the pain. We are going to San Francisco to have this baby!"

Baldie agreed with Isaac and told her sister, "That is the stupidest and most foolish thing you have come up with."

The day Mother was released from the hospital after my birth, my father had to work, so Baldie drove to San Francisco to pick us up. She came into the hospital with a beautiful pink blanket. Before leaving the city, we stopped at a store and Baldie and Mother did some shopping. Baldie carried me, wrapped in the pink blanket, on my first shopping trip in San Francisco.

• • •

A Black real estate agent in Oakland, Viola Taylor, had worked on selling my parents their first house. She was a few years older than my mother. Mother was surprised one Christmas Day when Viola stopped by for a visit with an invitation to join her in helping more Blacks become homeowners.

Mother understood the value of being a property owner from growing up on the Forty-Acres-and-a-Mule farm in Oklahoma. She had survived the experiences of migrating to Richmond with her family, living in poor conditions, and watching Blacks struggle to better their lives. She noticed how people respected her father-in-law and brother-in-law, who both owned property. She was forever grateful to her father-in-law for loaning them the down payment money and was determined to repay him quickly. She was also impressed with Viola. Acquiring her first house planted the seed, and Viola ultimately led my mother down the path to a career in real estate. Mother was motivated not only to help her parents purchase a home in the neighborhood but also to help other Blacks establish their own domains.

Once she decided to accept Viola's invitation, Mother began taking real estate classes. Both of her mentors, Viola Taylor and Ruby Bims, were well established in Oakland real estate business. Occasionally all three would attend North Richmond Missionary Baptist Church and sit together in the pews in their Sunday best, praising the Lord. After-church activities included getting together for lunch, hosting an open house, or meeting to discuss the plight of Blacks who wanted to become homeowners. These three ladies began to open up unknown opportunities in the Black community to purchase land. After becoming a real estate broker, my mother launched her own agency, Petgrave Realty, but her relationships with Viola and Ruby were solid, and they continued to develop new projects together.

Mother was aware that the 1944 GI Bill guaranteed low-interest mortgages to all World War II veterans. She fought local banks that had a history of discriminating against Blacks, and less than seven years after migrating to California, she had helped her parents, her brother, and other Black families purchase homes in her neighborhood. By 1950 all members of the Williams family were living in their own homes and adapting to life in Richmond.

The community Mother served comprised prosperous, hardworking, and supportive Black families. She was one of the youngest women to become active in the Hoffman District Home Owners Association (later Hoffman Homeowners Association). Twelve Black women established relationships with other women in the community involved in Richmond politics, and became a force for the Hoffman Homeowners to have a voice in city issues that concerned them.

Within a few years, White homeowners had fled the Hoffman community. My mother believed that White flight in the 1950s was primarily a Black and White issue: Whites thought Blacks living in their communities would lead to socioeconomic decline. She would say we did nothing to drive Whites out; they just did not want to live around us.

Former First Lady Michelle Obama, speaking at the 2019 Obama Foundation Summit, stated, "White folks . . . were afraid of what our families represented." I believe Mother would concur wholeheartedly.

Mother felt that Whites moving out of neighborhoods where Blacks were moving in meant that the Whites would no longer defend their space with violence or intimidation. She would smile and say, "That was fine with me; I didn't have to worry about another white cross placed in my yard."

New Black homeowners were determined to not let their communities suffer as a result of White flight. The twelve Black women in the Hoffman Homeowners Association became a political force with their husbands by their sides every step of the way. They were united in their vision for safety, good schools, and a decent place to raise their children. The neighborhood did not deteriorate; it became a community they were proud of.

Sixty years later, living in different and diverse communities, women of the Hoffman Homeowners Association would still get together and share memories of living in the Hoffman community. My mother's parents resided there for the rest of their lives. I remember Mother saying, "The Hoffman community has a history of heart and soul." She was loyal to the neighborhood of her first homeownership.

• • •

While I was growing up, one block away from our house was Jack Newell's, a grocery and liquor store. Within walking distance were a Black-owned dry cleaner and an elementary school. The neighborhood hummed with people busily going about their days. All the men had jobs or a hustle, and neighbors were family members or friends. Everyone knew each other and created an environment that was supportive for children. All the families had young children around my age. My grandparents were one of the oldest couples in the community and were respected as such.

Each year, a big carnival would come to Hoffman Boulevard, one block away. It seemed so magical to transition a large piece of vacant property into an exciting and amazing place for kids—with roller coasters, Ferris wheels, game and food booths, haunted houses, and a merry-go-round. The carnival was a gathering place to see friends and families having fun, laughing, talking, and socializing, and was a special event the children looked forward to each year. It was like Disneyland come to Richmond and brought the communities together for a few days.

I liked going to the carnival with my parents and watching my mother greet and talk with folks; her conversations often swung to living situations and property, and she then passed out her business cards. My father didn't think talking about real estate and passing out business cards was appropriate to do at social gatherings, but that didn't faze my mother, although throughout their marriage, the subject would result in arguments.

* * *

When my mother was taking real estate classes, my maternal grandparents, who lived three houses away in a two-bedroom house, would babysit. My grandfather was a short man, with long, straight, silver hair and a caramel skin tone. He was handsome, a hard worker, fun to be with, and full of wisdom and stories. He definitely had strong Indian features, and his behavior and actions reflected the Muscogee Creek Indian culture. He had a large backyard and the most beautiful vegetable garden, fruit trees that produced sweet apples and plums, and a gorgeous rose garden that he had created for his wife. He was the best grandfather and devoted special time to be in his grandchildren's lives.

Growing up, I spent a lot of time following my grandfather around his backyard as he tended his garden. He often spoke about the horrible farming conditions he had endured in Checotah. Soaring temperatures, well into the evening, made it uncomfortable to sleep, and they hung wet clothes around the house to cool it. They dealt with intense periods of drought and the economic and environmental impacts associated with the Dust Bowl. Many of his family members and friends had to abandon their farms, unable to grow crops. Some of his friends passed because of difficulty with breathing, referred to as "dust pneumonia."

Those who visited my grandfather's backyard always commented how beautiful his garden was. The rows of vegetables were perfectly straight. The corn grew tall and bountiful. Tomatoes, beans, squash, cucumbers, greens, a variety of fresh produce—all so plentiful. His backyard mirrored, on a small scale, the farm he had left behind in Checotah, and he devoted hours in his backyard to working the soil, watering, and manicuring his garden. As he tended his crops, he would say out loud to himself, "Got to treat the earth well!"

Grandfather stressed the importance of closeness with nature and a love for the earth. He stood in a lineage of men successfully farming and raising livestock in Checotah. He knew the benefits of planting, growing, and selling food, and the values taught by his ancestors about working the land to sustain his culture through agriculture were embedded in his mind and spirit.

He built a row of rabbit hutches in the rear of the yard and raised a variety of species in different colors. When the rabbits had babies, listening to him and watching him take care of the bunnies was like a science lesson.

He was always busy doing something in his old shed, and neighborhood men and family members would come to visit, share stories, or help him with whatever he was working on. He was always speaking about his experiences, tradition, and culture. His ongoing message to his grandkids was "Get an education, because that's the only thing the White man can't take from you."

Often I would sit on the grass, eating an apple from a tree full of beautiful and tasty apples planted by my grandfather, listening to his words: "It's a blessing for a man to own land, but the desire and beauty in life is to die on your land."

Looking up at the sky, I'd see a large doll my grandfather placed in the tree to serve as a scarecrow. After Grandfather passed, our family found a stash of his savings in the tattered and worn doll, money hidden there for years. For thirty years that scarecrow doll had hung in the apple tree, swinging and swagging with the breeze of the wind, raindrops dripping from its hair. A few months after Grandfather passed, my grandmother told me that some of his tools and equipment came up missing out of the shed, backyard, and garage. But his were the last fingerprints on that old doll, and it was his immediate family who found his savings.

* * *

One story Grandfather told with much intensity was about the destruction of Black Wall Street. Also known as the Greenwood District, this Tulsa neighborhood had thrived after its founding in 1906. Shortly after Grandfather returned from completing his military service, in his early thirties, came the event that changed everything, leaving an indelible mark on his brain.

It all started on May 31, 1921, with the accusation that Dick Rowland, a Black nineteen-year-old shoe shiner, allegedly assaulted a White seventeen-year-old elevator operator, Sarah Page. She eventually declined to prosecute. But in the meantime, many White people in Tulsa called for his lynching.

This incident was the impetus for the Tulsa Race Massacre, which took place in this vibrant area with a majority Black population. The Greenwood community was burned to the ground; residents were tortured and feared for their lives. Black Tulsans were imprisoned and, in the wake of this domestic terrorism, up to three hundred deaths occurred. Many of my grandfather's acquaintances survived the massacre, but their lives forever changed. And fear of the White man heightened to a new level.

He was puzzled by the fact that he had served faithfully in the military, only to return to steadily growing tensions surrounding the Great Migration of Blacks from the rural South to the cities of the North. Blacks were incurring most of the damage, with the destruction of whole Black communities and many Black lives lost.

• • •

My grandmother used to say that you can't do much when you visit other people's houses. And you were always supposed to be doing something—either go to school or go to work, or do sewing or cooking or canning. You don't belong in someone's home just visiting, and things that go on in some of your friends' houses may place you in harm's way. During my teenage years, my grandmother would hear my mother fussing at me about my choices of friends or the bad decisions I was making. My grandmother would say, "Those who lie down with dogs get up with fleas." Mother took her mother's wisdom to heart throughout her life and did her best to instill the same in me.

My grandmother loved to make preserves, clean her house, and attend church services. She was always reading her Bible, quoting Scriptures, and encouraging her family to live by the Ten Commandments. Often, she would say, "Sometimes it feels so good to just sit by myself, and not talk to anyone but God." She was very active in the North Richmond Missionary Baptist Church and held Deborah Circle meetings in her home, where church sisters would gather, read the Bible, discuss Scriptures, sing, and pray. Refreshments were always served, and Grandmother's best china was used.

On some Sundays, my grandmother and I would go to church; when my mother wasn't working or showing property, she would join us. For special occasions like Easter, Christmas, or church events, Mother would take us shopping and buy us new attire. North Richmond Missionary Baptist Church provided my grandmother with religious continuity and a sense of community and faith, lending stability to her new living conditions. But Roy, Son, and Baldie seldom attended.

I was baptized and active in youth activities at St. Luke Missionary Baptist Church, across the street from the store. Most of the Black families in the neighborhood attended St. Luke. I sang in the youth choir, leading solo songs. I could not hit any notes and had no harmony, yet Mother was always in the pews when I sang—my biggest cheerleader. I attended vacation Bible school and flourished attending church events. My mother would provide food and snacks for church events and would attend services at St. Luke when she could, but like my grandmother, she remained a member of North Richmond Missionary Baptist.

My grandmother was a Baptist churchgoing lady who didn't get involved in messy situations. When her daughters would meet up at her house, they would begin to gossip about what they had heard about neighbors, church folks, or friends. "What's right is right, and what's wrong is wrong, and talking about other people is wrong, so don't bring that here," she would admonish them.

She was careful about whom she welcomed into her house and encouraged her daughters to do the same. She said, "When you let the wrong people into your house, stuff will come up missing . . . like peace and faith."

If drama popped up, Grandmother would shut it down. Even though my grandfather and their adult children would cuss when she was not around, they all respected her, and they were careful how they spoke in front of her. My mother said, "Everyone in the family knows that it was through those Forty Acres and a Mule that we survived and prospered. She was able to hold on to her acres, and for that your grandmother should be respected! She had enough sense to hold on to her property, work the land, and make a living. The White man or Indians couldn't swindle her out of nothing, and they tried, but she didn't take any wooden nickels. She saved her pennies and worked hard."

• • •

Son lived with his parents until he married. After working hours and on weekends Son was frequently visiting his sisters' businesses, driving a new car—always shiny as a new penny—inside and out. Reflecting on her brother's life, my mother said, "He would marry, get his own house, then separate and return to our parents' house. I think he kept returning to our parents' house because Dad would get up and cook his breakfast every morning! I used to think, 'Golly, he has it easy, because I have a family and I am also working.' So, I think that's why he kept coming back home." Son worked at S&W and lived periodically with his parents until he passed from a heart issue at thirty eight years old.

• • •

One of Grandmother's favorite things to do was go shopping at Goodwill stores or in downtown Richmond on a Saturday morning with her daughters and grandkids. Downtown Richmond businesses were thriving with energy and activity at that time. High school boys would have fun cruising up and down Macdonald in their cars. Art's Records sold 45s and LPs, and the Fox movie theater was crowded with neighborhood children during the weekends. We would go to the Fox Theater for an all-day affair: we could watch the movies over and over again, and no one would hassle us.

Richmond residents supported downtown Richmond. There were dentists' and doctors' offices, clothing and shoe stores, bakeries, Milens Jewelers, JCPenney, S. H. Kress, National Dollar Store, F. W. Woolworth, a shoeshine shop, a magazine shop, a drugstore, and banks—all within a three-block walking distance. Buses were rolling down Macdonald every few minutes, with people hopping on and off, creating an atmosphere of prosperity that Grandmother loved.

Blacks were moving from the Canal Projects, sometimes sharing homes with other families in areas where Blacks had previously been unable to rent or purchase property. They were becoming homeowners, purchasing commercial properties, and opening businesses. Racial profiling existed, but obstacles were being fought. Black real estate agents were joining forces, fighting for the right of Blacks to purchase property, and rising up and raising hell against the practice of mortgages being denied outside of minority-dominant neighborhoods.

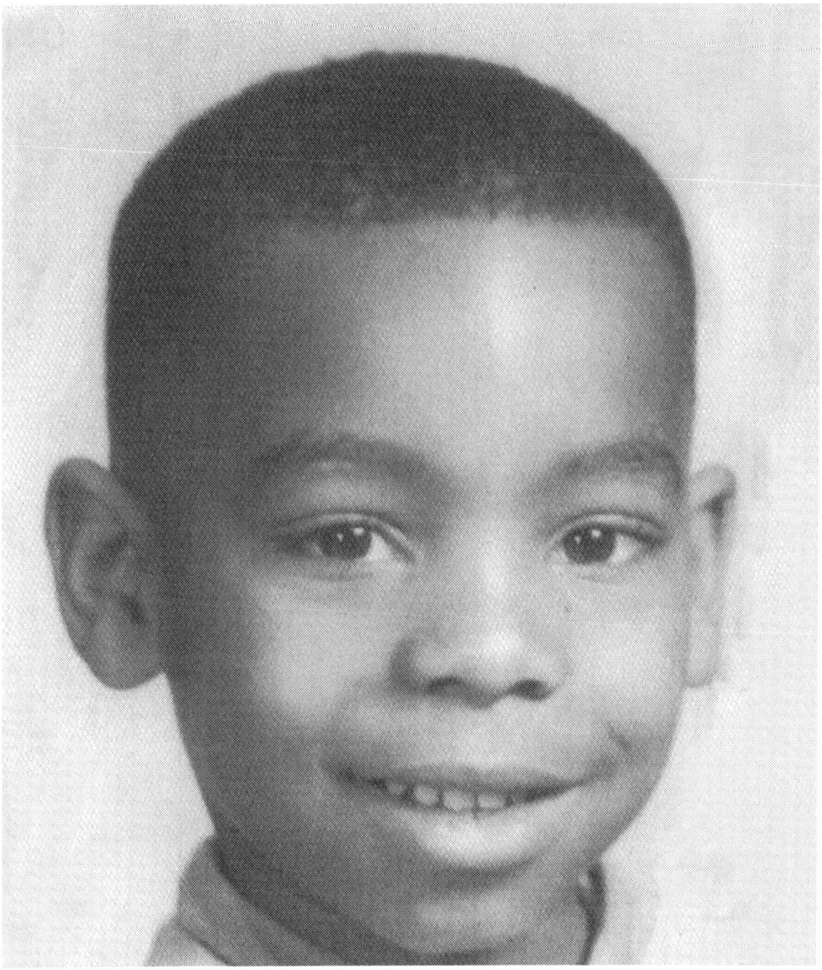

Larry Strickland, my sidekick for walking the railroad tracks through Richmond

Yvonne Strickland, the baby in our family

GAME CHANGER 9

THE DOWN BEAT CLUB

Baldie, Mother's younger sister, was naturally pretty, about five foot three, and well-liked; she didn't put on airs, was very popular, and enjoyed good company. In 1948 she married San Francisco native Larry Strickland, who was twenty-one years older than she. She was happy and content with her life and new husband.

The Strickland family had moved to North Richmond in 1918. A gentle soul, Larry owned the Down Beat nightclub in North Richmond. He was known throughout the community as "the Boss man," but we called him "Big Larry."

With expansion of paved roads through rural and urban areas during the 1930s, and the construction of the Interstate Highway System during the late 1950s, trucking businesses began to flourish.

In 1949, when Baldie was twenty-one, she and Big Larry purchased two big rigs and started Strickland Trucking. Baldie obtained her commercial driver's license from the DMV to operate an eighteen-wheeler, and Strickland Trucking was licensed by the Public Utilities Commission to transport materials and goods across the state of California.

Baldie was often on the road by herself with large loads. At one point, an employee of the commission told her that she was the first woman to drive a big rig full-time. My cousin Larry remembers his parents working as a team to get loads to their final destination.

They carried fruits and vegetables, Christmas trees, and lumber. Big Larry would take one big rig and pick up a load of lumber from Eureka in Northern California. He would return home with the load, and Baldie would take that same load to Los Angeles and deliver the lumber to its final destination. Meantime, Big Larry would be in their other big rig on his way to pick up another load.

As you can imagine, as a child, riding in the big rig with Baldie felt romantic and exciting to me. Cruising through the streets of Richmond, with my cousin Larry tooting the horn in response to children on the sidewalks who were smiling and making that familiar pulling hand motion—it put us in the spotlight. We had no idea how hard this work was for the adults.

* * *

At twenty-five, Baldie had her first child, a son named Larry, and three years later, she had a daughter, Yvonne. She no longer drove trucks and was focused on the Down Beat Club, taking college courses, and raising her children.

The Down Beat was a popular club where R&B greats such as B. B. King, T-Bone Walker, and other Black celebrities from the 1950s performed. The club was Baldie's wheelhouse—she solicited top entertainers, initiated gambling, and worked side by side with her father, Roy, to run the business.

One of several nightclubs (Minnie Lou's, Club Savoy, Do Drop Inn, and Tapper's Inn) in North Richmond, the Down Beat smelled of cracklings and beer; a strong bar odor prevailed. There were few windows downstairs, and the bar and dance room were always dimly lit. The interior stairs at the back of the bar led to a second-floor space that resembled a ballroom, with a large pool table used for gambling. On rainy days, that same space became the children's playground, where we rode bikes, played ball, and had fun around the pool table. On the opposite side of the stairs on the same floor was a three-bedroom unit occupied by Baldie and her family.

When I was growing up, staying all night at Baldie's house was exciting. I looked forward to spending time with my younger cousins, Larry and Yvonne. North Richmond and the Down Beat had a far different flavor from where I lived, above the S&S store on South Seventh Street that my parents bought in 1954.

The Down Beat became the place where male family members and friends congregated during the weekends. Son, for one, spent a lot of time at his sister's house and socializing in the club.

Baldie loved to play cards and dominoes, smoke cigarettes, drink coffee, and have fun. She always had visitors sitting in her kitchen, eating and talking. Baldie stayed up late, and she slept in. Mother would get upset when she visited her sister in the afternoon and Baldie was still in bed. She would tell Baldie, "Get up, the early bird catches the worm," and an argument would begin.

Baldie would say, "I'm not interested in catching no worm, because I've been up all night dealing with the Down Beat."

Mother, on the other hand, a loner by nature, never learned to play cards or dominoes, and she considered those activities a waste of time. She was a closet smoker and loved to drink black coffee, but she didn't indulge in drinking alcohol. She didn't dance, either, and didn't like the fact that her husband was spending time at the Down Beat during the weekends, or that Baldie was always entertaining people. Neither one of them held back from expressing her dislikes and opinions. For instance, Baldie never hesitated to tell her sister, "This is my life, and I am not you. Just because you don't like to have any visitors at your house, don't come over here telling me what to do."

• • •

Under cover of darkness, dancing, socializing, and gambling, fighting occurred frequently at the Down Beat Club. As a child, I remember looking out the window at my cousins' house and seeing and hearing acts of violence that seemed like something from a movie script. There were frequent anonymous calls to the county about the violence and crime occurring in the North Richmond neighborhood, pointing the finger at all the nightclubs in the area. Grandfather told of occasions when the Down Beat was raided and the family discussions and decisions made to deal with the consequences following each raid. The county believed that the Down Beat was a meeting place for criminals and eventually rescinded the club's business license, forcing it to close down in 1960.

Living in homes above our parents' businesses, Yvonne and I grew up fearing the violence that frequently occurred within our space. There was always some uncertainty in our living environments, and peace could suddenly change into outside forces bringing danger. We were conditioned to watching our parents' clients react to conflict in a threatening manner. We often witnessed individuals respond aggressively as a form of self-defense or to do harm, and from my perspective these altercations were scary and produced persistent fear. I had moments of being traumatized, but my family restored a secure environment as quickly as possible to relieve immediate distress and repair my sense of safety.

• • •

My mother admired Baldie's husband, Larry, and respected him as a businessman. He was well-known in North Richmond and enjoyed drinking a glass of wine socially, but he was strictly business-minded. He was a people-person and used the social aspect of the Down Beat to find more trucking contracts from movers and shakers in the Bay Area, who often came to his nightclub.

Larry had several contracts to haul lumber, Christmas trees, fruits, and vegetables and always kept his fleet of trucks on the road. He hired Black men from the neighborhood to work as truck drivers and taught them how to drive long-distance hauls. He was a really hard worker and an entrepreneur kind of guy. He was like the dean of the Black truckers, because he started buying big diesel trucks and hauling for big lumber industries.

His last contract was with Judson Steel. In June 1972, he passed out at the steel company and died on the job. His doctor had told him not to go back to work because of his heart condition, but he slipped out, got in his truck, and drove back to work, right to the end of his life. He was quite a provider for his family. My cousin Larry had just graduated from John F. Kennedy High School and, at eighteen years old, immediately stepped into his father's role of running the family trucking business.

North Richmond Missionary Baptist Church

S&S Market Little League Team

Ermestine and her mentor Ruby Bims visiting New York

GAME CHANGER 10

S&S MARKET

One morning as a small child, I woke up to the purr of my father's truck and knew he was headed for work. My father was a hardworking man whose mission was to provide for his family by advancing to higher-paying positions at American Standard. I could hear my mother in the kitchen, preparing oatmeal and talking on the phone about a meeting she was going to attend later in the afternoon. I wondered whether I was going with her to the meeting or to my grandmother's, which was my preference. After breakfast, it was clear I was going to the meeting, because Mother told me to put on my dress and patent-leather shoes and find my little purse and gloves.

My parents didn't have babysitters other than our grandparents, so the norm was for me to go with Mother wherever she went. She created a little box with crayons, coloring books, and storybooks; everywhere we went, that box was with us. In time, the contents of the little box changed to *Ebony*, *Jet*, and *Life* magazines, chapter books, newspapers, maps, and a calculator.

Sitting in the meeting, Mother was dressed in her best Jacqueline Kennedy attire, facing two White men—bank executives.

It was the 1960s and she believed it was a fashion mandate to wear white gloves every day; she never attended a meeting without them. Mother started acquiring a collection of gloves, some fabric, some leather, and always kept a spare pair in her car and briefcase.

The younger man asked her where she was from.

She responded, "Oklahoma."

He smiled and said, "So you're an Okie."

She did not respond to his comment but slowly began removing her gloves, finger by finger, folding the gloves neatly and placing them on her lap.

The older man was thumbing through some paperwork and said, "Unfortunately, there is no financing available. The federal government won't insure a bank loan to you."

She pulled out her folders and responded, "I am a Negro woman with money, and I want to purchase this store."

She started negotiating, smiling occasionally and eyeing me frequently while talking business. That was the first time I saw my mother square off with White men; she was so smooth with her responses. She raised her voice level, looked the men straight in the eye, and said her piece, then began putting on her gloves and gathering her belongings. Meanwhile, the older man sat quietly behind his desk, organizing some papers.

Then she said, "You know, even a small mouse has anger. Did you know that?" I had heard her make that same comment to her mother, when my grandmother was trying to calm her down about one problem or another.

The man didn't say a word, just nodded his head and said, "Nice talking with you, Mrs. Petgrave."

She added a comment new to my ears: "Well, I am a pretty brave woman from working on Forty Acres and a Mule, so I'm telling you point-blank, I am angry, because you are treating me unfairly. Come on, Gloria."

On the way home, she passed by S&S Market, pulled into the parking lot, and said, "This is going to be our new home and store."

She pulled off her gloves, picked up a writing pad, and began drawing a diagram of the building. "This is where I am going to open my real estate office," she said, pointing to the garage. "Those White folks are going to know who I am, and I am not an Okie. My mother owned her land, and she probably owns more land than they do. These White men are not going to restrict me or cut me out of the legitimate financing that is available."

We sat in the parking lot for a while, and she considered changes and repairs she wanted to make to the building. After surveying the building and thinking out loud about possibilities, she slowly cruised through the neighborhood, identifying other businesses, churches, schools where people she already knew lived and worked within the community. She was excited about the possibilities and more determined than ever to purchase the store.

• • •

The zoning for the surrounding area was commercial, light industry, and residential. Across the street on Ohio Avenue were railroad tracks and blocks of light industrial businesses. Around the corner of Eighth and Ohio was the Richmond School District building, bustling with employees. Across the street on Seventh and Florida was St. Luke Missionary Baptist Church, a gathering place for neighborhood children who participated in youth activities provided by the church.

As she cruised the neighborhood, Mother would stop and talk with people outside, ask questions about who they were, where they lived, where they worked. She would shoot questions so fast, they didn't have a chance to inquire about who she was. Every day after picking me up from school, she would continue surveying the neighborhood and passing out her real estate business cards.

She would always end these conversations with, "If you are interested in selling or buying property, or know someone who is, get in touch with me." Mother basically introduced herself to the entire community before knowing whether she had successfully qualified to purchase the store.

• • •

After Mother's meeting with the loan officers at the bank, she told my father she felt that they were trying to redline her from buying the store. She was openly upset.

"They don't want to give Black people the type of loans they are giving Whites, but we're not going to buy that store the way they want us to."

My father asked her, "Why do you think that?"

She responded, "Just like that cross that appeared in our front yard means something to me, I believe I am encountering racism, trying to exclude us from having legitimate mortgages. We are going to buy that store. Your sister keeps saying I'm an Okie, and both of you were raised in Richmond. So you don't see it the way I do. But believe me, I see it and I feel it. But I am Tressie Williams's daughter. They just don't know who they are dealing with."

Not long after that, my parents signed a mortgage contract to purchase S&S Market. They excitedly talked about the possibilities, and my father was 100 percent on board. Mother was proud of herself for taking a stand and demanding the same interest rate as Whites. I am not sure if the mortgage came from that same bank we visited, but she was certainly becoming well known within banking institutions throughout Richmond.

Moving to our new home, and opening the store and real estate office, was an adventure. One morning while reading the newspaper, Mother found an auction that was selling store equipment that day. It was a "dress, patent-leather shoes, gloves, and purse" day for me, for sure. A variety of used store equipment was for sale: shelving, meat counters, cash registers, produce counters. The auction was full of White men.

Mother was dressed in a pencil skirt that showed her legs, a tight-fitting sweater, pumps, and gloves—dressed up, but not in a flamboyant way. She kept putting her gloves on and taking them off, writing down the items she had bid on and their prices. Pretty soon Mother was feeling good about her accomplishment at the auction: getting all the equipment she needed to open the store, along with some office furniture (desks, typewriters, adding machines).

She did worry about her husband's reaction to spending so much money. My father didn't share the same vision as my mother and didn't always agree with her decisions, but in the end, he supported her efforts while continuing to work at the factory. Mother was operating the store and the real estate office, becoming a businesswoman as well as being a wife and mom.

Above the store were two living units; the smaller one, Mother rented to a pastor who worked in a local factory and left for work and returned home about the same time each day as my father. His stay-at-home wife and young son, who was a few years older than I, were visible through our kitchen windows as they went about their daily activities. Because he was a preacher, church folks were always visiting their apartment. These were my parents' first tenants.

My mother's store was truly a one-stop community asset; it carried at least one of any item you could find at Lucky or Safeway, including household goods, medicine, hosiery, groceries, beauty products, toiletries, meat, produce, and toys at Christmastime. I loved going with her to the Oakland Produce Market in the Jack London Square neighborhood. The Produce Market was a hustle-and-bustle environment, with lots of loud talking and activity.

The streets surrounding the market were always humming with sounds of forklifts and teeming with the smells of fresh fruit and vegetables. Groups of small business owners walked around crates and pallets of fresh produce speaking a variety of languages. Storage rooms were packed to the brim with a variety of produce. We would spend hours walking around, selecting items to load into our pickup truck and sell at our store. They had the best cherries. During trips to Jack London Square, my mother always dressed very professionally, but she often had to lift boxes and put them onto the truck. Sometimes the men who worked at the Square would help us, but she didn't depend on that. We would head back to Richmond, happily eating the delicious cherries, and I would read a storybook out loud while she drove.

• • •

Every morning after I got dressed for school, Mother would take me into a little storage unit behind the cash register counter and comb my hair, stopping to wait on customers. Neighborhood customers were always coming in and out, and Mother had become well known throughout the community. The store became a focal point where customers would come in with the neighborhood gossip and discuss politics, community efforts, schooling, housing, you name it. Mother let neighborhood residents get merchandise or food on credit when they were going through hard times. Once her real estate office became famous, clients from other neighborhoods began to seek her out while trying to become homeowners or rent apartments.

Mother was a talker, was incredibly curious, asked many questions, and always thought outside the box. She would soon know everything about your life and your goals and would quickly sum up her viewpoint of who you were. After listening to both Black and White customers share their experiences of becoming homeowners, she recognized just how unequal the playing field was. She knew that Blacks were being schemed against and discriminated against.

One comment that would send her into a rage was when someone referred to her or her family as Okies. During conversations while she was grilling some folks, they in turn would ask about her and where was she from. If they responded with, "Ooh, so you're an Okie," that would end every conversation very quickly. She would sometimes proudly use the term herself to mean a smart, fearless, and determined woman, but if someone used it against her, watch out.

• • •

The neighborhood kids were Black children and White children who attended Nystrom and Lincoln Elementary schools, with working fathers and stay-at-home mothers, living in a supportive community. The store became the neighborhood spot for children to gather and play in the parking lot. I would go into the store and sneak out candy bars, ice cream, and snacks for my friends to enjoy. We would sit for hours on the exterior stairs, watching customers come and go, talking and playing.

My parents were happy and content with achieving their goals, with family members intricately integrated into their daily lives, and living in communities where Black economic opportunities and property ownership opportunities were on the rise.

Nystrom Elementary School, Richmond, CA Class Picture, 1956-57

Alonza Hill, a rebel for the Nystrom Elementary School community

Gloria as a sixth-grade student in Mr. Hill's class

GAME CHANGER 11

MR. HILL

As a child, I attended Nystrom Elementary School and loved it. I walked just three blocks to school with my friends, whom I would join as they passed our store every morning.

Blacks in the community believed that the school board did not care about Nystrom Elementary School. Blacks were well aware that upper-middle-class children living in El Cerrito and attending the "hill schools" performed much better academically than children in segregated Black schools. Black schools were characterized as inadequate, both physically and educationally.

My sixth-grade teacher was Mr. Alonza Hill, a moderately short, handsome Black man with a professional style and demeanor. He was always suited up in work attire, with a tie complementing his suit. He was well-organized, motivated students, and elicited maximum teacher respect.

I never forgot the moment my classmate David, who lived around the corner from us, was talking while Mr. Hill was illustrating at the blackboard. Mr. Hill paused and threw an eraser across the room toward David. Everyone in the room froze. He walked toward David, picked the eraser up off the floor, and walked a few feet away. Standing in the middle of the classroom, he said to everyone, with his eyes sternly looking at David, "Your parents send you to school every day to learn, and that's what you are going to do! David, you know our class rules; I expect you to follow them."

Mr. Hill returned to the blackboard and resumed illustrating a math equation. I glanced at David. He was my friend and frequently helped me with my chores at the store. The teacher had David's full attention from that day on, and David began to behave quite well. Most teachers would doubtless choose a different approach than eraser throwing, but in this instance I suppose it had the desired effect.

At the end of fifth grade, Mr. Hill had appointed me captain of the Safety Patrol, which had strict requirements, procedures, and responsibilities. Mr. Hill had high standards and expectations for everyone on the Patrol, and I was proud of my position. I was the only one wearing a Captain's badge, took my job seriously, and, like Mr. Hill, expected respect for that role from my friends.

Directly in front of the school, close to the crosswalk, was a serious drainage problem. On rainy days the drains would back up so much that crossing the street required wading in knee-high water. Mr. Hill secured funds to buy the Safety Patrol knee-high boots, new raincoats, and helmets. On rainy days, the Safety Patrol (and sometimes Mr. Hill himself) would carry small children across the pond of water to dry land. We aimed to please and never knew when Mr. Hill might be watching us.

One day, Mr. Hill stopped by the store. Minutes before his arrival, Mother had been fussing about my spelling test grade. While paying for his items, Mr. Hill smiled at me and said, "Mrs. Petgrave, your daughter is an outstanding captain for the school's Safety Patrol!"

I had been in a cloud of gloom a few seconds before, but upon hearing his words, both my mother and I were smiling and proud.

Mother started firing off questions about Mr. Hill's family and history, as she was known to do. What college did he graduate from? What did his wife do? How many children did he have? What schools did they attend? Where did he live?

After Mr. Hill left the store, I knew about him on a personal level. Mother said, "Glo, you are doing well in some areas but have much work to do in others. Where is your spelling test? We are going to learn all the words you got wrong."

I practiced spelling those words until I went to bed.

The next morning, while combing my hair in our secret, out-of-view-from-customers space, Mother said, "Mr. Hill is an excellent teacher and cares about his students. There may be one, and only one, Mr. Hill in the district. I am happy he is your teacher. Pay attention in class, act like you have good sense, and learn from him."

She quizzed me on how to spell the words again before I left for school. She was a teaching mother, with high expectations for her daughter, and she always demanded that I strive for the best.

Mr. Hill will forever be a wonderful memory in my mind. He demonstrated high expectations, was creative with teaching strategies, showed compassion, and gave both students and parents respect. He cultivated a sense of belonging and was always quick to give praise and recognition. He was able to create a learning environment that emphasized that everyone could be successful, and he demonstrated flexibility and patience.

Mr. Hill was one of the few teachers who left a positive impression in my heart and brain. I believe he made a lasting impression on most of the students he taught at Nystrom Elementary School. He was, in fact, a model of the teacher I later strove to be for my students. He was a mirror of the teachers I wanted, searched for, recruited, and treasured during my principalships.

Mr. Hill eventually became principal of Nystrom, and for many years after I graduated from elementary school, he would periodically stop by the store, buy some snacks, and talk with Mother.

They would discuss discrepancies in school budgets, the quality of teachers, and evidence of low expectations for certain schools, and talking with him refueled Mother's desire to purchase a house in the El Cerrito hills. He also engaged in conversation with customers, children, and parents entering and leaving while he ate his snacks. Everyone in the community admired and respected Mr. Hill.

Mr. Hill taught students based on solid values and truth. He used his magnetic leadership skills to advocate for his students' success. Mr. Hill's shoes were too big for his students to fill, but their shoe size was perfect for his expectations. And his support continued after school hours. Periodically, on Saturday mornings he would pick up four male students in the Nystrom neighborhood for a mentoring day. Before returning them home, he presented every student with a new white shirt to change into and took them to a sit-down dinner at a nice restaurant.

And then there were Nystrom's annual talent shows, which gave students a chance to show off their special skills, involved the community, and were exciting and fun. Mr. Hill was always scouting talent. All students in his sixth-grade class participated. No experience was required for student actors, comedians, singers, dancers, musicians, artists, writers, or builders as well as those in behind-the-scenes roles. Students chose a performance piece, rehearsed consistently after school, and performed in the standing-room-only school auditorium. Under Mr. Hill's leadership, students planned and created props, sets, and costumes, and had fun doing it. Mr. Hill choreographed a dance and rehearsed with us until we were confident performing it. I remember my friend David was my partner, and we were awesome!

• • •

Maritime Child Development Center, located next to Nystrom, had been created during the war so White women could work around the clock at the shipyards and sleep overnight with their children if they chose to. As a student walking past the building to and from school, I knew that none of my Black friends attended, and it seemed common knowledge that Black children were not welcome there. But I was clueless that it was racism and discrimination that blocked my feet from entering. It was also common knowledge that Richmond School District's schools were segregated, based on the community the school was located in, and the race and socioeconomic class of the residents.

Despite or because of this exclusion, Black residents bonded together and networked with their family members, friends, and neighbors to ensure that working parents' children were taken care of. Mr. Hill stood with Black families at the forefront of the struggle for equality and did not allow imposed racism to handicap his goals.

The first time I stepped into Maritime Child Development Center was when I was on the Richmond Community Foundation board of directors in 2016. I was given a tour of the facility, a historic building brought back to life with the royalistic characteristics of its past in place. The beauty of the modernized historic building was captivating with the fallout shelter revitalized. My father's business a block away, my mother's store, about three, from a historic building that had meaning for Blacks.

During the tour I examined the fallout shelter to reduce casualties in a nuclear war. Events during the Cold War heightened the awareness of fallout shelters. During the late 1950s construction of fallout shelters was part of the civil defense program. None of my family members or friends had home shelters in place.

The cost could be very expensive. President John F. Kennedy recommended, "A fallout shelter for everybody, as rapidly as possible."

When shelters were being constructed, it was recommended that inhabitants remain in the space for at least two weeks following a nuclear blast and sleep in the shelter for at least three months. There were also public areas designated as fallout shelters and eventually converted to other uses.

Maritime Child Development Center located in the center of the Nystrom community was off limits for Blacks. I imagined hearing the sound of a bomb alert and folks sliding down to secure safety. And I also thought of Blacks living in the community with limited accessibility to safety during fearful times of war. No, that safety was not for us.

In time Americans began to accept that fallout shelters probably did little to protect them from a nuclear disaster and began using them for other purposes, storage, wine cellars. Fortunately, nuclear bombs were never dropped because Blacks may have been hard-pressed to find protection and this story would have had a traumatic ending.

• • •

One day, while I was riding through the El Cerrito hills with Mother as she evaluated potential real estate for her clients, she pointed out a corner house in a premium location on Arlington Boulevard, with a fence that provided complete privacy.

She said, "Glo, that's where Mr. Hill lives with his family. He achieved his goals. I am proud of him. He has a house in the hills, and one day I will, too."

Blacks moving to the El Cerrito hills, from her perspective, were indications of accomplishment, success, and overcoming discrimination. Through the years, I passed Mr. Hill's house frequently. Thinking back to how I saw him as a sixth-grade student, he reminds me of former President Barack Obama. Stylish and handsome, Mr. Hill selected his words deliberately to deepen one's understanding.

As a student, I had no plans of following in Mr. Hill's footsteps to become a teacher and principal. And when I did eventually become an educator myself, I never threw an eraser across the room. But there were many situations when I wanted to shake up students' thinking about teaching and learning. I also wanted to shake up the community's thinking about opportunity gaps, parenting, and active involvement by using a community approach to educating students. I wanted to shake up my staff with high expectations, a belief that all students can learn, and a healthy environment for teaching and learning. To embrace the community as a support system.

In 1984 Mother called me, extremely emotional, and sadly told me of Mr. Hill's death. Mr. Hill was fifty-six years old and the principal at Stege Elementary School when he died.

Ironically, I was principal of Stege Elementary School when I retired from West Contra Costa Unified School District in 2004. I had truly followed in Mr. Hill's footsteps. His shoe size was bigger, but my feet fit perfectly. Not surprisingly, student talent shows were an event I spearheaded as a teacher and principal at every school and community I worked in.

Fun time in the Down Beat (Big Larry and the Ellison brothers)

Ermestine at work

Dad, second from the right, a few months before spinal cord injury

GAME CHANGER 12

DANG LUCK!

One Friday evening, my parents and I were sitting at the kitchen table finishing dinner. Dad went into a top cabinet, pulled out a box, and returned to the table. He told us, "I bought a gun for our safety. Let me show you how to use it."

Moving her chair closer to Dad, Mother smiled and said, "Don't forget, I grew up on a farm and my dad had rifles."

Dad responded, "Maybe so, but I want to show you how to use this pistol."

He demonstrated step-by-step details of the gun and how to load, hold, aim, and fire it. He gave my mother an opportunity to explore and practice.

Early the next morning, my parents dropped me off at my grandparents' house and said they were going to practice shooting. When they returned to pick me up, my grandfather asked my father, "How did Sister do?"

My father responded, "Pretty good. With more practice, I won't worry when she is working in the store by herself."

"Pretty good?" Mother chimed in. "I can aim and hit a target almost as good as either of you, and you've both been in the Army!

Tell him, Dad—tell him that you taught all of your Okie kids how to shoot guns and that I was the best shooter. I don't need to practice anymore."

My grandmother, who was listening to the conversation silently, said, "Ermestine, practice shooting with your husband some more. You really need to know what you're doing. When you guys get home, hide the gun where you can quickly get to it."

On the way home, Dad decided to purchase another gun, so one would be hidden behind the store counter and one was upstairs in our residence. I was given explicit instructions about not touching the guns. Mother agreed to go for more shooting practice the next Saturday.

* * *

Returning home from school, I would change out of my clothes and go downstairs to the store and sit in the small, relatively quiet space behind the counter doing my homework while my mother waited on customers. My friends would come into the store to buy penny candy or something for their parents. I would hear their voices and come out to socialize.

After I finished my homework, the work began. At an early age, I was taught how to work the cash register, wait on customers, stamp prices on canned goods, clean and store returned soda bottles for pick up, and organize things on shelves. Mother didn't believe in idle hands. If my friends came into the store to visit, she would have them working with me while we were talking, and then she let them choose anything they wanted to eat. She made working fun, always talking about learning, and my friends loved to visit me in the store.

One day a White man who lived with his family across the street in front of the railroad tracks came into the store to buy his weekly supply of liquor. He was already a little tipsy when he entered the store and, as usual, my mother started asking him questions. Where is your family from? How long have you been living in your house? What do you do? How many kids do you have? The man slurred and stuttered his responses. But for some reason he clearly articulated the words "Blacks would rather be by themselves, so we are planning to sell our house soon."

Mother was quick with her rebuttal: "What are you talking about? Are you drunk or something? We don't want to live in these run-down government projects. You can get a loan to move on; we have to fight for loans, pay a higher price, and get unfair interest rates. Take your liquor and get out of here, talking ignorant."

The man, a little older than my mother, took his money out of his wallet, grabbed his bag, and stared at my mother. After she gave him his change, he said, "Thank you, Mrs. Petgrave," and stumbled out of the store.

Mother looked at me and said, "Lord have mercy, I can't stand ignorant folks."

She had lived in the Canal Projects, and she was right—nobody wanted to live in those dilapidated war-housing ghettos.

As another customer walked into the store and greeted my mother, I stepped out and watched that White man walk across the street and stumble up his stairs. His daughter and I were friends, and we frequently played together. I knew she had older brothers and that her mother didn't have a job. Her brothers, well known in the neighborhood, frequently came to the store and were always outside talking with their friends. Her mother was never seen; she would send her children to buy items. If her daughter hadn't shared with me bits and pieces about her mother, I would not have known that she lived in the house. Their daughter was my only White friend, and we had fun spending time together. I really liked her and was sorry to hear that they were going to move. But, as luck would have it, we ended up moving before them, and her father continued to come into the store years after to buy his liquor.

* * *

My parents' life took a chilling and dark turn in 1957, when they decided to paint the store. They hired painters who used a scaffold to paint the two-story building. That Friday, Mother and I were working in the store. I heard Dad's pickup truck returning home from work. He came into the store, put his lunch box on the stairs leading into the house, and said he was going to tell the painters to move the scaffold so that the neighborhood kids wouldn't play on it over the weekend. Mother continued to work behind the meat counter serving a customer, and two other customers were shopping with their kids.

A few minutes later, there was the sound of a loud bang and voices screaming. Everyone ran outside, where a tragedy had unfolded. My father was lying on the ground with the scaffold on top of him. He was not moving, unresponsive; everyone was in shock. While my father was helping the painters move the scaffold, a wheel had come off, and the scaffold fell right on his back.

Mother ran into the store and called 911, and a small crowd of neighbors began to gather. The ambulance arrived and transported Dad to Brookside Hospital. I will never forget the fear in my mother's eyes. At the age of thirty-five, my father had suddenly become paralyzed. He was unable to continue his career with American Standard. From that day on, my mother and I spent hours and hours every day visiting Dad in the hospital, and she always encouraged him to keep his spirits high.

* * *

Mother decided to hire employees to work in the store so she could spend more time at the hospital with Dad. One of the employees she hired was Shirley, a White lady who lived in the neighborhood. Shirley stood five feet four inches tall and weighed over three hundred pounds, and she had a very distinct and pungent body odor, but she had a unique personal style, always thoughtfully put together: Her hair was always in a bouffant, with every strand in curls neatly held in place with hair lacquer. Shift dresses and muumuus in bold prints were her favorite garments, accessorized with a sash tied into a bow around her neck. Her look was completed with flawless makeup and a flower in her hair to match her attire.

Shirley had been renting an apartment in the neighborhood for years. From listening to her share bits and pieces of her life, I recall that she was childless and divorced from a man who had mentally and physically abused her. Shirley never spoke of family members or friends. I believe that for many years, we were her family. She was friendly but didn't take any mess from customers. She quickly became a valuable, loyal, and long-term employee to Mother, worked long shifts, and was a good babysitter for me when she worked in the store. Overall, a hardworking lady.

Throughout the years, Mother trained and hired many store employees but trusted few. She trusted Shirley completely, however, and appreciated Shirley's work ethic.

Now Mother did not worry about leaving me at home while she attended meetings or worked in real estate, since Shirley was there working. Whether in the real estate office, the store, my bedroom, or outside playing, I was always within earshot of Shirley's voice calling my name. She regularly inquired about my homework and gave instructions to complete it before she would allow me to engage in other activities.

Shirley was my unofficial nanny. I would ask her permission to do things, and I followed her directions while Mother was busy taking care of business. Twice, when the store was robbed, Shirley and I were working behind the counter together and were later subpoenaed to go to court. Her court attire was the same as her work attire: a colorful dress accessorized with jewelry that matched perfectly, perfume, and lots of makeup.

Shirley was sympathetic to Mother's situation and very supportive. She didn't own a car and would walk to work during the day, or else Mother would pick her up in the morning and take her home in the evening. Years later, Shirley was fatally stabbed in the back while walking home one evening. I had not seen Shirley for years before her death, but memories of spending time with her in the store, her smile and mannerism, remain vivid in my mind.

• • •

Dad was transported to Veterans Administration Hospital in Long Beach, where he remained for more than three years. At least twice a month, Mother and I would drive to Long Beach to visit him in the hospital. The trip took over seven hours one way, with Mother sharing memories of her past, making me read a school textbook out loud, and then asking me questions to check my comprehension skills. We would also eat on the trip, and that little box of activities for me would always be in the car. After that long drive, we would remain at the hospital for hours, my mother talking business and future plans, my father inquiring about family members and what was going on in my life.

It was an unforgettable experience to see, firsthand, war veterans wounded from enemy action or from operational activities in war zones. I witnessed injured veterans lying on permanent gurneys, limbless, with metal penetrating their heads, paralyzed from the head down, the waist down, missing body parts, distorted faces.

My father was one of the oldest patients there, and in bad shape, but there were so many younger men in worse situations.

My father acquired friends while living in the hospital. When my mother and I would visit, they would pass by in wheelchairs, lying flat on gurneys—smiling, laughing, and trying to move forward with huge new challenges.

"Hey, Ike, game of dominoes later?"

"Ike, I didn't know your wife was visiting."

My mother, in her natural manner, began asking questions about their lives. Where were they from, what did their parents do? Were they married, did they have kids? One question I never remember her asking is "How were you injured?"

I remember one young man in particular. He had stopped by Dad's bed and began sharing his story. He left his wife and two children and joined the Army, thinking it would provide better opportunities for his family. He was now a paraplegic and, once he returned to the United States, discovered that his wife had had a new baby with one of his best friends. While he shared his story with my mother, tears were rolling down his cheeks. He said that he was twenty-two years old, with a broken heart and a broken body.

I remember glancing at my mother; she, too, had tears streaming down her face. The young man shook it off, wiping tears away, and said, "Ike, we're planning a domino game tomorrow; you in?"

Dad, who loved playing dominoes, nodded yes and said, "I'm in."

And with that the young man rolled his gurney down the hall. The three of us watched him and my mother said, "That was so sad to me."

My father responded, "Everything in this place is sad and hard to swallow."

• • •

My father's life had changed in an instant and would never be the same. At thirty-three, my mother had to assume all responsibilities for running the store and real estate office as well as raising a child. My grandparents' visits to our house occurred more frequently. Grandfather provided support to both daughters, running the Down Beat at night and helping in Mother's store during the day.

Grandmother provided spiritual support and encouragement and helped her daughters with household chores. There were always tasks on Mother's to-do list. I remember my grandmother's unflinching, straight-in-the-eye contact while very firmly telling her, "God has always shown up for me when I was going through severe storms in life. I had faith that he would take me through the storm. God and God alone will get you through. Take time for God. You are not honoring the Sabbath! Keep it holy! Get into God's words and spend time with God. Instead of working in the store or your real estate office on Sundays, make sure you have a good relationship with God."

I focused on Mother and her response. Her eyes teared up, and tears trickled down her cheeks. Very emotionally, shaking and crying, she said, "Mom, you just don't understand the roads I walk, the struggles I face."

Grandmother stepped into Mother's space and looked directly into her eyes. "I am not saying to settle for the road with less resistance. I am just saying trust in God to guide the path you walk. Everything that glitters is not gold." Grandmother embraced my crying mother in a hug.

I left the kitchen, headed for my bedroom with tears flowing, and Mother went to bed earlier than usual. I got into bed with her, no words spoken, just loving smiles. Emotionally drained, she quickly fell asleep. I stared at her for hours, thinking about what she was going through, before going back to my bedroom. That night I saw her fear and understood the journey she was frightened of from a more adult view.

From that point on, more frequently than not, the three of us sat side by side in church pews. Mother did not drift aimlessly day to day but remained focused on a long-term direction: finding a way to balance her life and attend church with her mother.

While her husband was hospitalized, Mother continued to follow her innate drive to do better for her family and her community. She decided to invest in properties to help enable Blacks to be property owners in their own communities and have the ability to rent in locations of their choice.

It was a challenge for her to do without her husband's salary, but she was determined and wouldn't take no for an answer. She refinanced the first property, bought the liquor license, and hired more employees to keep the store open later hours, and the business continued to grow.

Mom's real estate mentors with William Martin, migrants to the Bay Area, fighting throughout their lives for the rights of Blacks to become homeowners

Doug Ellison, Richmond Police Department, hired in 1946

S&S Market, the family home and store

GAME CHANGER 13

FEAR

In the dead of night, I woke up to the sound of glass breaking. Running toward Mother's bedroom, I saw her pull the gun from under her mattress then race to the living room window. She grabbed a hammer that she kept in the piano stool, broke the window, and began shooting down toward the store while yelling for whomever it was to go away and leave us alone.

On another occasion, someone broke into the real estate office and managed to get into the store from there to rob us. My mother woke up and heard voices downstairs. She came into my bedroom and shook me awake, then put her finger to her mouth, signaling me to be quiet. When I saw the gun in her hand, I knew there was trouble. We tiptoed into the kitchen, and she dialed 911. My mother and I hid in my bedroom closet, fearful that the burglars would come upstairs. We remained in the closet, holding each other, scared and crying, until we heard the police sirens.

• • •

During this time, the Richmond Police Department was hiring more young Black officers. In 1946 my Aunt Lillian's brother-in-law,

Douglas Ellison, was hired, becoming the second Black police officer on the Richmond force, and he eventually rose through the ranks to become sergeant. He owned several pieces of property and lived in North Richmond. His wife, a strikingly beautiful, soft-spoken person, raised their two sons.

Doug had an athletic physique and a lovely smile, and he was a professional fighter. In uniform, he was regal, purposeful, and dedicated to serving the community. During his days off, Doug would be dismantling cars at Study Boys' wrecking yard, at home, or fishing. He would spend his leisure time fishing with my grandfather and talking about life. Around family members, Doug was pure-hearted and a fun guy, a big brother who did not tolerate nonsense.

It was comforting when Doug would arrive on the scene of a crime—strong, fearless, and reassuring us that everything would be all right. The police officers were always able to calm Mother down and restore a sense of peace.

Mother let it be known that she was going to protect herself and her daughter with her gun, if necessary. The police officers repeatedly told her that if she were to shoot someone for breaking in, she could be held liable. Douglas Ellison told her to think about getting a guard dog that would bark and make us aware of unwanted activity around us. A few days later, we went to the dog pound and found a miniature salt-and-pepper poodle. Mother named him La Chant. After transitioning into his new home, La Chant would bark and alert us to visitors. He slept on my bed every night, and I felt much safer with him around.

Thirty-year-old patrolman Arthur Lee Johnson (also known as Lee Arthur Johnson) was younger than Doug, and he was kind and reassuring. My first encounter with Arthur Lee Johnson was when I was eighteen, and he responded to my 911 call. Two men had started fighting each other inside the store, knocking products off the shelves and scuffling on the floor. Angrily they followed each other into the parking lot and continued fighting. After an intense battle, each bleeding and stumbling, they parted ways before Arthur Lee arrived.

I was in awe when he walked into the store. Tall, with a unique swagger. Confident, with a calming tone of voice and a beautiful smile, for my mother and me he exemplified strength, courage, and safety. After I graduated from high school, Mother began leaving me in charge of the store more frequently for short periods of time while she showed property to clients or dealt with other business-related matters. Leaving me alone in the store promoted a sense of becoming an adult, but the fighting incident made me afraid to run the store by myself.

Mother began to think that burglaries were happening frequently because most people knew that she and I lived alone in the apartment above the store. As females, we were intimidated and felt very threatened. I think we were viewed as easy targets. Mother also felt that some viewed the location of our liquor store as a deprived area, and a lack of security precautions increased the risk of our being victims of crime.

We continued to struggle with repeat victimization. Most of the burglaries occurred between one and six in the morning, and burglars would enter the store by forcing door locks or breaking doors or windows. Their target goods were cigarettes or bottles of alcohol. Only one door separated our residence from the store, and our fear was always that one day burglars would get into our house. I was afraid of having to look into the eyes of a nervous person pointing a gun, demanding money.

Doug and Arthur Lee frequently monitored and patrolled our store, to show a police presence and make my mother feel safer. I still remember the persistent fear of burglars invading our home and my nightly prayers for God to watch over us.

* * *

Pastor Davis and his wife and son were still tenants in the unit next to ours; it was comforting to have them nearby. One day, however, Pastor Davis went to work and never returned. He was burned to death at his job at the factory. His wife and son continued to rent the unit for many years after the accident. Mother respected their privacy, and seldom did they visit one another, but we all knew we were there for each other.

I really liked spending time with another next-door neighbor, Josalind Hall. Her father went to work every day, and her mother was a housewife. Josalind had siblings who were younger fraternal twins. I was a few years older than she was but loved to visit her house. It was rare that I went inside any of my friends' houses; Josalind's house was the only one that my parents gave me permission to enter. From my young viewpoint Josalind had the perfect family, and they were the first occupants of a brand-new home. I always smelled the aroma of a baked cake as we walked down the hallway to her bedroom, and there was a fireplace in the living room that I wished we had at our house.

And then there was the tea party celebrating Josalind's twelfth birthday. Four girls in stockings and high heels, with special hairstyles and touches of makeup for the occasion. We sat in Josalind's living room, eating delicious food on her mother's best china. Mrs. Hall was teaching us to be young ladies while creating an unforgettable moment on her daughter's birthday. She had a way of crafting pleasant memories by making special gifts and presenting them to surprised friends and neighbors.

Josalind and I would spend hours sitting in her family's parked car in front of the driveway, people-watching, talking, and eating snacks that I had snuck out of the store. But none of those snacks compared to the buttery popcorn balls Mrs. Hall made or the desserts she prepared. Those were my special treats.

* * *

About three years after my father's accident, he returned home from the hospital in a wheelchair. A water-powered elevator was installed, so my father could come and go as he pleased. He would take Josalind and me to the drive-in theater. He had to have been so bored, but the three of us sitting in his car, eating and watching the newest movies to hit the screen, was fun for me.

During the work week, Dad spent his time taking me to school or picking me up in the car, watching TV in the kitchen, cooking, cleaning, and playing dominoes with visitors. Mother felt that he was not doing all he could do to learn to walk again. She wanted him to show more effort. He tried to please her, but after a while both of them came to the realization that he would never walk again.

One evening my father and I were sitting at the kitchen table, watching the *Amos 'n' Andy* TV show. I was doing my homework, with schoolbooks scattered in front of me, but my focus was on watching TV. My mother came into the kitchen and observed what was going on, became angry, and yelled, "Turn off that TV. The *Amos 'n' Andy Show* is demeaning toward Blacks, and there is nothing to learn from watching them."

She walked over, turned off the TV, and said, "Gloria, do your homework."

My father reached over and turned the TV back on and said, "Gloria can do her homework after this show is over. We're both watching it, and the show will end soon."

Mother was standing near the stove. She grabbed an iron skillet, threw it through the TV, and said, "She won't be watching this TV. Now do your homework!"

My father, who was a peaceful, quiet, and calm man, was shocked—and so was I. He looked at the TV, put his wheelchair in motion, picked up his car keys and coat, and said as he left, "You are crazy!"

I remember watching him go down the ramp to the elevator and thinking, "What about me? Wait, take me with you!"

I began opening my schoolbooks and doing my homework. Mother ranted and raged while cleaning up the mess made by her breaking the TV. She made it clear that, in order to be successful and get somewhere, I needed to concentrate on homework and learning, not on *Amos 'n' Andy*. And for the first time, I heard her pass along my grandfather's advice to me, "Get an education, because that's the only thing no one can take from you."

She preached to me for over an hour about the importance of learning, working hard, and making good grades to go to college.

"Damn *Amos 'n' Andy*," she yelled on her way downstairs to work in the store. "Oh, and tomorrow after school, put on your dress, patent-leather shoes, and get your purse. You are going with me to a meeting to take care of some business."

The next day, we went to Mechanics Bank, where she met with the bank manager, a professional-looking older White man; we met with him frequently as the years went by. He greeted her with a big smile, "Hello, Mrs. Petgrave. Please have a seat; it's always a pleasure to see you!"

By 1962 my mother had decided to purchase vacant lots and build and invest in multifamily apartment buildings; this way she could continue to help enable Blacks to rent or buy property. She had become a businesswoman functioning on her own terms and fighting hard to achieve equal rights.

At the time it was not uncommon to see whole houses lifted off their foundations, loaded on giant dollies, and moved to different locations. Sometimes you might see Mother cruising behind her house to its new location. She knew how to make it happen.

Her primary reason for meeting with the bank manager on this day was to purchase three more vacant lots and buy houses to relocate to those lots. Two hours later, she signed the necessary paperwork. On the way home, she shared her plans to buy more real estate. She said, "One thing I've noticed is that, if you have an education, money, or property, people treat you a little differently."

Mother had an innate drive to push herself, her family, and her community. During business meetings with powerful White men, she refused to back down and was quick to respond to racial barriers with angry words that left no doubt how she was feeling. She supported and was active in the Neighborhood House of North Richmond and the NAACP. Her goal was always to create opportunities where none existed.

That weekend my father and I went out and bought a new TV for the kitchen. Sitting in his wheelchair, waiting for the salesperson to put the TV in the trunk of his car, he looked at me, smiled, and said, "That Okie is not going to tell me what to do!"

I was happy he was buying a new TV, but I also knew he would never say that in front of my mother. We both knew that her response would not be good. She could be an exploding firecracker, creating an array of sparks surrounding you.

My father was very thrifty with his spending, but he purchased a much nicer TV than the one Mother had smashed with the skillet. When we returned home, he sat outside our store until a customer he knew passed by, and he asked the man to carry the TV upstairs. He set up the TV for Dad, put the antenna on top, and the three of us watched TV for some time.

From that point on, the living room was where I did my homework. My TV-watching time came after Dad had checked my completed homework; we secretly watched *Amos 'n' Andy* when my mother wasn't around.

The show began in 1928 as one of the first hugely popular radio comedy series, and it was created, written, and voiced by two White actors playing the roles of Black men.

In 1951 *Amos 'n' Andy* was adapted to television and used Black actors in the main roles. The NAACP protested, describing the show as "a gross libel of the Negro and distortion of the truth," and consequently the television show was canceled in 1953. But my father and I loved *Amos 'n' Andy* and found it very entertaining. Whenever we heard Mother's footsteps as she came up the stairs from the store, we quickly changed the channel so we could keep peace and harmony surrounding us.

Cousin Larry and Grandmother Tressie after church

First introduction of half-sister, Geneva. Family women: Grandmother Tressie, Yvonne and her mother, Baldie, half-sister Geneva

GAME CHANGER 14

CLICK-CLACK TRACKS

I loved to open my bedroom window to feel the fresh air and listen to the birds chirping, or see and hear the trains rolling down the tracks across the street. My dog La Chant's favorite spot was curled up at the foot of my bed, but he always joined me in observing from the window. We would watch each train on its journey, and I would fantasize about where it began and where it was going to end. Trains to me were a strong force of energy, noisy but peacefully entertaining. They came to signify even more after my cousin Larry's young friend was killed while playing on the train tracks. On the day of the tragedy, Larry was visiting Aunt Lillian's brother-in-law, King Ellison, whose grandson was Larry's friend. Larry was watching cartoons at the time of his friend's violent death on the train tracks.

We struggled to comprehend this loss through reoccurring conversations about the sequence of events. Larry spoke often about his friend's death, retelling the freak train accident, believing he could have saved his friend's life instead of choosing to watch cartoons. From that point on, my observations out my window would be more bittersweet as, like clockwork, the trains would flow down the tracks, still noisy, still entertaining, and now also representing violence, suffering, and guilt.

I spent many an hour looking out my bedroom window or sitting on the exterior steps, eating an Oh Henry! candy bar, my grandfather's favorite, with no concerns about my chubbiness. I could see the store parking lot, with people coming and going, and hear their voices. I could see my school friends walking to the store, and after getting their attention I would rush into the store, where we would talk and laugh while they shopped. We would have fun and play games, like jumping rope and jacks. Our favorite activity was dancing. My friend Flo often got into trouble for taking too long getting back home, so I always walked her to the end of the block, dancing all the way. As soon as she crossed the street, she would begin running as fast as she could. We always had so much to talk about and enjoyed each other's company.

As an only child whose upbringing was predominantly led and shaped by where my parents came from and their own family culture, I valued spending time around my peers. My young mindset said, Life should flow smoothly like a train on a track. Of course, it didn't. For one thing, Dad's injury was a train wreck in our lives. And my world seemed different than that of most of my friends. I lived above the store with a Jamaican father, very humble in a wheelchair, and a mother proud of her Creek Freedmen heritage, transformed into a well-known businesswoman on a crusade for justice.

As a small-business owner from a marginalized community, Mother established relationships with banks to acquire loans. When Mrs. Petgrave walked in the door, bank employees knew who she was. She was bold and unapologetically unaccepting of underwriting based on her net worth, which—like that of many Blacks—was lower than the average for Whites. Quick minded she was, always calling out institutions in power while securing opportunities to use her property as collateral for loans in communities where property may have been redlined and have diminished capital. Fully embracing her new role and any controversy that came with it, she was not always politically correct in her mannerisms and in representing the side of the railroad tracks imposed on her.

As I stared through my open bedroom window, I often thought about my parents, their uniqueness and their connection through experiences co-creating their understanding of life. I practiced connecting dots through their past: Mother dealing with systemic racism, redlining, and economic disenfranchisement as a businesswoman. Dad creating a new life as a paraplegic trying to find a way to happiness. I looked for places that their stories intersected, intertwined, and separated again.

• • •

As an only child, I imagined that having sisters and brothers like my cousins did would be awesome. I thought they were lucky to have someone close to play with and spend time with. I looked forward to sleeping over at my aunts' houses. Aunt Lillian's daughter, Clarice, was a year older than I and had two older brothers. I loved spending time with her; my father and I would pick her up almost every Saturday, and we would ride around the Bay Area, eating, laughing, and discovering new places.

Clarice and I started getting interested in boys at about the same time. We got in trouble together on several occasions, and my mother begin to object to us hanging out together. Once, Clarice was going to spend the night at my house. We told my parents that we were going to walk to her friend's house. But our plans were really to connect with a couple of boyfriends and go to San Francisco. The guys picked us up from Clarice's girlfriend's house and we went to North Beach.

We had a great time, and this was my first experience of being around guys with a car, having fun. Needless to say, we didn't return home at the time my parents expected us. We asked the guys to drop us off around the corner from the store.

As Clarice and I were getting out of the car, my mother's car pulled up behind us. This was one of those dreadful moments. Clarice and I knew that trouble was ahead for us. As soon as the guys realized my mom was behind us in her car, they drove away, barely giving me time to close the car door; one of the guys was still in the back seat.

My mother lowered her car window and said, "Walk home and go straight to the kitchen table."

Clarice and I only had to walk around the corner, but we walked as slowly as possible, trying to get our story straight. After about an hour of interrogation and chastising from my mother and father, we were told to go to bed. But we knew this was not the end of the conversation.

The next morning, Aunt Lillian came to pick up Clarice, and the conversation began all over again, with more questions and more criticism about our decisions. After Clarice left, my mother was still angry, and she said that I would no longer be able to spend time with Clarice.

My father said, "Gloria doesn't have any sisters, and I think they should spend time together like sisters. Teenagers make mistakes. Let's hope they learn from this."

Mother screamed, "Gloria was born alone, and she will die alone," and exited the kitchen. I was confused and had a hard time understanding her message. Why was death thrown into the conversation?

After she left the room, my father looked at me, shook his head, and without saying a word, started flipping through the TV channels. I left the kitchen for my bedroom, where I opened the window and sat looking at customers coming and going. This time, when I saw my friends pass through the parking lot, I didn't holler at them to get their attention and engage in conversation.

I was deep in thought. Not only about the trouble I was in—I realized that a friend of Clarice's boyfriend, who was driving the car, had shown interest in me.

My father continued to provide opportunities for Clarice and me to be together. We still picked her up for our Saturday getaways. The three of us spent a lot of time together, and my father made sure we had a good time going from here to there. There were limitations to what we could do because he was in a wheelchair, but he could drive, so we would go from morning to night. We always ended up at Pearl's Soul Food and would sit in his car, eating and talking.

Father and daughter moments: Isaac and Gloria

Isaac and Baldie, brother-in-law and sister-in-law

Grandfather Roy retreats to his private space

GAME CHANGER 15

NOTHING LEFT TO HIDE

The last time I remember my mother and her sister-in-law being in the same room was a nightmare. Clarice and I were sitting at the kitchen table watching *Amos 'n' Andy.* My father was busy cleaning up the kitchen. Aunt Lillian came to get Clarice and started chatting with her brother. The last words she said were, "Ike, you guys haven't eaten yet?"

Next I heard the quick steps of my mother entering the kitchen. Clarice and I were focused on *Amos 'n' Andy,* so I didn't see what happened. All I know is that in a split second, Mother and Aunt Lillian were tussling on the floor. My father took the lap tray he always had resting on his knee, put it on the counter, and started yelling, "Hey, hey, break it up."

I was suddenly in the middle of a serious reality TV show.

Clarice was no longer sitting beside me but was instead hitting my mother on the head, screaming, "Get off my mother!"

Then came a big crash; my father was no longer in his wheelchair but lying on the floor in an unusual physical position. The loudness of his fall captured everyone's attention. Everything seemed to be in slow motion, they all froze, and no words were said as they released one another and got off the floor.

I rushed to my father to see if he was okay, kneeling beside him. Clarice and I helped him back into his wheelchair while Aunt Lillian watched. After evaluating the situation, Mother went back downstairs to work in her real estate office.

At first, no one said a word. Then Aunt Lillian said, "Come on, Clarice, get your things and let's go."

Clarice and I made eye contact as she gathered her belongings and left.

Dad put his lap tray back on and returned to cleaning the kitchen counter. I sat at the kitchen table, thinking about the drama I had just witnessed. Dad, who was by nature a quiet man, was clearly doing the same—reflecting and trying to figure out what had just happened. Finally, he spoke out loud.

"Do you think that just happened because I was letting you watch *Amos 'n' Andy*?" He knew I didn't have the answer. He looked at me, nodded his head in disbelief, and continued to clean.

After a while, I went downstairs to the store. Shirley had placed a "Be back in fifteen minutes" sign in the door window, and I noticed a couple of my friends standing on the ramp talking. I walked through the store and into Mother's real estate office. She was talking to Shirley about store business. I sat at a desk and listened to their conversation, but my mind was still playing repeat videos of what I had witnessed thirty minutes earlier. I imagined Shirley had heard all the commotion from our apartment and wondered what was going on upstairs.

The phone rang, and Shirley returned to the store. In her professional voice, Mother said, "Hello, Petgrave Realty. Mrs. Petgrave speaking. How can I help you?" After a brief conversation, she hung up, looked in my direction, and said, "The first time I met Lillie, she referred to me as an Okie, as if Okies are less-than. I can't ever forget that."

I remember staring out the window, trying to process what had happened. Mother glanced at me and said, "Glo, stop daydreaming. Go clean out the pop bottles and finish sorting them in the right containers for pickup."

That was my clue to get busy. I walked into the store and saw a neighborhood friend buying candy. We talked for a while and then she followed me into the supply room and sat on a box. We had a good time, talking, laughing, eating candy, and dancing while I cleaned out pop bottles.

Later that evening, Mother and I were on our way to visit her parents. I was quiet, and she, too, appeared to be in deep thought. As we turned the corner to park, she smiled, and with much confidence stated, "This Okie is going to try and make it, with or without a man."

Her words were etched in my mind before she even parked the car.

As I got out of the car, Grandmother rushed by me with a smile and handed my mother a small grocery list. Mother headed down the street to Jack Newell's store. Grandmother and I hugged each other before walking into the house.

Grandfather was eating ice cream in the kitchen as I entered. He looked up and said, "Come on in here, Glo, and have some ice cream with me. I heard you been having some drama at your house."

Grandmother had resumed reading her Bible at the dining room table. I was standing at the kitchen counter and heard her voice loud and clear. "Roy Williams, don't bring no gossip to our house. I don't want to hear it!" There were a few minutes of silence before she began to read the Bible out loud.

I glanced out the kitchen window and saw Mother walking to the porch. Grandfather washed out his ice cream bowl then quickly headed to his bedroom retreat to watch sports programs and finish packing his suitcase for a trip to Oklahoma. Grandfather frequently returned to Oklahoma to visit his other children, family, and friends. He was happy about his trip and eager to remove himself from more conversation with his wife about gossiping.

Mother walked into the kitchen, put the bag of groceries down, fixed a bowl of ice cream, and sat at the dining room table next to her mom, eating and listening to her mother reading from the Bible.

Pulling into the store parking lot later, as if reflecting on her day, Mother said, "Well, everything is now out in the open. There is nothing left to hide." She closed the car door, started talking to a customer who was parking her own car, and headed inside the store.

I got out and went straight into our house to see what my father was up to. But her words lingered in my ears. I was connecting the dots and realizing that a divorce was on the horizon.

My parents were extremely different in their temperaments, goals, and aspirations. Mother was very opinionated and headstrong. In the blink of an eye, she could become a powerful force of energy swallowing up your space. Dad was cool, calm, and collected. Never did he display aggressive traits or manners. The only time I saw a different view of him was when he was interacting with Mother in conflicts regarding business-related issues or about his sister.

My parents lived together until 1962, when Dad decided that he was ready to move into his own house. When he stopped asking, "Where is your mother?"; when Mother stopped worrying about where he was going or where he had been—that was the sign they were moving on to begin new chapters in their lives.

After their divorce, at the age of thirteen, I became a property owner. Instead of paying child support, my father gave one of his properties to my mother and a corner house on Nineteenth Street to me. Tenants lived in the house for years, and my mother collected rent on my behalf. The house was four blocks from my parents' first home and had similar features, including a white picket fence. Driving past the house, my mother would smile and say, "Glo, that's your house. Your father is taking care of you the best way he can."

Yes, the house was mine, but I didn't feel like a homeowner until I purchased my own house in Richmond Annex in 1977 at the age of 28. I didn't realize the significance of my father's gift toward generational wealth. I didn't connect to his commitment to leave a legacy for his grandchildren through real estate. The structural racism my parents encountered to acquire the property was beyond my viewpoint and understanding until much later in life.

• • •

In 1977, sitting in court attending an estate sale of property auction with Pop and Mother—the only Blacks in the courtroom—and I was outbidding others interested in buying the property.

I remember how awesome my emotions were when the judge's gavel indicated I was the new owner. The house was not in move-in condition, but it belonged to me and it had a view of the bay. Located in Richmond Annex with the zip code I needed for my daughter to attend the desired schools. After remodeling, we moved into our home a year later.

• • •

There are moments of clarity. As my mother said the day I realized my parents were going to get a divorce, "Everything is out in the open now, nothing left to hide"—and, I will add, "or say." But sometimes the truth really hurts, and no one ever spoke again of the incident in the kitchen with Aunt Lillian. My father was determined for Clarice and me to be treated as sisters. The love he instilled in us for each other prevailed. But I will always remember Clarice on top of Mother, my mother on top of Clarice's mother, and my father—all lying on the floor.

Clarice remained a constant throughout my life. She was indeed like my older sister, and we enjoyed spending time together. Most of the time we were doing things undercover. Some of my fondest memories are about Clarice and I getting into trouble while having fun, and then dealing with the consequences together.

My father moved into his own house, owned by his father. There were three houses on one parcel of land; the other two my grandfather rented to tenants. Sitting at my father's kitchen table, watching TV or doing homework, looking out the window, I would see his tenants or their friends coming and going. Each of us beginning a new phase in life. Exploring what could be and learning how to survive apart. Pushing beyond boundaries and discovering all that life had to offer.

Incidents and experiences from our past were the game changers affecting our way of thinking and doing.

Words expressed by mother years after the incident with Aunt Lillian had a profound effect on my psyche.

"Clarice was on top of me trying to help her mother. Where were you? Why didn't you try to help me?"

I never had a response, nor did she seem to expect one. Her message was crystal clear and let me know her thoughts and feelings regarding the matter, years later.

She was not angry with me at the time she spoke these words, just out of the blue she would convey that my actions were puzzling to her. An incident hard for me to forget or understand was still on her mind and I am sure my father's as well. And in response to her questions, I will never have an answer because I honestly don't know.

But now I think the dynamics of their sister-in-law relationship could have been influenced by the fact that mother was pregnant. Some sisters have a special love for their brother, and can feel like they are being trapped into marriage, or taken advantage of, turning what could have been a good sister-in-law relationship into a sour one from the very beginning. But at this point, why does it matter? Why do thoughts regarding this matter still dance around in my mind?

In high school, once again Clarice and I broke curfew. Fearful of the consequences, I talked Clarice into running away. We were discussing where we would go, what we were going to do. At that time her parents were adding a second floor level to their home. Clarice and I snuck up the ladder into the construction area, still planning what we were going to do. Ever so slightly we could hear her parents' voices below. It seems we had been hiding for hours before hearing movement on the ladder. Uncle Birt appeared and said, "What are you two doing up here? Get in the house." He slowly backed down the ladder and Clarice and I were in trouble again. I believe Mother would have liked more distance between Clarice and I. We were both academically good students but we were also into boys.

Birt and Lillian had four other children besides Clarice—Richard, Burt, Bruce, and Sonya.

Family time with grandchildren always a priority for Pop (William Martin)

My first home purchase, for me and my daughter Kim, later converted into Annex Child Development Center, after I married Al Scoggins

My grandparents' home, three houses down from my parents' first home. This is the home that Son kept returning to throughout his life, even though he owned his own.

PART THREE:

MAKING A NAME FOR HERSELF

Petgrave Realty Co.

SALES – EXCHANGE – REFINANCE

ERNESTINE PETGRAVE – Broker

112 South Seventh Street
Richmond, Calif. 94804

(415) 235-3328

Ermestine Petgrave, real estate advertisement

Isaac behind the counter in the Paper Shack

The Paper Shack in 2021

GAME CHANGER 16

THE PAPER SHACK

In 1960, my father opened his own business, the Paper Shack, a small store on Eleventh and Ohio Avenue, four blocks from Mother's store. In this tiny space, about the size of a two-car garage, he sold a large variety of candy, books, magazines, school supplies, greeting cards; nearly everything in his store was made of paper. The Paper Shack was a wonderland for neighborhood children, who loved to go there and buy candy. I would walk to the Paper Shack to visit my father. I loved joining him behind the counter as he sat in his wheelchair, interacting with customers.

Across the street from the Paper Shack was a Black-owned, popular, and thriving barbershop called Smitty's. Most neighborhood Black men came into the Paper Shack before or after getting a haircut or shave.

Both businesses provided a space where Black men would gather to relax, talk about events of the day, and become more knowledgeable about the world they lived in. The two businesses were a social and cultural environment for exchanging stories, analyzing what was occurring within the community, and discussing obstacles Blacks were encountering. Treatment of Blacks by the Richmond Police Department was a constant topic of discussion at Smitty's and the Paper Shack.

A visit to the Paper Shack was an opportunity to learn about the universal struggles of Blacks by reading books, magazines, and newspapers attractively displayed in the entrance of the store. My father used every wall and every corner of the store. Two or three revolving book racks contained all kinds of paperbacks: everything from dime novels to James Baldwin and Langston Hughes. The first magazine or book on display always showed evidence of being read repeatedly.

Visitors would come and spend time there, eating and reading while engaged in conversation and expressing opinions about topics they were reading about. My father would always tell clients to purchase the magazine or book behind the first copy, since it wasn't as worn.

• • •

My father assigned me to specific weekly chores in the Paper Shack, but I spent as much time as I could hanging out with the kids who came in to shop for candy, or listening to my father's customers talk about life. Dad sold Iceberg Slim novels, and when I could get away with it, I would secretly read them. I found the perfect spot beyond father's view to stand and read books for sale.

One day, I was organizing greeting cards on the back aisle of the store, and I overheard my father tell one of his close friends, "The best thing was to get a divorce from Ermestine. She is still a young woman who desires, and deserves, to enjoy life."

My father faced emotional hurdles and physical limitations. With that injury his entire life had changed in a few seconds. Rather than wallowing in what he couldn't do, he opened the Paper Shack to develop a new source of income. He adapted to his disability and conquered many challenges, instead of moping around, feeling sorry for himself.

I don't know if she ever told my father, but I know Mother was proud of him for becoming a business owner. She was a strong advocate for Booker T. Washington's belief that economic development was the best path to racial advancement, and the means to challenge Jim Crow prejudices. We would ride past the Paper Shack and she would smile and say, "Look at your dad, Glo. He is taking care of his business and is in the hustle, despite his injury. That's what you have to do, find your hustle and go for it."

• • •

Sometimes, at a moment's notice, Mother would demand I go to live with my father. When Mother would call him, ranting and raging about something I had done to upset her, he never hesitated or rejected my coming to live with him. My life continued in an ordinary manner whether I was living at his house or at Mother's. Things weren't that different from when my parents were living together above the store, except he was now working in the Paper Shack and there was much less drama.

When I was about twenty and living with my father, I had a horrific experience. His house on Hoffman Boulevard was near a busy highway that led to San Rafael. Parking in front of his house was dangerous because semitrucks rolled back and forth consistently. My parking spot was on a dimly lit side yard with no houses, just land. One evening, not late but already dark, while I parked my car, a woman appeared out of nowhere. She was bleeding, crying, and screaming, "Go, go, go!"

I couldn't move, couldn't think. I glanced around, checking our surroundings. Then she was suddenly sitting in my passenger seat, screaming, "Go, go, please go. He is going to kill me. Please, please drive!"

This moment was like nothing I had experienced. I didn't know what to do. I looked around but didn't see anyone. She was still crying and screaming, blood dripping down her face. I pulled off in a daze, trying to figure out what was going on.

I was driving a lady and I didn't know what she looked like, how old she was, who she was, crying and bleeding with her sweater pressed against her head, covering the wound, covering her face. I had no idea if the man she was fleeing from was following us.

I was in so much shock that I don't remember how long I drove or where we went. But eventually, I returned to my father's house for help. I remember him sitting in his wheelchair trying to help and comfort the lady. Finally I had the opportunity to really look at her. She wasn't much older than I was, and she was scared. About an hour later, her mother came and got her.

After they left, Dad said in a stern voice, "Don't ever do that again. Don't let strangers get into your car and drive off. Don't bring strangers to this house."

His tone and facial features indicated this was serious business. He would say what he had to say and be done. Nothing to discuss, no debate. This reflection of him I only witnessed while he was dealing with conflicts with Mother. By his demeaner, I knew he meant it.

I was still trying to process the whole ordeal. It was like stepping into the *Twilight Zone* for an episode. Back in reality, I wondered what I would do if it happened again. I didn't feel heroic; I felt terrified. I had never experienced being beaten up by a man. I felt her fear and could see her pain.

Later that night, while my father was in the bathroom, I called Mother from the kitchen phone. It was pretty late, and I could tell by her voice she was tired and sleepy. I shared my experience with her from beginning to end, and she listened attentively and didn't interrupt.

Curiously, she asked, "Did the lady call the police? Did anyone call the police?"

"No," I responded.

There was a long pause before she continued, "Well, I'm glad it worked out how it did. You are okay, and let's pray that the lady is okay. I understand what your father is saying; your grandmother always says the same. Don't let people into your house. But I think you did the right thing. I don't know what I would do in that situation. I am happy that you are okay.

"Pack your belongings and plan to come home tomorrow. We have some things to do this weekend. Say your prayers and go to bed. Tomorrow is another day."

Before going to bed I told my father that I would be returning to Mother's house to live. His response was a smile and, "Good. Your bedroom is always here when you need it."

I was looking forward to going back to Mother's house and putting this episode in my life behind me. I couldn't stop replaying the image of the lady getting in my car and the fear instilled in my body, wondering how I would react if it happened again.

• • •

The kitchen was the focal point in Dad's house. I would spend hours sitting at the kitchen table doing homework and watching TV while he cooked, cleaned, watched TV, or played dominoes. When I complained about not understanding my homework assignment or being unable to complete a task, his response was always the same, "Glo, my only limitations are the ones I put on myself, and your limitations are the ones you put on yourself."

Recuperating at the Veterans Hospital was a pivotal time for my father. He had established lifelong friends whom he talked to frequently on the phone, and sometimes they would come to the

Bay Area to visit. They would play dominoes, smoke, and talk about life. Ron, who was from San Diego, would drive up often to visit Dad. He, like my father, had adjusted to being a paraplegic. Through the years he had become bitter because he felt that the rich could dodge being drafted, but he and his family members didn't have the same options.

The images on TV illustrated the reality of the Vietnam War and summarized for me why America should not be at war. The civil rights movement had made me aware that the less affluent and less educated made up a large percentage of the troops assigned to combat.

This is not to say that service did not have its positives; my grandfather, father, and uncle were all war veterans, and they were proud to wear the uniform and the medals and ribbons that represented their bravery. But as I dug deeper, I became more convinced that the military men in our family found that their service did not remove racial inequities once they returned home. Blacks in Richmond were subject to mistreatment, violence, discrimination, and racism at every step in accomplishing their goals of prosperity.

Martin Luther King Jr. publicly voiced his opposition to the Vietnam War on moral grounds, citing the disproportionate number of Black casualties. Muhammad Ali resisted being drafted, served prison time, and received a three-year ban from boxing.

I was among the growing number of young people who were totally into the antiwar movement. My views were influenced by meeting men who had been wounded in war and were recuperating at the Veterans Administration Hospital in Long Beach. I was personally touched in my soul and heart. I felt the direct, deep-down pain and sorrow they expressed.

* * *

The length of time I lived at my father's house varied, as unexpectedly my mother would call and say, "You need to come home so I can . . ." (either *wash your hair, take you shopping for a special occasion, attend an important event with me,* or *express concern about your report card).*

I was not an easy child for Mother to deal with. My personality didn't quite match hers. I disliked being the center of her attention, although she nurtured my experiences and supported my efforts. She did not always agree with my choice of friends or the events and places we went to, resulting in conflicts. As a teenager, I was constantly flexing my boundaries for more independence.

On the other hand, I was an easy child because I clearly understood my mother's expectations and was never defiant. I always wanted to please my mother and myself as well. My relationship with Mother mirrored the relationship she had with her sister, Baldie, although I was less vocal in my resistance.

• • •

In 1978, the proposed Hoffman Freeway (the John T. Knox Freeway, Interstate 580) was designated as part of the interstate freeway system. State and federal funding for the project was attained in 1982, and work was begun on the freeway, which ran right in front of my father's house.

Highway construction and redevelopment (otherwise known as "urban renewal" or "Negro removal") targeted Black neighborhoods everywhere, with over ten thousand people displaced from West Oakland alone.[5] This particular construction forced my father and his sister, Lillian Ellison, to relocate after living in their homes for decades; my father had lived in his home since coming to Richmond in 1928 as a young boy. Both had upgraded and modified their homes to meet their personal needs, expecting to live the rest of their lives there. As my father was now a paraplegic, his house was designed to accommodate his disability. His sister had added an entire second level to provide more living space for her children. They both owned their homes outright, and neither had any desire to move. But with the redevelopment they were forced to accept below-market rates for their homes, and finding suitable housing was daunting, with virtually every comparable home costing more than the amount they received for their home.

With the purchase of replacement homes, they incurred new mortgages in their sixties, and the possibility of retiring had to be put on hold. Children of some of the first Black families that migrated to Richmond, they were now dealing with health issues and losing hope. The land their father purchased after arriving in Richmond, the home where they grew up, and the land their father farmed to feed his family on Hoffman Boulevard were unfairly taken away. The other Black homeowners who lived within the construction area of the John T. Knox Freeway experienced a similar fate of displacement. After years of saving and sacrificing to become homeowners, they found themselves in a state of financial insecurity, devastated and forced out of their homes.

I remember so clearly a conversation when my father shared his experience in dealing with the demands of the Redevelopment Agency. His voice radiating concern about his own well-being, he said, "I think God is giving me a test of faith."

My father was not one who spoke of his religious beliefs or attended church. At this point, I knew he was putting faith in the Lord to direct his decisions and to ease his worried mind. I knew my father was trusting God in his day-to-day journey.

Ermestine in London, learning about real estate and acquiring goals, from a different viewpoint of the world.

Ermestine and her mentor, Viola Taylor

GAME CHANGER 17

PETGRAVE REALTY

My mother's one-room real estate office in the back of our store was called Petgrave Realty. Here is where I learned to type, answer business calls, file, and greet clients in a professional manner. Basically, my mother trained me to be her office assistant. I was also being educated in civil rights advocacy; our conversation topics included redlining and supplying subprime loans with unrealistic terms—racial policies and practices initiated by federal, state, and local governmental and financial agencies that intentionally segregated and discriminated against Blacks.

My mother would boast, "The law is not on our side, and never will be. As my father always said, 'It's just the way of the world.' These California White folks support discrimination, but I'm an Okie from Checotah, and we own Forty Acres and a Mule. My parents own more land than these White folks ever will. We are Creek Freedmen. I am not going to let them prohibit us from buying or renting wherever we want to live."

• • •

Visits to the City of Richmond's planning and building departments had long been weekly events. When I was a child they were routinely planned for days after Mother picked me up from school. Well prepared with document folders in her briefcase, carrying tightly rolled building plans, Mother was always confident that she had done her research and was ready to move forward with projects. Dressed professionally, with beauty and elegance, she entered the building with her protective shield, ready to go into combat if warranted.

Upon entering the building, she was always recognized immediately and greeted with, "Hello, Mrs. Petgrave [or later, Mrs. Martin]. You look beautiful today. How are you doing?"

Everyone at the City of Richmond who interacted with Mother in one way or another knew that she was from Oklahoma and that her family owned Forty Acres and a Mule. She was proud of her heritage.

Mother's feeling that she was not being taken seriously because she was a Black woman was no doubt realistic. Almost every project she brought to the table met with resistance in a matter-of-fact way.

"They think I have half the brain they have," she'd say.

Mother believed that knowing is half the battle when dealing with new employees who were not in the know of what they didn't know. We spent a lot of time at the Richmond Public Library, I in the children's room, she researching all she could about real estate in the other side of the building. Our visits were so frequent that the librarians greeted us by name.

• • •

As my mother acquired multi-unit apartments, more and more clients came to Petgrave Realty searching for apartments to rent.

She didn't have disqualifying factors for prospective tenants, and she required only a commitment to pay the agreed-upon rent. But she definitely had standards she expected from all tenants; poor housekeeping, poorly behaved children, and being a nuisance to other tenants were unacceptable. She would talk to tenants in a matter-of-fact manner to encourage the good-neighbor policy.

While signing rental leases with tenants, she always articulated her three Rs: *Respect me* by paying your rent on time, *respect your neighbors* by not becoming a nuisance, and *respect the property* by not destroying your apartment.

I heard those same words over and over again and watched eager tenants agreeing wholeheartedly. Some lived up to the three Rs; some didn't. If they could not follow through with the Rs, they would be asked to begin looking for another residence. Mother would say, "I don't want to lose you as a tenant, but you are not hearing the nature of my words. You've got to do better. If you do, we will get along just fine."

It was rare for tenants to come to the office to pay their rent without it turning into a more personal visit. Mother asked questions about the tenants' lives, their families, and their children, and shared her experiences growing up on those forty acres in Checotah. She went out of her way to make it possible for tenants to succeed.

It was important to her to provide housing for Blacks, because she knew White landlords were discriminating against them. Black families were dealing with a severe housing shortage, due to both discrimination and unfair and unjust renting practices. White families could rent from the private market, but Blacks were dependent on neglected and congested housing projects.

* * *

In 1961, when I was twelve years old, a flyer circulated throughout the community and was posted in the store and real estate office. It announced an organizational meeting to be held in St. Luke's Church, across the street from the store. The flyer posed four questions: (1) What makes a neighborhood a slum area? (2) How can we prevent our neighborhood from becoming a slum area? (3) What makes a neighborhood a desirable place to live? and (4) What will it cost you?

At the meeting, Mother was the elected secretary of the Santa Fe Neighborhood Council, and thereafter she attended every meeting, participating in discussions about perceived problems in the neighborhood. The Santa Fe Neighborhood Council worked to improve the livability, safety, and appearance of Black neighborhoods.

The meetings occurred during the week, and I had a designated seat within Mother's view. My box of school supplies and books by my side, I completed homework, daydreamed, and listened to hours of discussions addressing residents' concerns, goals, and determination for equal rights.

My education continued wherever I accompanied Mother. I remember frequent nights, sitting on a box crate, reading out loud while Mother painted vacant units. She never expected me to help paint. My job was to read and then respond to her questions while she was checking my understanding of the words I had read. We spent hours of uninterrupted time in vacant units, painting and reading, or just talking while planting flowers and doing yard maintenance on her properties.

Going to court with my mother was also a frequent event. I wore a dress and patent-leather shoes and watched her go before the judge in eviction cases (without an attorney) or attend court hearings for people suspected of stealing from or robbing her store. Employees at the City of Richmond, the courts,

Richmond School District, and the county knew who she was. But they couldn't predict how she was going to react or respond to their comments.

* * *

Black-owned family businesses were numerous and thriving throughout the Bay Area in the sixties. Mother, Viola Taylor, and Ruby Bims were purchasing and selling properties—three beautiful professional Black women, joined as a team, focused on helping Black families rent in desirable locations and become homeowners in the Bay Area. They were knowledgeable and supported one another in meeting their goals. The Bay Area was a vibrant community of activity for Black business, and Petgrave Realty was a big part of it.

It seemed that Mother was always meeting and discussing projects with Black contractors, plumbers, electricians. Most of these meetings happened in her store or real estate office. She was a good negotiator and was respected as a businesswoman.

My mother made it her personal business to know about and meet White realtors whose offices were in the Downtown Richmond area. In her quest to learn more about the real estate market, she befriended a local White agent. He was an older man, short and chunky; when he was in the area, he would always stop by Mother's office to chat. His favorite candy bar was Three Musketeers, and she would tell me to go into the store and get him one.

He lived in El Cerrito, and his two daughters were attending UC Berkeley. He wanted them to graduate from the university and feared the possibility of being kicked off the real estate board for engaging in contracts with Blacks. He talked about the challenges of serving Blacks in the community, and he said he was looking forward to retiring.

My mother had heard the rumor that many real estate agents had a fear of being blackballed by other realtors if they sold a home to Blacks, and now it seemed the rumor was confirmed.

My mother had begun thinking about buying a house in El Cerrito so she could enroll me in a hill school. She knew that she would be on her own as far as acquiring property in that area, and she was prepared for the challenge. I heard her frequently say that she couldn't remember the last time a White man ever tried to make her life easier.

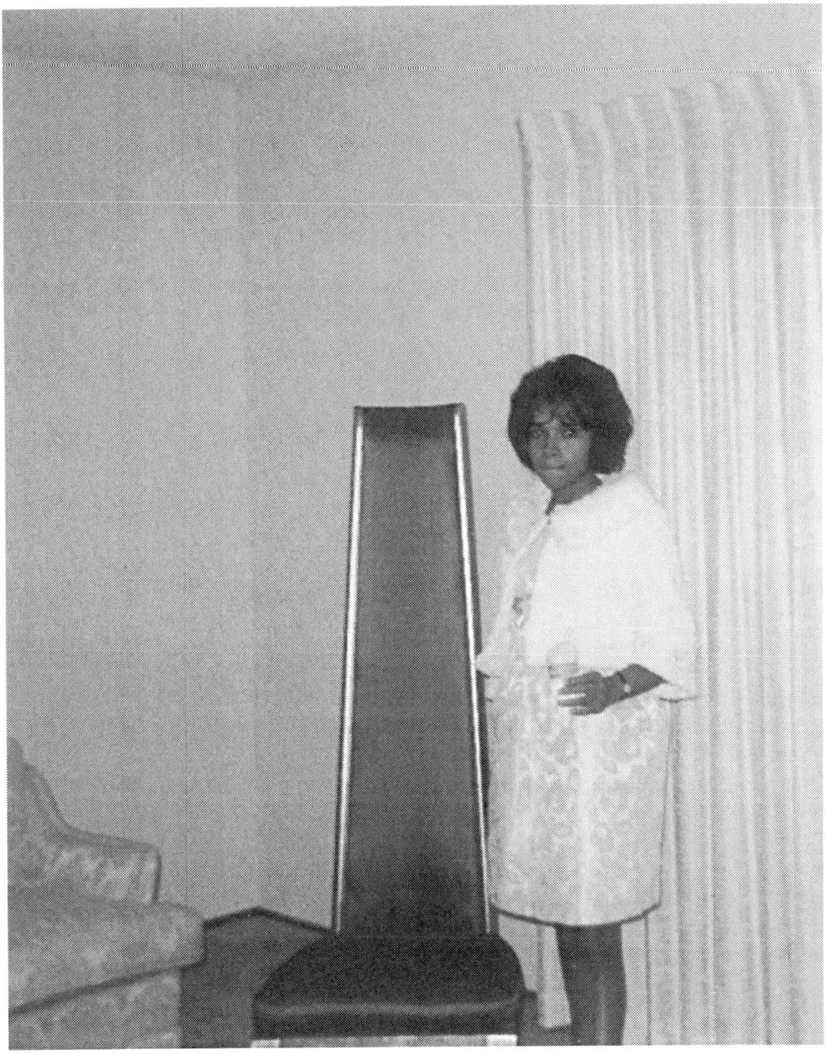

Gloria in ninth grade, posing near Ermestine's favorite royal blue chair

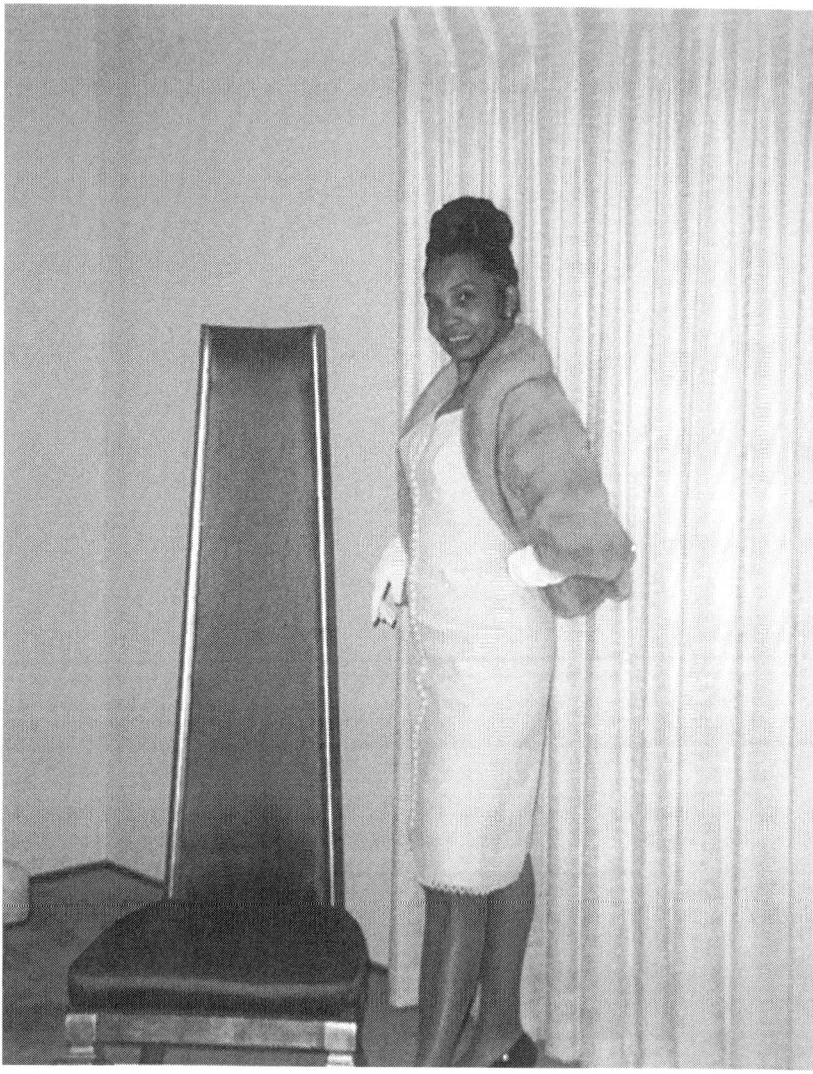

Ermestine posing before attending a business social event with Gloria in San Francisco, circa 1964

GAME CHANGER 18

JUNIOR HIGH SCHOOL

In 1963, Martin Luther King Jr. shared with the world his dream that "little black boys and black girls will be able to join hands with little white boys and white girls." But the dream was far from realized.

Affirmative action was beginning to open the door for more Blacks in my generation to achieve success and obtain a college education, but my mother knew well that Richmond's Black communities and its segregated schools were the result of a long history of deliberate public policy. Segregated housing was supported by local, state, and national law directly financed by the federal government.

I attended Roosevelt Junior High School, less than two blocks from my mother's store. Roosevelt was a predominantly Black school, with teachers and staff who embraced the community, encouraged and supported students' efforts and talents, and created an environment conducive to learning. But my mother learned that Whites believed segregated Black schools were filled with the most disadvantaged students and had the lowest academic performance.

In contrast, Mother had listened to Whites boast about the educational opportunities their children were receiving at private schools and the hill schools such as Portola Junior High and El Cerrito High, which had higher college acceptance rates. She wanted me to have the same opportunities. Private schools were never a consideration for me, but getting me into Portola became my mother's goal.

My mother searched for and found a lot in Richmond Annex that had a run-down, uninhabitable house. She purchased the property and used this address to enroll me at Portola, striving to better my chances of getting the best education possible.

• • •

The transition from Roosevelt to Portola Junior High was challenging for my parents, and especially for me. We Blacks were small in number and stuck together. I was, more often than not, the only Black person in my classes, filled with White children who shared stories of their family vacations and lived a life so very different from mine. To get to school I was transported by my mother or father, or I walked to Macdonald Avenue and caught the bus. After school, I, along with most of the Black students from the Stege neighborhood, walked down to San Pablo Avenue to catch the bus home. A few Black students whose families had recently moved to homes in the El Cerrito hills took a different bus home.

One day, a Black teacher who taught at Lincoln Elementary and lived in Parchester Village stopped in my mother's store with her daughter Linda, who was using a friend's address so she could attend Portola. I listened to the teacher tell my mother that she knew firsthand that the children attending hill schools performed much better academically than the children at Lincoln and Nystrom. She shared that most of her teacher friends sent their children to the hill schools so they would be better prepared for success in college.

Our mothers hatched a plan for Linda to ride to school with me every morning. Linda was living in Parchester Village, and I was living in South Richmond. We were both new to Portola and were traveling a long distance to get to school. Every morning Linda rode with her mother to Lincoln Elementary School and walked a block to my home to begin our journey to school together. I was happy to have a new friend at a school where I had none.

Linda and I were often tardy together; one day the school called the number listed on Linda's emergency card, which was for the friend whose address she was using. The maid answered the phone and said, "No child by the name of Linda lives here." As a result, Linda was kicked out of Portola and returned to her neighborhood school. Soon afterward, she was attending a private school.

I, on the other hand, continued to attend Portola. My parents put a new plan in place. I was going to catch the bus on Macdonald Avenue every morning to ensure I would arrive on time. But frequently I would miss the bus and walk back home, and my father would take me to school. Being tardy was an ongoing occurrence that signaled a red flag and prompted the school staff to drive by the address listed on school records. They discovered that the address was an abandoned house, and I was sent back to Roosevelt. Oh, happy day!

• • •

I was so glad to return to my neighborhood school. I loved it. I belonged there with my elementary school friends. The atmosphere was so supportive. My ninth-grade neighborhood friends (including David) and I practiced our dance for the school talent show for hours at my house—two boys and three girls. Then we walked to Downtown Richmond and selected red and white clothes for all of us to wear. We still followed our sixth-grade teacher Mr. Hill's teachings and took full responsibility to become professional in our style and performances.

We had to audition for that talent show, and our group was one of those selected to perform. When a friend sang "My Guy" by Mary Wells, I realized what a beautiful voice she had. The auditorium was full of parents, family members, and friends. My father in his wheelchair and my mother next to him were sitting in the front row.

Being back at Roosevelt made me *so* happy. However, my mother didn't feel the same, and she expressed her feelings to Richmond School District officials that they were discriminating against her.

The School District Administration Building was within walking distance of our house on South Seventh Street, and my mother became a frequent pop-in visitor at the superintendent's office. During visits, she was always asking school district staff members about the school boundaries, where staff lived, and what schools their children attended.

When my mother dropped in, the superintendent was never available. During appointment visits, when she was able to talk with the superintendent in person, he always greeted her cordially. But she felt he had a strong allegiance to the school board, to local business, and to White Parent Teacher Association parents who were leaders in the better schools.

The school district staff soon knew my mother by name. They were respectful and friendly and encouraged her to attend school board meetings. That was on her agenda; we attended whenever she could. She never addressed the school board but instead sat quietly, listening and taking notes. She was learning the dynamics of the school district, the policies, and which players made the decisions.

While working in the store or real estate office, Mother felt it important to share with her customers and tenants what she had learned at school board meetings. The discussions always seemed to trigger fears that the superintendent was part of the administrative bureaucracy and was manipulating Blacks to believe school policies were cast in stone. Rumored statements by board members shared within Black communities indicated the intent to keep the schools racially segregated.

My mother never stopped trying to get me reenrolled at Portola. During her phone calls and visits to the superintendent's office, she consistently expressed her desire for me to have the same opportunities as his children. In her mind, owning that dilapidated house and property within the Portola boundaries gave me, her daughter, the right to attend Portola.

But historical policies and practices were firmly in place for segregation to continue within the district, and her efforts to get me reenrolled were blocked. She recognized that the political landscape was absolutely focused on keeping Black children in segregated schools.

I remember vividly our last visit to the superintendent's office. It started with a friendly welcome. "Hello, Mrs. Petgrave. You look nice today, as usual."

He was sitting behind his desk, smiling at her. I sat down in a chair.

"Get up, Gloria, we won't be here long," Mother said briskly. I already knew she was angry by the choice words she had used while we were on our way to the administrative building.

She stood in front of his desk, slowly and unsmilingly starting to take off her gloves, and said to him, "I own the property that allows my daughter the right to go to schools in El Cerrito. I am paying taxes—just like everyone else. I just stopped by to tell you that, with all deliberate speed, I am going to hire contractors to build my home on the Richmond Annex property. You have definitely flexed your political muscle, but you haven't won. My daughter is going to attend El Cerrito High in the fall!"

She didn't wait for his comment, and she left his office without saying good-bye. I followed right behind her, hearing the click-clack of her high-heeled pumps as we walked down the hall.

Mother was walking so quickly and furiously that she lost her balance and had to brace herself against the wall to break her fall, dropping her purse and gloves. A young White man stopped to assist her, and I picked up her items. She shook off the incident, and we continued out of the Administration Building.

She walked slowly down the steps and said, "You *will* be attending El Cerrito next school year. I am not asking them to give you bus tickets or provide transportation. I own that land, and they can't stop me. Well, *he* can't stop me."

We drove in silence to the Richmond Annex property, parked there, and sat for some time people-watching while she made a diagram on one of her business folders.

I remember that visit to the superintendent's office so clearly. This was when I became aware of Mother's plans to build on the Richmond Annex property. I knew from her tone of voice and body language that she was serious.

I was blindsided by her commitment for me to go to school in El Cerrito. I couldn't ignore the thought that this might be the last year I would attend school with my neighborhood friends, whom I'd been close to since kindergarten. I was so relieved to be back with them at Roosevelt and was not feeling good about this situation. She had flipped the script.

• • •

When my mother and I would attend school board meetings, there were never many Blacks in attendance. She made it her business to introduce herself to members of community groups and organizations who were voicing their concerns and attempting to break down historically accepted racial policies.

Store customers, real estate clients, and fellow parents would share their experiences of being called Okies and Arkies and not being welcomed in the community, and those words were like someone had pushed a sword into her heart. She hated being referred to as an Okie. Those were fighting words, a direct attack on her intelligence and ability.

She believed this prejudice was the source of the resistance to her request to get me back to Portola. During their first meeting, the superintendent had inquired how long she had lived in Richmond and where she was from.

Mother knew that most Blacks who had migrated to work in the shipyards were from Oklahoma, Arkansas, and Texas. She vividly remembered that white cross being placed in her front yard, and she had listened to my father and other Blacks who were among the first families to live in Richmond talk about being called obscenities. These pioneers had learned to survive by ignoring this deep-seated hatred. But Mother couldn't ignore injustice.

• • •

During the early 1960s, more opportunities arose for Black families to buy in El Cerrito because Black real estate agents and brokers were selling property to Blacks in El Cerrito Hills.

Most of the Black students I met at Portola Junior High had recently moved into the El Cerrito hills from Berkeley or were living in the all-Black community surrounding Stege Elementary school.

I was the only Black student living in South Richmond, which most considered the ghetto. Many of my new friends were also new to Portola and El Cerrito High School culture.

Within six months of Mother's angry visit to the superintendent, she had an apartment building constructed on the Richmond Annex lot, with an extra-large unit for us. She had not been successful in purchasing a house in the hills, but we would live within the school boundaries so I could attend El Cerrito High School. She fought—and overcame—the obstacles the City of Richmond tried to impose to building a fourplex.

My mother felt a sense of accomplishment in forging ahead and building the apartment building. She talked continuously about how she never allowed obstacles to stop her.

No one could outsmart my mother as she fought racial discrimination during the civil rights movement. White men in high-powered positions were no match for her wit; plus, she could outcurse them. On most occasions, they would tell her, "I need to talk with the owner; I need to talk with your boss." Then she would respond with rage, as if they had called her an Okie. My mother *was* the boss.

She understood that most whites thought she was incapable of achieving the projects she was pushing so very hard for, and she vigorously opposed the White man's view that Black women were less than. Over and over again, she fought—without a blueprint!—the injustices she saw around her.

Gloria's graduation from El Cerrito High School

Ermestine showing property

GAME CHANGER 19

EL CERRITO HIGH SCHOOL

Despite my desire to attend Harry Ellis High School with my old neighborhood friends and my cousin Clarice, it was still exciting when my mother and I moved to our new house in the Richmond Annex. I loved our new home because it was brand new and modern—it even had a fireplace in the den.

My first day of tenth grade, I remember Mother driving me to school. She was backing out of the garage when she remembered that she had forgotten her briefcase and some folders she needed for a scheduled meeting. She stopped in the driveway and got out of the car to get them. While I waited, I turned the radio to station KDIA. She returned and placed her briefcase on the back seat. Sam Cooke's "A Change Is Gonna Come" began playing.

As we rode up Fairmont Avenue, she said, "Glo, *I* had to fight like hell to get our house in the right neighborhood for you to go to El Cerrito. Now *you* have to study hard, make good grades, and go to college. Pick and choose your friends carefully."

She added, smiling, "I like that song by Sam Cooke. I am going to give you some money to buy the record for me this weekend!" She parked in front of El Cerrito High School, gave me some money, and said, "Here is some spending change. Remember what I said. You are here to get an education and go to college. Have a good day! I will pick you up after school."

As I got out of her car, I heard, "Hey, Gloria is back!"

In front of the school was a small cluster of Black students I had met and made friends with at Portola. Mother looked at me and said, "I hope you heard what I said: You are here for one reason only. To get your education."

The small group of Black students walked toward me, smiling. It felt good to be welcomed and excitedly greeted with, "Girl, it's good to have you back!"

This was my new posse! They would become my college buddies and adult friends. I knew that through Mother's determination and effort, this is where I would graduate from.

• • •

My first day at El Cerrito High School was uneventful. Afterward, I made my way to the front of the school and saw Mother's car parked across the street. As I got in, she looked up and asked, "How was your day?" I began sharing with her about my classes, teachers, a summary of my experiences. Then I turned on the radio; James Brown was singing "It's a Man's World."

After the song was over, she said, "Glo, this *is* a man's world. But I have the guts to fight like a man, and you need to learn how to be strong and do the same. This may be a man's world, but right now I don't have a man in my life, and maybe I never will again."

On our way home, she stopped by the record store. We bought three records: "A Change Is Gonna Come"; "It's a Man's World"; and "My Girl," sung by the Temptations. Then we went to the Albany Bowling Alley for dinner. Mother pulled out a folder with documents the City of Richmond had given her, which stated reasons for denying her plans for a project, while I thumbed through my new textbooks. I didn't have any homework, but Mother had assigned me the task of looking through the textbooks to see what the courses were going to be about.

While we were eating, she began talking about the need to fight to accomplish things that White men can get through City Planning easily. "But this Okie is going to pioneer my way through and not allow them to stop me," she said with determination. After dinner, we went home. I played our new records while reviewing my textbooks.

This was the first time Mother had expressed an interest in the songs I loved to listen to. She was not into music, other than listening to gospel songs on the radio. Now Mother sat across from me at the kitchen table, reading through the City of Richmond's documents, strategizing her game plan. She talked about how the City of Richmond made it almost impossible for Blacks to be successful; she believed their intentions were a deliberate scheme to block her. "But I'm not going to sit there like a bump on a log," she affirmed.

Later that evening, a high school senior called me. He had gotten my phone number from his next-door neighbor, a girlfriend I met at Portola. Mother answered the phone and interrogated the guy for about twenty minutes: Where do you live? Where do your parents work? Where is your family from? Do you have any brothers or sisters? What junior high school did you attend? How long have you attended El Cerrito High School?

I sat there, listening to her routine and systematic questions. Eventually she said, "Okay, here's Glo. She can't talk long, because she has some reading to do for school."

I had not personally met this guy yet, didn't know who he was or what he looked like. I just knew he lived near my friend Maria. After a few minutes on the phone, Mother told me, "Say you have to go back to studying."

I thought, "Wow, you talked to him longer than I did." But I also felt good about the fact that he had gotten my phone number on my very first day of school. El Cerrito might not be as bad as I thought! I put "My Girl" back on and continued to thumb through my books, but my mind was on the phone call.

• • •

At Roosevelt, I had received the academic knowledge and skills for success in high school. The teachers doubled up to teach and prepare us for success in a culturally enriched environment. At Portola and El Cerrito, however, I was enrolled in Home Economics, Typing, and Accounting classes. Based on my face and race, they had predetermined my opportunities for career choices. When Mother would talk to counselors about the classes I was assigned to, their response would be "Sorry, Mrs. Petgrave, the other classes are already filled; these are the only classes available."

I didn't see the bigger picture and the impact on college opportunities. I didn't realize that the classes I was being assigned to were limiting my ability to choose the career of my choice.

All I knew was, I didn't have to study hard to make good grades because my mother had already trained me in those subject areas while I was working in the store and the real estate office. In eleventh grade, because my mother was persistent in her request to the counselor, I was enrolled in college-prep classes, and my mother had to hire tutors for me to catch up and get good grades.

• • •

At least twice a week, Mother would pick me up from school. The night before, she would be specific about what I was to wear to school, because afterward, I would be going with her to a meeting. My meeting attire was a skirt, white blouse, and white tennis shoes refreshed with white shoe polish. During every meeting, I had a textbook open and was supposedly reading. But most of the time, instead of being focused on my book, I would watch people in the meeting, or think about my school day or my friends, or be bored and ready to go home.

While speaking at a professional meeting, Mother had a way of taking her gloves off in a very sophisticated manner—slowly taking out each finger and folding the gloves neatly before placing them on her lap. The meeting usually consisted of White men listening, asking questions, and then telling her why she couldn't do whatever it was she was planning to do. When this happened, she would end the meeting by slowly putting on her gloves and telling them they didn't know whom they were dealing with.

She never backed down in what she wanted to do. She felt that her future was bright, and anything she wanted to do, she had the determination to accomplish. She had a mission and a dream pushing her forward.

Honoring Doug Ellison

My uncle Son and friend

Son at Veterans Hospital, a few days before he passed

GAME CHANGER 20

TROUBLES

Son had strong and respectful relationships with women throughout his life, with periods of retreating to his parents' house to regroup. His work ethics were strong, his desire for acquiring property wealth was solid, and his search for finding the right woman was everlasting. He also struggled with alcoholism. Grandmother believed in her heart that the Army was the reason behind Son's drinking problems.

In 1965, Son was diagnosed with a hole in his heart, and his health slowly but steadily declined. He passed at the Veterans Hospital in Martinez, California, in February 1966.

Mother and I visited him frequently at the hospital, but our visit on the day before he passed was the most memorable. On the way home, Mother began reminiscing about their childhood in Checotah and journeys after leaving Oklahoma. She concluded with, "My God, Son has a hole in his heart. How could he not have known that all those years? My brother wanted a good wife and children. Although all the women he was ever with loved him, they just couldn't seem to get it right. Hmm, so my brother really had two holes in his heart. Lord have mercy."

Clouds were turning grey as we realized death was knocking at the door. The family storm was approaching, and our faces and behavior exhibited our fear. Mother started singing "Precious Lord," while I rode in silence. This was my first experience with the death of a close loved one.

Mother paused her singing, saying, "I have to stop and pick up my rent check from a tenant, then stop by the store and your grandparents' house."

I was daydreaming about Son's life and praying for him. I thought about visits to one of Son's homes; I was always fascinated by a large fish tank under his television set. The tank resembled one seen in doctors' offices, restaurants, or commercial buildings. It was memorable, exotic, soothing.

I remembered hearing Mother share about one day she was washing dishes and looking out the kitchen window, when she heard the familiar sound of Son's Harley Davidson motorcycle. He was living with their parents down the block and frequently passed in front of our house. She looked outside, expecting to see him go by, but instead, Son turned into her driveway and plowed straight through the garage door. Mother was shocked, startled; she ran to the garage, screaming, "Oh my God, oh my God." Son was shaken up, but unharmed. This was the moment when Mother realized without any doubt that her brother was an alcoholic.

I looked down at my ankle, remembering the day Son came and picked me up for a ride on his new Harley. I was proud to be riding behind my uncle, waving at folks he knew along the way. However, that ride turned out to be a very painful experience because the motorcycle exhaust pipe burned my ankle severely. The wound became infected, and the healing process took months, while the scar took years to disappear. That was the last time I ever rode behind anyone driving a motorcycle! Men in our family, including my husband, proudly owned Harley Davidsons, but never were my arms wrapped around their waists. Although that motorcycle ride with Son ended up unpleasant for me, the time spent with my uncle was always awesome.

I recalled one evening I broke curfew and returned home to find Son and my mother sitting in his parked car. Worried about me, she had called him. He was not feeling well but got out of bed to calm his sister down and to make sure I was okay. I remember my friend Priscilla pulling up in front of my house and everyone in the car saying softly at the same time, "Gloria, your mother is outside waiting for you." I was totally freaking out, not sure how my night was going to end. Possibly I would be sleeping at my father's house for a few days.

Years after Son's passing, when Mother was upset about something I did, she would say angrily, "And my dead brother got out of his sick bed once to find you! When are you going to get some sense in your brain?"

• • •

During the summer of 1966, in the midst of the civil rights movement, Mother found out about a four-week program at Tuskegee University in Alabama for high school students. I was accepted to the program, and she also convinced the mother of one of my friends to enroll her daughter, Priscilla. I was happy to hear that Priscilla was going to attend, because I was dreading the possibility of being away from home for a month by myself.

In preparation for attending the Summer Program, Mother and I spent hours in the library researching Tuskegee University. A historically Black university, it was the former home of botanist George Washington Carver and World War II's Tuskegee Airmen. In 1965, Tuskegee University was identified as a National Historic Landmark for the significance of its academic programs and its pivotal role in higher education for Blacks. Mother was sold on the belief that Tuskegee University was where I needed to be—at sixteen years old.

Our mothers drove us to the airport separately and said their good-byes. Priscilla and I were off to a new adventure on our own! It truly was an earth-shattering experience, living in the dorms with other teenagers from a variety of Southern states. We encountered a new culture of thinking, dressing, behaving. Priscilla and I were engulfed in a completely new world. On our own, we were attending classes at Tuskegee, finding joy in eating at a chicken café near campus, and meeting new friends throughout our journey.

• • •

Before leaving the Bay Area, I shared with many people my upcoming summer plans in Alabama. Lots of friends stopped by my house in Richmond Annex in friendly gestures of saying good-bye. But one friend had a different motive: to unlock the sliding door to the downstairs balcony.

Mother and I never unlocked that door; we had endured our share of fear living above the store and were always in prevention/security mode. Returning home from the airport, Mother discovered that our house had been vandalized! Her mink coat, jewelry, money hidden under the mattress, gun—all were gone. She immediately called the police and reported the incident.

During our next telephone conversation she angrily said to me, "Your friend Dwayne came back to our house after we left for the airport and robbed us."

I couldn't believe what I was hearing—Dwayne? No, she must have gotten that wrong. Couldn't have been Dwayne.

She was adamant about how she thought he had vandalized our house. Highly agitated, Mother said, "Your grandmother always says to keep visitors out of your house. There is truth in her message. Both of us have to keep people out of our house. You see what can happen!"

During this point in my life, I was more of a people-person, like Baldie and my grandfather. No longer living above the store, I was alone a lot after school while Mother was working at the store or the real estate office.

Occasionally, after school, girls and boys would accompany me home in secret. My friends knew they weren't supposed to be at my house and often asked, what time is your mother coming home? They knew my mother, and she knew them. They did not want to be there when she arrived, and I wanted them to be long gone. My friends and I would do teenage things to have fun: talking, laughing, dancing, putting on makeup, restyling our hair, just hanging out. But always, always we were focused on when it was time for them to leave—before Mother returned home from work.

Sitting in my dorm room, I reflected on Mother's ways. She never had male or female company in our house unless they were family members. She engaged with other people within the boundaries of her store and real estate office. Mother was quite angry when she hung up the phone, and I was happy that I had four weeks of away time before returning home. And I was struggling to believe that Dwayne had actually burglarized our house.

A few days later, Mother told me that she had contacted Dwayne's parents and retrieved some of her belongings. I was so pleased to hear that most of her things were back. Needless to say, that was the end of my friendship with Dwayne. We never communicated again. Later in life, I heard that Dwayne had passed in his twenties.

Two of my high school male "friends" taught me early in life that some people look for ways to commit crimes, and Mother and I were easy targets for theft or violence. Crime is widely thought to be committed by youth who live in poverty. But Dwayne (who burglarized our home) and, a few years later, Duane (who robbed the store) were children of affluent Black families. It wasn't that they didn't have access to money. But under the disguise of friendship with us, both of these young men had planned ways to do harm, create fear, and bring sorrow into our lives.

Mother was struggling hard to make an honest living, working long hours to achieve her goals. I, on the other hand, was unwittingly bringing danger right to our front door and into our house through so-called friends. The actions of these two young men created much grief and another layer of conflict between Mother and me.

After my parents divorced, Mother did not date until she met William D. Martin. There were many years in between of her being happily single, uninterested in men, and focused on me and her careers.

I learned well what my mother and grandmother always preached to me, "Keep people out of our homes." My grandmother always said, "People do not always mean you good! Stay in your house, and let them stay in theirs."

Mother's cousin Gladys, Gloria, Tressie, and Ermestine attending the Links Cotillion—a night to remember

Gloria, the debutante

GAME CHANGER 21

LINKS COTILLION

In 1965 my mother's older cousin, Gladys Jordan, who was a member of Alpha Kappa Alpha Sorority, invited me to be a debutante in the Links Cotillion. This was my first introduction to cotillions and becoming a debutante. I didn't know what to expect, but my mother made it clear that this was something I was going to do. No expense was too much to make us fit into this new reality of the people around us. The experience forever altered our lives.

The activities leading to the cotillion were a game changer and expanded my friendships, awareness, and exposure to the greater Bay Area. I met Black teenagers whose parents were doctors, lawyers, college educated, well known, career minded, and professional looking, living in the hills of El Cerrito, Kensington, Berkeley, and Oakland. Parent meetings associated with being a debutante provided opportunities for Mother to meet and form relationships with professional Black parents, pass out her business cards, and network more widely. One of the debutante's fathers worked at HUD and provided knowledge and guidance for my mother to expand her real estate opportunities.

For several months before the cotillion, we debutantes were taught about and groomed for charm, etiquette, elegance, social grace, and self-esteem. In preparation for our debut, we were taught sisterhood, career-planning strategies, the importance of community service, and lifelong skills in order to develop into strong, intelligent, sophisticated young ladies who understood the importance of serving our communities.

In the cotillion ceremony, we debutantes would be escorted by our fathers. My father was in a wheelchair, so my mother decided that a cousin around her age would represent my father. I remember feeling jealous watching the other girls practicing with their fathers in what seemed in my eyes to be a father-and-daughter moment. I was practicing with a man I hardly knew, and I resented the fact that my father was not there because of his disability. (My father, grandfather, and Aunt Baldie did not attend the cotillion.) I was escorted by two gentlemen, and I don't remember their names and faces or know anything about their lives. They escorted me through one of the most significant experiences in my life.

The cotillion turned out to be my Cinderella moment. A white, towering Christmas tree provided the atmosphere in which thirty-two young women were presented at the Links Cotillion. The San Francisco Hilton Hotel's Continental Ballroom was transformed into a winter wonderland, with mounds of snow and frosted pine boughs bordering the archway beneath where each debutante bowed. As each debutante's name was announced, we descended the stairway of the platform and joined our father or close male relative for the promenade.

The debutantes were dressed in white formal gowns, carried lighted wands, and wore white fur wrist bands accented with red carnations. We danced the intricate steps of the traditional minuet and then were joined by our escorts in the cotillion waltz.

The formal cotillion presentation concluded with the debutantes' grand promenade accompanied by their escorts, who formed an honor guard. I didn't meet my peer, Don, until the first cotillion rehearsal. He was the son of a family Cousin Gladys knew. Then the evening of dancing and festivities was opened with the debutantes and escorts waltzing to the music of the Rudy Salvini Orchestra. At the end of the cotillion, the debutantes and escorts traveled across the Bay to Frere Jacques in Oakland for post-dance festivities and breakfast at dawn.

The Links Cotillion will forever remain in my mind as an uplifting vision of beautiful Black girls in gloves and white formal gowns, a season of etiquette classes and peer social events, and my mother proudly and elegantly smiling and happy. My mother, grandmother, and Cousin Gladys were dressed in lovely long formals and gloves.

Participating in the cotillion while a junior in high school encouraged me to pursue higher education and civic involvement. While preparing for the event, I experienced a wide array of social and cultural activities and opportunities for personal development and growth. Steeped in rituals and tradition, the cotillion marked my official joining of a new society.

I was a debutante who didn't live in the hills of El Cerrito, Berkeley, or Oakland, with parents who didn't graduate from college, and I benefited from the Links Cotillion on so many levels. The cotillion also opened up new doors and opportunities for my mother to expand her real estate business and create more opportunities for Blacks.

Gloria, second from left, front row, working in a Title 1 school in Oakland Unified School District, in 1982-83. A composition of staff unseen from my viewpoint today.

John Stewart, far left, owner of Stewart's Rose Manor Funeral Service

Sarita Ellison, Richmond Police Department

GAME CHANGER 22

SHIFTING GROUND

In Mother's attempt to understand more about her new home, she was always probing my father about the history of Richmond, since his family was among the first to settle in the city. Father often reminisced about his life, sharing both positive and negative aspects. He peeled back layers of his history that had a common thread of strong work ethics, determination, and true grit.

As my father lived with his sister and father on Hoffman Boulevard after he arrived from Kingston, Jamaica, at the age of six, his prewar years were strikingly different from Mother's. Clearly, he had witnessed a different climate between Blacks and Whites than that of the migration years, when a new fear of the Black man fostered an atmosphere of anger and hate within a community where folks had previously gotten along quite well. Racial lines were drawn with the influx of Blacks into Richmond, and North Richmond was clearly defined as the land Blacks would be forced to live on. The diverse North Richmond community did not welcome new migrants with open arms.

According to my father, a small group of Blacks lived in North Richmond before World War II, and they loved living there.

Portuguese, Italians, Japanese, and Mexican Americans resided in the area. Father remembered North Richmond as an isolated, densely populated agricultural area with makeshift housing. The soil there was known to be rich, and Japanese families owned plant nurseries within the community. Streets were unpaved and prone to flooding; there were few streetlights; and the garbage dump was nearby. North Richmond had inadequate fire and police protection.

In 1940 Henry J. Kaiser opened a shipyard in Richmond to build *Liberty* ships for World War II. Recruiters were sent through sections of the South, paying for train tickets and giving expense money to prospective workers. Blacks—primarily from the rural areas of Texas, Arkansas, Oklahoma, Louisiana, and Mississippi—migrated to Richmond for jobs in the shipyards. Whites were recruited from the same states, bringing historical and cultural hostilities from the places they left behind.

Migrants arrived in Richmond to several dilapidated "war housing" projects in a city that had identified, controlled boundaries. In the 1940s, most of Richmond's Blacks were concentrated in and around North Richmond, some within Richmond's city limits; neighbors residing just across the street were in the unincorporated areas of Contra Costa County. North Richmond quickly spiked into an overpopulated shantytown for Blacks, both during and after World War II. Black migrants began to create a cultural and political identity new to Richmond, sparking social tensions.

As a Black military veteran who believed that serving in the Army was the right thing to do, Father returned to a new Richmond after the war. In less than five years, North Richmond had grown from a rural town to an overcrowded community of hardworking Blacks who had very little control over their living conditions and were not welcomed by Whites. Residents were battling about housing, education, and police protection.

Services and conditions were poor, and other ethnic groups left North Richmond, resulting in the racial segregation of Blacks.

* * *

Mother's high school goals of graduating from Langston University and becoming a member of Alpha Kappa Alpha were left behind when she joined her family on their journey to California. They traveled to unknown territory, believing that jobs were available and that new adventures were on the horizon that would lead to accomplishing their goals.

Mother left Langston University and stepped out—on faith—into a world of uncertainty. She relocated to the beautiful Bay Area, in a state with job opportunities and an unbelievable climate, with her new personal lists of what she desired to do and accomplish. Unfortunately, their new living environment in the Golden State had far worse conditions than those her family had left behind in Oklahoma.

Families like mine left their land and their homes in their special part of the world, where they were surrounded by a familiar culture and comfortable style of living. Navigating challenging journeys, they planned for and dreamed of a better life. Black men and women, with or without money, many with young children, took risks, inspired by hope. They also sought safety from violence and crime.

What the migrants didn't envision was being viewed as a threat to the safety of others in the cities where they decided to make their new homes. They arrived to find segregated, neglected living conditions and were deprived of equal opportunities to acquire property wealth, education, and jobs. Words like *Okies* and *Arkies* signified "disrespected," "less than," "unwanted." Black families had arrived, and now, surrounded by railroad tracks, they had to bond together for survival.

• • •

One of the first Black morticians to open a business in Richmond was Charles Williams. Rose Manor Mortuary on Fifth and Nevin quickly became known throughout Black communities for serving Blacks at critical times in their lives.

Williams passed early in life from leukemia and was John Stewart's mentor. After Williams passed, John continued as proprietor of Rose Manor Funeral Service on Nevin. In the early 1970s he purchased property on Macdonald Avenue in Richmond, directly across the street from Harry Ellis High School. Loyal and faithful John continued to serve the Black community. His fights with the City of Richmond to achieve his vision and goals were intense, given the discrimination practices in place to create unimaginable obstacles. He persevered and fought against the racist practices preventing Blacks from acquiring property and owning businesses.

John personally knew most of the families he served—their struggles or hardships—and provided personalized service to Black families in their time of need. Dignified in his approach as a community leader, participating in community events, engaged in and actively supporting Black churches, and belonging to a variety of political and professional organizations, he was well known throughout the Richmond community. Charismatic and talented, he often shared humorous stories with a warm smile.

John was respected and appreciated by my family. He captured the essence of professionalism in a compassionate and caring way, making the loss of their loved ones easier to bear.

John, like Mother, sponsored Little League baseball, and upon greeting each other, their conversation quickly escalated to expressing pride in the S&S Market team and Stewart's team. But they'd always delve into the business aspects of their life, the challenges Blacks faced in achieving their goals.

• • •

I wasn't into baseball, even though the TVs in our homes were always set on the channel showing baseball games. I knew the males in our family were proud of Willie Mays and that he was someone important.

At some point while sponsoring her S&S Little League team, Mother met Willie Mays. I remember how excited she was when he began purchasing large quantities of merchandise from her store.

She would say, "See Glo, he's floating money back into Black communities. That's a smart man." I didn't understand the powerful message behind her words and his actions. Willie Mays was committed to helping Black communities.

A Willie Mays autographed portrait "To Ermestine" was framed and placed in the real estate office in full view and remained displayed in her office for years.

The picture I see now is crystal clear. Blacks were supporting Black businesses, and money was flowing into Black communities, increasing economic growth. I remember her words but didn't get the significance of the message between her words. Willie Mays was giving back to the Richmond community while inspiring youth in positive and meaningful ways. He was giving of his time and engaged with Richmond's Little League teams, floating cash back into Black communities, spending time with Richmond's youth, and spreading his wealth.

• • •

Soon after my mother and Mr. Martin moved to El Cerrito, John purchased his second El Cerrito home on Barrett Avenue. This was a house I knew so well from the outside, glancing at it in fascination while riding public transportation to junior high school, always wondering who lived there. This house was like a mansion to me, a reflection of luxury living by Whites like I would see on TV. Once Mother parked outside this house and we looked at it for a few minutes. She of course was proud of Blacks moving to homes in El Cerrito, gaining personal satisfaction from knowing the history of their struggles.

Stewart's Rose Manor Funeral Service is one of the few Black businesses in Richmond today where a family member still owns the land and the business. Lydia Stewart, John's daughter, a graduate of the University of California at Berkeley, taught English to middle and high school students in the Los Angeles Unified School District before returning to Richmond and teaching at Kennedy High School. After her father passed, Lydia resigned from the district and in 1997 took over the business to continue her family's legacy.

Lydia acquired additional property neighboring Stewart's mortuary, expanded the business, and continues to provide clients with her father's personal touch. Her clients are more diverse than her father's, and her commitment, loyalty to the community, and passion for the city remain strong. By maintaining the business and the land, she is honoring her father, a trailblazing Black pioneer who followed in the footsteps of his mentor, Charles Williams.

* * *

And then there is Sarita Ellison, the granddaughter of Aunt Lillian and great-niece of Doug Ellison. Lillian and Doug were children of the first Black families to settle in Richmond years before the migration to the Bay Area, and Doug's parents hailed from Temple, Texas.

Sarita, who is close in age to my daughter Kim, joined the Richmond Police Department in 2015, and she is currently a sergeant. I remember watching her tag behind her older brother and cousins at Aunt Lillian's house. Always curious, mostly quiet, but distinctly opinionated in expressing her thoughts. She was the baby girl in the family, but the other children knew not to mess with her.

I know Sarita to be a loving, kindhearted, humorous woman with a heart of gold. She demonstrates courage, strength, and determination to improve Richmond communities, showing no fear of what she may encounter. When Mother was in distress during the early 2000s and called for police assistance while dealing with tenant problems or property break-ins, often Sarita would arrive for her 911 call. Mother always made clear her appreciation of the strength Sarita possessed, her courage and style. Never backing down from confrontation or attempts at intimidation, Sarita is a reflection of Ellison dignity demanding respect.

And closer to my heart . . . while Mother was living with me and her Alzheimer's was at its worst, she would not recognize me and would go into panic mode. I remember her saying, "Who are you? I need to call Sarita to come see about me. Do you know Sarita? Call her for me. I want to go home, I don't know you."

When Hercules Police responded to her 911 calls, they could calm her down for the night. But she was searching for Sarita to help her. She couldn't remember my name, but Sarita was deep in her mind.

While Mother and I lived above the store, Doug Ellison and Lee Arthur Johnson provided her with comfort when she was in distress. During the end of her career, Sarita was her comfort source.

In 2001 Sarita started working in law enforcement at the Martinez Detention Facility, and over the years she became known by inmates as "no-nonsense Ellison." Working for the county as part of the sheriff's department, she was a deputy from 2001 to 2004, a corporal from 2004 to 2011, and a sergeant from 2011 to 2015.

She clearly demonstrates the strong characteristics of Doug Ellison, flashing a Hollywood smile but making sure the nature of her conversation is understood by all. Sarita is standing solidly on the shoulders of her migrant ancestors, and their vision of hope for Richmond remains the same. She merits my admiration for choosing to work in Richmond, for dealing with dangerous, unpredictable situations with no fear of the unknown.

* * *

During the 1950s, Parchester Village, a new development in Richmond envisioned as an integrated suburban community, evolved into an all-Black middle class. Many of the first-time homeowners there were veterans with good jobs in Richmond's shipyards, and with pride and purpose, they happily left North Richmond behind.

Cousin Gladys was one of the first homeowners in Parchester Village. She was politically astute, solidly middle class, active in AKA Sorority, and committed to the Richmond community.

Another middle-class Black family we knew was the Fullers. My friend Chester Fuller's grandparents had arrived in Richmond in 1942 from Pine Bluff, Arkansas. Chester's maternal grandfather, Paul Linsy, was a skilled and experienced carpenter making a pretty good living and finding consistent work. Chester's maternal grandmother, Lee Ethel Linsy, was a Rosie the Riveter and contributed to US military success in World War II. The entrance of Black men and women into war industry jobs did not happen naturally. There was great resistance from labor groups to the hiring of Blacks for anything except menial service positions.

To defeat our enemies by keeping our industries strong, millions of women were encouraged to take over jobs previously done by men. Women responded to the country's need by stepping up to fill these positions. Black women contributed to the war effort in factories that focused on the construction, manufacture, and assembly of ships, aircraft, vehicles, and munitions. When men began returning home from the war, the government instituted propaganda campaigns that urged women to return to being housewives. But being able to support the soldiers by helping make useful products to win the war made women feel accomplished and proud.

After being discharged from the Army in 1946, Leroy Fuller followed his wife's parents—Paul and Lee Ethel—and arrived in Richmond with his wife, Juanita. Leroy had been a tech sergeant in the Army and believed in hard work. Upon arrival in Richmond, Leroy and Juanita rented from Willie Foster, a prominent Black man in the community. Leroy worked for the city, picking up dog poop at Nicholas Park. He decided this was not the right job for him and began working for an established construction company, learning to become a professional carpenter, like his father-in-law. He and Juanita opened a small store on Battery Street in 1951 and lived behind the store.

In 1952, Leroy and Juanita purchased a vacant lot on York Street and constructed a business from the ground up: a store on the first floor and a hotel on the second floor. At twelve years old, Chester worked beside his family to build eight one-bedroom units, with a communal kitchen and living room and shared bathrooms. They did this with the help and expertise of Black electricians, plumbers, and architects, all under the supervision of Chester's grandfather. During Chester's high school years, his parents built a duplex, and again he was actively involved, learning the basics of construction and working beside his family.

Many of the celebrities who came to North Richmond to play in local nightclubs rented rooms from the Fullers during their stay, although most of the rooms were rented by longer-term tenants. On a daily basis Chester and his brother, Anthony, were responsible for hotel chores, like cleaning the kitchen, bathroom, and common areas of the hotel, as well as store-related chores.

The Fullers brought a hustle to make it in Richmond, and they were good at it. The family owned six different businesses within Richmond. The parents were the head of the family team; their boys were businessmen working hard so the family would prosper.

In 1952, the Fuller family purchased a house in Parchester Village, using Leroy's GI Bill benefits, and resided there until 1970, when they bought a beautiful ranch-style house on Pebble Drive in the El Cerrito hills.

In 1972, in partnership with her friends, Carolyn and Ted, Juanita opened CJ's Lounge in the Mercantile Center, a new shopping center, a block away from my parents' office. CJ's quickly became a location for Blacks to meet and discuss business and network while enjoying a cocktail and scrumptious food. Occasionally while working in the office, I walked to CJ's to talk with my father about one thing or another. His demeanor would be serious when discussing business or joyful when talking with friends. CJ's had the perfect atmosphere to strategize, mobilize, and create vibrant thriving communities to live, work, and succeed.

I remember working in my mother's store while I was in high school and seeing the Fuller truck, packed with watermelons, cruising down the street. Sixteen-year-old Chester had created his own watermelon business. He would drive by, smiling and yelling, "Watermelons, watermelons." I thought that was so cool!

While visiting Baldie's house, Larry, Yvonne, and I often walked to the Fullers' grocery store. Chester and Anthony would be busily working side by side with their parents. Mother would always tell me, "You see those Fuller brothers? They are hustling for their family. That's what you need to do, too, instead of spending time with your friends. Life is all about having a hustle."

Willie Mays, supporting Black communities

Sarita Ellison and her dad, Richard

GAME CHANGER 23

BLACK PANTHERS AND COWBOYS

During the 1940s, the Richmond Police Department faced rapidly changing conditions. During World War II, the building of the ships *Liberty* and *Victory* in the Bay Area caused Richmond's population to explode. Thanks to federal funding, Richmond hired seventy-five additional police officers in the summer of 1943.

In 1954, *Brown v. Board of Education* brought with it challenging periods of integration. New civil rights and human rights were established for Black people. Affirmative action policies, originated by John F. Kennedy and signed into law by Lyndon B. Johnson in the Civil Rights Act of 1964, promoted diversity and equality in job hiring and college admissions. Johnson sought to end discrimination and improve opportunities for Blacks.

Richmond's Black migrants were frustrated with the high level of poverty in their community, and they fought for educational opportunities for their children. They flipped the script on the secret story that Whites had written for Black lives. Some families were able to achieve economic success, educating themselves to secure better jobs and purchase homes beyond North Richmond or Parchester Village. In the Golden State, they were shaking the chains that forced them to live only on land neglected by everyone else. As a result, class divisions raised their ugly heads.

By the 1960s, race riots were happening in cities across the United States; Blacks were fighting for their civil rights. In Oakland, California, in October 1966, the first draft of the Black Panther Party for Self-Defense program was created. In all-black attire, wearing ebony-color berets, flaunting closed and raised fists, carrying unconcealed weapons, strong Black men became visible in the streets surrounding the Bay Area. The Black Panther Party invaded our consciousness with the illusion of power to protect our neighborhoods and our families from harm and injustice.

Initially, the Black Panthers' main objectives were to protect and promote the civil rights of oppressed people and combat police brutality. Soon, however, their principles of self-determination, service, and self-defense were also associated with their vision.

On the other end of the spectrum, the actions of renegade White police officers brought attention to the life of Black migrant families living in North Richmond. These were bad elements within the police force who endangered the lives of Blacks living in Richmond. They were accused of brutality, unnecessarily aggressive conduct, verbal escalation of situations, and abuse of power. Some people within the Richmond Police Department looked the other way and tolerated the violence and unfair treatment these renegade officers brought to North Richmond; no real consequences for their bad behavior were ever revealed. The North Richmond community felt that the county and city of Richmond had failed to deal with this "deviant cult" of violence-prone officers.

In 1968, the Guardians of Justice was formed. This group of Black police officers was standing up and testifying, both in court and within communities, to stop the deteriorating relationship between the Richmond Police, the Sheriff's Department, and the

Black community. The Guardians wanted the police force to halt the long-standing misconduct they witnessed on the job.

In April 1967, Denzil Dowell, an unarmed Black resident of North Richmond, was shot and killed by sheriff's deputies at Third and Chesley. A coroner's inquest ruled the shooting justifiable.

The Black Panther Party responded to a request from the Dowell family for protection from police harassment within the North Richmond community. The first issue of the *Black Panther Community News Service* was published with the headline "Why Was Denzil Dowell Killed?"

• • •

In 1966 I was a senior in high school focused on graduating, friends, fashion, and Motown. I was a debutante, living a new and exciting life, with friends in the El Cerrito hills, whose parents bought them new cars for their sixteenth birthdays. My mother and I no longer lived above the store in fear of violence or theft. Our relationship with the police was trusting and solid; they had responded to our being victims of crime by establishing a positive relationship of safety and concern for our well-being.

In May 1967, when the newly formed and visibly armed Black Panthers led a protest at the California State Assembly to protest a bill that would have outlawed openly carrying loaded guns, I joined other Black students at El Cerrito High School in supporting them. Although few in number, we identified with "say it loud: I'm Black, and I'm proud." Whether we viewed the Black Panthers as revolutionaries or criminals, they were strong Black men, fathers, brothers, uncles, sons fighting for Black communities and risking their lives to do so. Different generations had different ideologies, but we shared the common thread of civil rights.

Our communities were proud of the Black Panthers for their exhibition of unapologetic Blackness and their fight for Black people's rights. We all knew that allegations of police brutality and aggression against Black people in Richmond were rampant and alarming.

My family had varying degrees of connection with the Black Panthers. Baldie and her family were still residing in North Richmond, and family visits were frequent. Larry stood in front of a North Richmond neighborhood grocery store to sell the *Black Panther Community News Service.*

Baldie was affiliated with the Peace and Freedom Party, a left-wing antiwar and pro–civil rights organization. First organized in California in 1967, the party opposed the Vietnam War and supported Black liberation, farmworker organizing, women's liberation, and the gay rights movement. In 1968, the party held a statewide founding convention in Richmond, and Black Panther leader Eldridge Cleaver was nominated as a presidential candidate.

Meanwhile, the local newspaper, the *Richmond Independent,* portrayed the Black Panthers as a hate group. Other media flipped stories from black and white to grey, labeling Black Panthers as a "Black nationalist" group full of criminals and violent sociopolitical misfits rather than local residents developing supportive community programs and defending Black communities against racial violence and police aggression. Black rights were aligned with criminality, which government leaders said needed to be met with "law and order." The Black Panthers were moving targets for law enforcement, and the police and FBI were able to provoke them, effectively criminalizing what the organization was doing.

In an internal FBI memo in 1963, Dr. Martin Luther King Jr. was branded by J. Edgar Hoover as "the most dangerous Negro of the future in this nation." At the same time, the Southern Christian Leadership Conference, the civil rights group headed by Dr. King, was deemed too passive by Malcolm X and the Black Panthers. Again, different ideologies, but a common commitment to civil rights.

* * *

In 1982, renegade White police officers in the Richmond area became known as the "Cowboys." The experiences of Blacks in Richmond communities were affected by the Black Panthers and the Cowboys alike. The voices and actions of Medgar Evers, Martin Luther King Jr., and Malcolm X, W. E. B. Du Bois, Frederick Douglass, Muhammad Ali, and Madam C. J. Walker filtered our thoughts, our actions, our way of thinking, our way of living, our values, and our hopes for our children. Black migrants had to rise above a systemically racist society whose policies entrapped Blacks in a world of struggle, unfair treatment, and harsh financial consequences.

In 1968, some friends and I attended a "Free Huey" rally held at the Oakland Auditorium on Huey P. Newton's birthday. Stokely Carmichael, Ron Dellums, and the Peace and Freedom Party participated. We brought so much pride and supportive energy for the Black Panthers. We knew from personal experience that high-ranking Richmond police officials and some officers were seldom disciplined for their involvement in police brutality. We knew from listening to our parents about police and government corruption, unfair policies and practices destroying our rights for equal opportunities. Our trust in the law was eroded by what we knew, heard, or read, and we seized the momentum to support our Black communities.

Like the Black Panthers, Mother aligned her values, intentions, talents, skills, and actions to promote opportunities for Blacks. She educated herself and created her own road map for shifting the old, stale paradigms of education, housing, and equality.

Her weapon of choice was her voice. With a broad understanding that hardworking Black men and women were being entrapped within a justice system of unfairness and discrimination, she forged ahead.

• • •

In 1982, the National Association for the Advancement of Colored People (NAACP) filed a lawsuit against the Richmond Police Department. According to Brandon Kooi's *Seven Highly Effective Police Leaders: 1895–Modern Times,*

> During the trial, Richmond's general population was 48 percent African-American and 40 percent white. The 161-member RPD was 20 percent African-American, and the trial showed the divisiveness between the white and Black officers. The civil suit alleged that the defendants all failed to address a pattern of misconduct and reckless unprofessionalism by a deviant subculture of white police officers on the swing shift who referred to themselves as "cowboys" because of the Western-style boots they wore. Attorneys entered into evidence a photograph of the officers on horseback holding a confederate flag. Several Black officers broke rank and testified at the trial . . . They claimed that an unwritten code of conduct condoned the rogue cowboy violence . . . The Black officers represented a group they referred to as the "Guardians of Justice" . . . The lawsuit resulted in the most significant judgment for racially motivated wrongful death in the U.S. history at that time."[6]

In 1984, my father and I watched a CBS *60 Minutes* segment on the civil rights problems of the Richmond Police Department. The show presented arguments about alleged brutality by White officers; it described patrolmen, mostly White, as "Cowboys" and the night detail, primarily Black officers, as "Guardians of Justice." Black officers recounted instances of unwarranted brutality by swing-shift officers. A representative for the Richmond Police Department called the show "one-sided" and "accusatory."[7]

Dad was clearly agitated by the spokesperson for the police department. He knew firsthand the shenanigans going on targeting Blacks. Doug Ellison, Aunt Lillian's brother-in-law, often described examples of the Cowboys' bad intentions. Doug Ellison was a resident of North Richmond for many years after becoming a police officer. He knew the faces behind stories of aggressive behavior and disrespect.

After watching the *60 Minutes* show, I repeated the story my mother had shared with me so many times about the white cross placed on their yard and how she never understood why my father didn't get bothered by it. Dad listened, his eyes on the television, sipping a cup of coffee and smoking a cigarette. I waited for his comment, but there was none, and I resumed focusing on the television. When he spoke, it was after he had reflected for some time. He shared the real fear the cross had brought to his manhood and his doorstep. His fear for his family.

He had lived in the community with his father and sister as homeowners since arriving in Richmond. They owned land and farmed their land, with animals and produce. No one bothered his family, and they were living a good life in harmony and peace.

"It wasn't until a larger number of Blacks migrated to Richmond that tensions, fear, and oppression entered my life," he said. "Your mother's anger at being referred to as an Okie, I understand."

There were moments when I felt overwhelming sorrow for my father. Becoming a paraplegic as a young man, life as he knew it never the same, the emotional challenge of how to put the puzzle pieces back together. This was one of those moments. Listening to his words, watching his face and the lap tray always on his lap. He drank his coffee, smoked another cigarette, and we watched television in silence.

I sat pondering his words as he rolled to the sink, designed for someone standing, and started washing his coffee cup and a few dishes. I said, "So you knew why my mother jumped on your sister."

He said with a chuckle, "Yep, I sure did."

A few days later, Father told me he'd heard news that a fight had erupted when two family members took opposing views of the *60 Minutes* program. After the show, one family member shot and killed the other.

I asked, "Did that happen in Richmond?"

"No, in Oakland," he replied. "That is such a tragedy for their family. I don't understand why or how it escalated to the point of violence. Do you?"

I shrugged my shoulders; that situation was way too deep for me to comprehend. Nonetheless, from an early age, I had observed Mother fighting for what she believed was respectful, right, and fair. Standing up for beliefs and turning family time into a battle zone was something I had witnessed. I recollected the scenes of the lady fleeing from her boyfriend, breaking into the security zone of my car; guns pointed during armed robberies in our store. I thought how differently those outcomes could have unfolded in a fraction of a second. In those moments, minds are racing, trying to figure out what is happening, caught in the moment—what should I do? Engulfed in fear and panic, unable to comprehend the danger of the situation.

One thing I knew for sure was that as children, Yvonne, like myself, grew up with some fear of the violence brought to our homes by our parents' businesses. A quick wrong decision could have changed our lives forever.

Flowers from tenants on Ermestine's birthday, May 5, 2005

Ermestine, property inspection

GAME CHANGER 24

THE LANDLORD

As Mother began acquiring more properties, she started driving by them frequently to see what was going on. If she saw garbage thrown around the front yard, people hanging out, cars parked on grass, or any visual damage to a building, that would result in an unexpected visit from Mrs. Petgrave. These visits started with a friendly greeting but could change quickly to address the concern that promoted the visit and clearly articulate her standards or expectations.

She had zero tolerance for tenants who did not demonstrate good-neighbor characteristics or who showed lazy or destructive tendencies. Underneath the image of being a tough landlord, she had a heart for tenants who were going through bad or hard times, struggling with unexpected circumstances, health issues, or financial challenges. She was lenient and allowed them to get food on credit from her store, or she reduced rent, or forfeited a month's payment.

My mother's tenants respected her and understood that when she addressed issues that were very disturbing to her, her message could be sharp, to the point, and sometimes delivered in an unexpectedly cold and hostile manner. One example occurred during my sophomore year in high school. My mother and I had spent a weekend planting new flowers at an apartment building, so she decided to drive by to water the plants. As we walked to the courtyard area, we saw that there were dirty baby diapers strewn all around.

"Oh, no, this is not going to happen," she said, and quickly started banging on a nearby front door.

A young man opened the door and said, "Hello, Mrs. Petgrave."

As I stood in the doorway, I could see his girlfriend sitting on the couch, holding a baby. He invited us in; the apartment was in a state of disarray. There were dirty baby bottles and dishes everywhere. We had to step on clothes and garbage as we walked toward the living room.

Mother quickly surveyed the living room and kitchen, sprung around, and said, "This is where I have to draw a line in the sand. Why are there dirty diapers all around the courtyard?"

The man responded, "Mrs. Petgrave, I'm doing my best."

Quick-witted, she smiled and said, "Well, your best is not good enough for me. You guys can't throw dirty diapers outside. It's not going to hurt you to pick up a broom and sweep your entryway. I can't take care of you. If you can't do better than this, you are going to have to move. I know your mother won't deal with this, and neither will I."

She glanced around the room again. "Clean up this apartment. Get up off your butt and clean this up. This is shameful how you are living in here. I won't have it!"

The young couple did not say a word while she clearly articulated her frustration with their behavior. It wasn't in her character to sugarcoat her feelings, and she let them know whatever came to her mind.

After she had said her piece, she looked at the young woman

and said, "You have a cute baby, but you are going to have to do better with housekeeping." She then turned and smiled at the young man and asked, "How is your mother?"

He responded with, "Mother is doing fine."

Mother said, "That's good to hear. Tell her I said hello. But both of you are going to have to do better. Clean up this mess!"

We started walking toward the front door, and as he turned to open the door, he said, "By the way, Mrs. Petgrave, I just lost my job and won't be able to pay next month's rent on time."

She stopped and looked at him. "Lord have mercy, just clean up this filthy mess. Get up off your butt while your girlfriend is taking care of your baby. You know why you're living here, don't you? Because your mother called and asked me to find a place for you and your new baby to live, and that's what I did. But you are going to have to do better if you want to stay here." As we walked out of the apartment, she turned and said, "Pick up these dirty diapers, and I don't ever want to see garbage in your entryway again! Clean this mess up now! You know, a lazy ox has to drink dirty water."

He followed us outside and responded, "Okay, Mrs. Petgrave, but what does that ox sentence mean?" as he began to pick up the dirty diapers. "Think about it," she smiled.

We stopped to water the new plants, and a bit later we noticed the young man picking up garbage around his area and sweeping his steps.

"Call me to discuss your job situation tomorrow, and tell your mama to call me," Mother said to him. When we got into the car, she said, "Gloria, let's hope for the best for that young man. I don't know. He may have to move back in with his mama unless he can get it together."

With that, we were on our way to do more drive-by viewings of her properties before heading home. She expressed her concerns about tenants taking advantage of her or mistreating property. I remained quiet, not really listening to her rant and rage, wondering how my own day was going to end after she saw the math grade on my report card.

After we got home, she asked me, "Didn't you get your report card today? Where is it?"

"In my lunch bag," I replied.

"Well, get it out and let me see it." From that point until I fell asleep, all of her attention was focused on me. Hearing her choice of words, I knew that she was not a happy camper. "Go sit down at the kitchen table and do your homework. Don't even think about watching TV for a while. This is ridiculous. You're going to have to do better than this."

I wondered if using the same response that the young man had used earlier, "I'm doing the best I can do," would get me the same reaction he had gotten from Mother. So I decided to say, "I just don't understand algebra."

"Well," she replied, "then I'm going to find you a tutor." She continued, "I told that messy young man that a lazy ox has to drink dirty water. What does that mean to you?" I sat there dumbfounded as she said, "Think about it. Lord have mercy! Just do your homework!"

Soon after, I had a tutor who came to our house twice a week.

* * *

One day an older lady came into the real estate office while Mother and I were working. Several neighbors around the unit she was renting had called with complaints regarding her grandson. He consistently had friends hanging out in front of the apartment building, littering and becoming a nuisance.

I had taken several of the complaint calls, and when the lady walked in, I diverted my attention to their conversation. I already knew Mother was unhappy about what she had been hearing from other tenants. Mother and the older lady greeted each other pleasantly.

Mother, calmly and without hesitation, said, "I don't need any distraction right now, so if you aren't in my life to help improve our community, I may not be the right landlord for you." The older lady didn't respond, and Mother continued, "Your grandson cannot be allowed to make your neighbors uncomfortable, with his friends drinking and partying outside in front of the building and trashing the place with garbage. That's something I can't stand. He needs to be in school or working somewhere."

The older lady remained silent. Mother shifted her attention to me, as I sat watching and listening to their conversation. "Gloria, what are you doing? Get busy. You need to pay attention to what you're doing."

She looked back at the older lady, who had not said another word after her initial hello upon entering the office. "You are right, Mrs. Petgrave, but my grandson, he doesn't listen to me. He does exactly what he wants to, as if I'm living with him and he's paying the rent. I need help; can you talk with him?"

My mother got up and poured a cup of coffee. "You know, I occasionally drive by my properties just to see what's going on. I drove by there the other day, and noticed your boy and some of his friends drinking in front of the building. I sat there watching. I saw cars cruise past and then stop. Your boy would approach the car and give them something, and they would give him money. Then the car would drive off. What do you think is going on?"

The older woman just sat there, listening, fidgeting with her purse. Not looking up, she was clearly uncomfortable with the conversation; her foot was bouncing up and down. After a few moments of silence, she responded, "That's what they do."

"Would you like some coffee?"

"No, thank you, Mrs. Petgrave. I am going to buy a soda in your store before I leave. But I do need help with my grandson."

"Well, I can tell you this—that may be 'what they do,' but they can't do it on my property. And if they continue, I'm sorry to say this, but you will have to move because I can't tolerate that. I am trying to improve the Black community. Sometimes I feel bad about selling alcohol in the community I live in. But that is legal, and I am making an honest living."

"Where is your grandson? Is he at home?" Mother continued.

The older lady looked through her purse and pulled out a money order. "I think so; he was there when I left. Here is the rent check."

Mother said to me, "Gloria, come get her rent and give her a receipt." She asked the lady if she was still working, and how did she get here?

"Mrs. Petgrave, today is my day off and I walked here."

"Okay, I will take you home and then talk to your grandson."

After I gave the older woman her rent receipt, my mother grabbed her purse and said, "Gloria, when I get back, I expect you to have completed that work."

The older lady smiled at me and said good-bye as they walked out the door. Most of the time, I didn't want to go with my mother to talk with tenants, but this time I did. I wanted to hear her conversation with the grandson. He was a few years older than I, a nice-looking guy, and he was popular with the girls.

When Mother returned, I informed her about the phone calls that came in and asked her, "What did you tell her grandson?"

She looked at the paperwork I was working on and said, "That's none of your business. Your job is to finish this work. Get busy; you don't have all day! We have other things to do."

She began returning folks' calls. Not long afterward, the young man in question disappeared from school, and my peers said that he had moved to Los Angeles to live with his father.

* * *

President Lyndon B. Johnson, in a 1965 commencement address at Howard University, said, "Negro poverty is not white poverty." That resonated with my mother. She felt that in the nation and in Richmond specifically, White men were imposing disadvantageous and ambiguous policies on Blacks, restricting where they could live and the opportunities they could pursue. The struggle was real, and in Mother's mind, part of that struggle was local: idle hands and wasted minds needed to get busy within the housing units she owned.

American Trust Building, 1001 Macdonald Avenue, Downtown Richmond

PART FOUR:

LIFE WITH MR. MARTIN

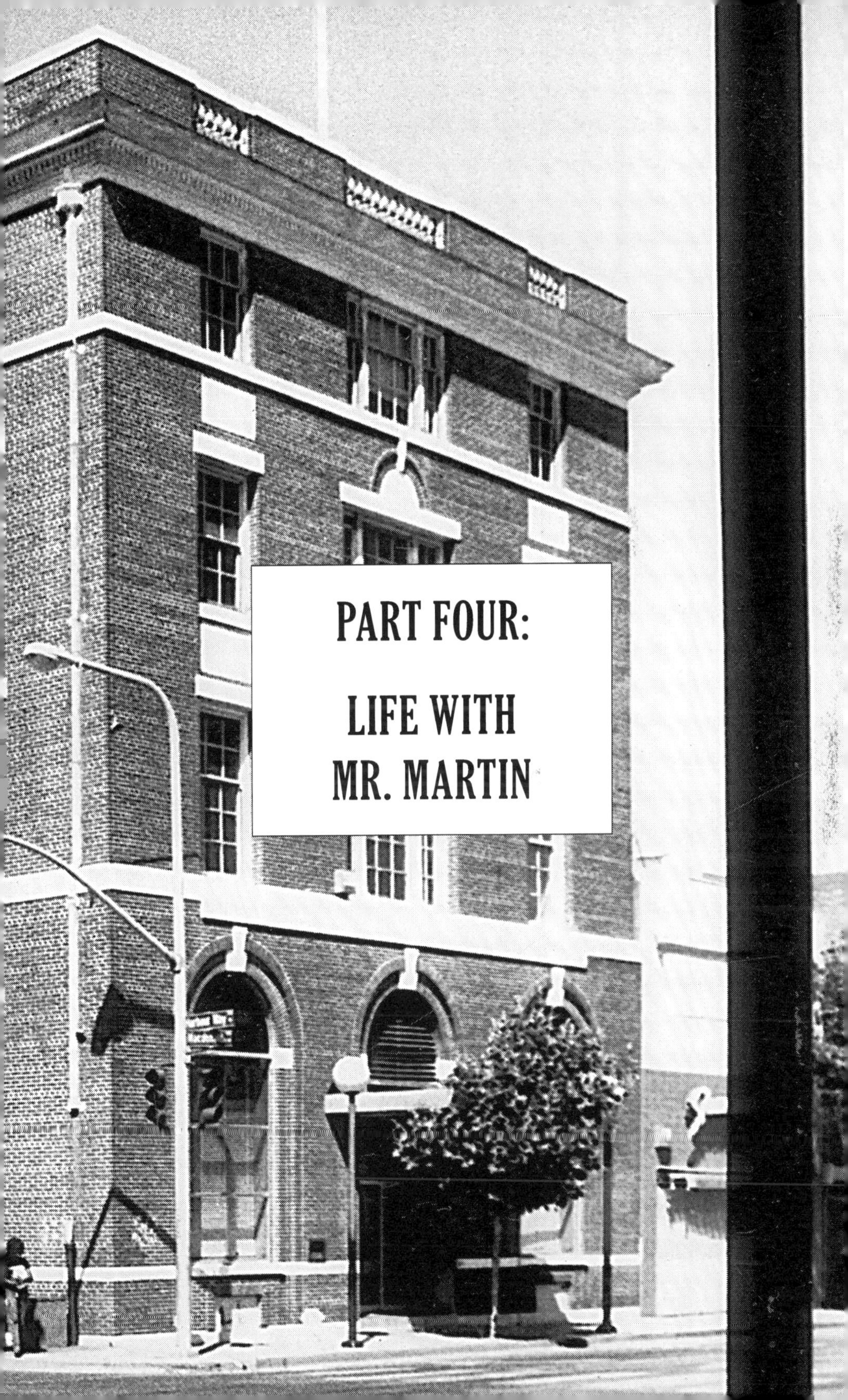

Ermestine and William Martin at a political event

GAME CHANGER 25

INNOCENT OR GUILTY

One day during my first year at Contra Costa Junior College, my mother called me, frantic and irate. She informed me that my friend Duane and a couple of his friends had robbed the store at gunpoint.

It so happened that they had parked the getaway car around the corner from the store, in front of the Richmond School District warehouse. A school district employee who visited the store often was in his office, looked out the window, and became suspicious of the young men sitting in the car. He watched them get out of the car and walk around the corner, then he wrote down the license plate number.

Duane and his partners had entered the store and pointed a gun at Mother's employee, demanded money, taken it, and then run out of the store. The school district employee noticed them as they ran back to the car and sped away. Soon after that, he heard police sirens arriving, and he went around the corner to see what was happening. He gave the police officers a description of the car and its license plate number. The robbers were caught and arrested when they returned to Berkeley, where they lived.

I met Duane while participating in the Links Cotillion activities and we eventually became a couple. An only child, he had graduated from St. Mary's College High School, an all-male private school, and lived in one of the more desirable areas in Berkeley with parents who adored him.

During his junior year, his parents bought him a new sports car. He would come pick me up with the top down, and I remember my mother saying, "I watched his little sports car going up Tehama; your hair was blowing in the wind. He is a nice young man."

Duane spent a lot of time visiting me and my mother at our house. We had no fear of him and welcomed him into our lives; he shared with us his goals for the future, including his intention to graduate from Howard University.

After graduating from high school, I still worked in the store. As my boyfriend, Duane would visit my house and drive me to work and stay with me for hours, helping customers. He would come behind the counter and into the storage room and the real estate office; he knew the whole building. So when he robbed the store, he knew just what to do. Ironically, the two guys I had a crush on early in my life, Dwayne and Duane, both hid their intentions behind a beautiful smile and loving words.

From that point on, my mother became even more cautious about which of my friends she allowed in her house or around the store. Duane and his friends were convicted and served time in prison. This was hard for Mother to digest. She had worked hard to put me in an environment where my friends were going to college, lived in the better communities, and their parents were attentive and hardworking.

• • •

In 1971, I had just graduated from college and was working in the store for the summer. I was putting some produce out when a nicely dressed Black man approached me.

He said, "Do you know who I am?"

I looked at him and said, "No."

He looked sternly at me and said, "You should! You sent me to prison for robbing this store."

I was speechless. He turned around and walked out of the store. I stood there, my mind racing, confused and dumbfounded. I didn't know what to think or how to process his words.

I began to think about the robberies that had happened while I was working at the store during junior high school. Talking to the police officers about the robbery, identifying the suspect, going to court, and testifying.

I had been subpoenaed several times while I was in elementary and middle school to identify Black men who had denied knowledge of or involvement in an armed robbery at our store. I wasn't alone when any of these robberies took place; there were customers and employees who also identified the suspect. But now, I began to second-guess what had happened in years past.

If he really was guilty of robbing the store, would he have come back to approach me? Had I sent an innocent man to prison? I locked the store and went into the real estate office in a state of confusion. I shared with Mother what had just happened. She listened carefully and said, "But you were not alone in your identification of him. Maybe he wanted you to know that he served prison time for the robbery and now has turned his life around."

I sat in the office, getting my thoughts together, as Mother answered the phone and started talking real estate business. I was thinking that maybe I had been swayed by listening to another person's opinion of who the suspect was. Did I help send an innocent man to prison?

This was during the civil rights movement, and I had become more aware of the injustices against Blacks. I was understanding and hearing the struggle of Black America through the Black Panthers, Martin Luther King Jr., and Malcolm X. My mother and I both wore Afros. She often attended political and business events focused on opportunities for Blacks. She was developing a strong, positive reputation in the community as a fighter for human rights who dealt with discrimination head-on and refused to back down. While in college, my friends and I often attended Black Panther political rallies and Flower Child events in San Francisco.

My heart sank as I wondered if an innocent Black man had served time in prison for a robbery he did not commit based on my misidentifying him.

I went over each moment of the encounter: he had come into the store dressed very professionally, walked through the aisles slowly, then stopped at the produce counter where I was. He definitely recognized me. Then, very smooth with his words, he looked into my eyes to deliver the words that jumbled my brain: "Do you know who I am?"

He had served years in prison. What were his feelings in court ten years earlier, listening to me testifying and identifying him as the man pointing a gun in my direction? How did he feel, what emotions were raging in his body if in fact he was an innocent man? I knew from my Black Studies classes that Blacks are overrepresented at every level of the criminal justice system, and now I was thinking about those serving time for wrongful convictions.

I looked at my mother behind her desk, dressed up and elegant. Why was she still on her business call? I wanted and needed to talk to her now. I went back into the store and unlocked the door for customers who were waiting outside. Perhaps she didn't want to talk with me about this incident, but I thought her mind, like mine, had to be rewinding the man's words.

I kept reminding myself, as Mother had, that I wasn't the only one who had identified him as the robber. But that didn't excuse my error, if it was one. After all, the cashier working in the store with me at the time was Angel, a White woman. It made more sense for her to misidentify him.

That evening, as Mother was driving us home after work in her new Cadillac, she glanced at me and said, "What's done is done." We rode in silence for a short time and then she said, "We've had a long, tough day, so what do you want to eat?"

While having dinner at one of my mother's favorite spots, the Golden Gate Lanes bowling alley in El Cerrito, she shared that she was considering selling the store because her conscience was bothering her about selling alcohol in a Black community.

That man never returned, and my mother and I never discussed this situation again, but the possibility that I had identified an innocent man as a robber lingered in my brain for years after, and his words "Do you know who I am?" will remain in my soul for the rest of my life.

Sergeant Lee Arthur Johnson, Richmond Police Department, circa 1974

GAME CHANGER 26

GUARDIANS OF JUSTICE

In 2006, after joining St. John Missionary Baptist Church, I learned more about the personal, religious, and spiritual side of Arthur Lee Johnson. From the choir he led those uplifting songs with his natural, beautiful voice and rhythm. Deacon Johnson held leadership roles in the church where his father, Robert Louis Johnson, served as pastor, and he worked in collaboration with my mother to build HUD housing in Richmond before he retired. But my first encounters with Arthur Lee were when he was a Richmond police officer rescuing Mother and me from harm and fear. A caring and inspiring man, he consistently fought to ensure equity and fairness of treatment for Blacks residing in the Richmond communities.

When Mother and I were victims of crime at the liquor store, Doug Ellison or Arthur Lee were the two strong, dark-skinned, regal, handsome, and caring men who most often showed up to our rescue. They were my heroes to look up to, because of their courage, their strength, and their heroic spirit as they spoke words of kindness and compassion to calm Mother down. I always marveled at their presence and the calmness it brought to my world.

Day and night, Doug or Arthur Lee periodically patrolled our store to reduce the incidence of crime. (Unlike burglars breaking in after store hours, armed robbery incidents often occurred during the day or just before closing.) Occasionally they would park the patrol car and come inside the store to say hello.

Both men had outgoing personalities and a very large presence. They were smooth operators, showing their true cards and their game plan. Everyone took Doug and Arthur Lee seriously.

Less known to me, the Cowboys of the Richmond Police Department served as one source of the racial injustice felt by Blacks, perpetrating acts of violence, brutality, and aggression. This was a sad reality that I had not experienced in my personal world. Incognito, they, along with other agencies, created unfair treatment and barriers for Blacks. The agencies forced deep poverty into Black neighborhoods as well as a fear of the law.

Law enforcement brought in train cars and used them to block train-track entrances into North Richmond at every crossing. They created barriers in and out of North Richmond for no apparent reason; there were no riots, no burning or damaging of properties to justify such action. The FBI infiltrated North Richmond as well, and with their presence a grey cloud of fear penetrated the community.

Blacks respected and loved their community, and they were tired of the Cowboys and their unjustified abuse. But no one knew how to stop them.

Black businesses in Richmond were supporting the Black Panthers' Breakfast Program and academic tutoring at the Neighborhood House of North Richmond. Bobby Seale and Huey Newton became part of the landscape, and they were responsible for creating a branch of the Oakland Black Panthers in the heart of North Richmond.

There were also efforts among Black law enforcement officers to improve local conditions. Doug Ellison and Arthur

Lee Johnson were two of nine Richmond police officers who formed the Guardians of Justice in 1972. Officer Marvin Richard Smith was the Guardians' first president. The others were Officers Ollie Glover, Otis Timmons Jr., Rudolph Johnson, Danny Nelson, Harold Redic, and Michael Nichols. They had an average of at least two years of college; they were well educated and trained for their jobs. The rest of the department had an average of one year of college. These nine exemplary officers knew that something needed to be done to confront and stop the serious police misconduct in Richmond.

Two of the nine officers, Douglas Ellison and Arthur Lee Johnson, were consistently part of the fabric of Mother's life. They were passionate about bringing change within the Richmond Police Department.

The Guardians' intent was to inform the community about their personal observations of misconduct by other Richmond police officers. We learned from them that within the Richmond Police Department, some officers were engaged in unlawful acts such as beatings, verbal abuse, and illegal detentions and arrests, primarily against Black young adult males. The officers justified this treatment by charging Blacks with offenses such as resisting arrest or interfering with the official lawful duties of an officer.

The nine informing Black officers wanted to create a collective plan and take direct action to bring about necessary change within the department. Routinely harassing and beating Black residents, treating Black males as suspicious targets, had to stop. Their hope was to stop police brutality, even at the risk of losing their jobs.

The Ellison brothers were very proud of Doug—one of the first Black police officers hired in the city of Richmond, he ranked up to sergeant by age forty-four. He was the only Black police officer in Contra Costa County above the rank of patrolman, and he was on the force long enough to qualify for his retirement pension.

Doug lived in North Richmond at the time, and around his brothers and family, he loved to joke, laugh, and also be serious in his unique, quiet way.

His brothers and close male friends encouraged him to try to stop other officers from enforcing illegal treatment of Black males. My father often repeated the story of an incident Doug had shared with him. While Doug was on patrol in Parchester Village, a predominantly Black neighborhood, he saw two White patrolmen engaging in illegal conduct, using unwarranted aggressive force. He ordered both officers to return to the police station. My father impersonated Doug's facial expression and voice as he told the story: "The two White officers told me that I cannot tell them what to do."

My father and grandfather were sympathetic to the situation Doug was in. Doug felt that actions directed at him from within the department were demeaning and insulting.

The Guardians of Justice's disclosure of police brutality by their White colleagues became controversial and divisive within the Richmond Police Department and the City of Richmond. Doug spoke out and accused fellow officers of forms of racist behavior he had personally observed in riots following the assassination of Martin Luther King Jr.

Riots were not expected in Richmond, and the unprepared police department found itself surrounded by incidents of such intensity that mutual-aid pacts with police departments in nearby communities were invoked. Most of these departments were composed almost totally of White personnel.

Clarice and I were in high school at the time, and after one of our outings with my father, Lillian walked over to the car when we were dropping Clarice back home. Chatting with my father, she mentioned Doug, her brother-in-law: "Ike, you know Blacks have been the target of illegal conduct by cops. I don't want my sons to deal with the treatment their father received. Doug is strong, and he will survive any on-the-job consequences from initiating the lawsuit against the police officers. You only have Gloria. I am concerned about my sons."

My father said, "You are so right."

In 1968 the nine Black Richmond police officers, represented by Henry Ramsey, Esq., stated publicly that within the Richmond Police Department, colleagues were regularly engaging in unlawful acts, including illegal detentions and arrests, beatings, and unjustified verbal abuse. Police misconduct had been committed largely by White officers and directed primarily against young Black men. In his memoir, *The Life Story of Henry Ramsey Jr.*, Ramsey confirmed that "rarely are police officers, Black or White, willing to stand up and be counted by publicly naming fellow officers who engage in such improper and unlawful conduct."

Richmond was ordered to provide sensitivity training to members of the Richmond Police Department. Other lawsuits filed resulted in a consent decree mandating that for each White officer promoted, a Black officer must be promoted.[8]

Sergeant Douglas Ellison retired from the Richmond Police Department in 1973, and Arthur Lee Johnson retired as a captain in 1992. Arthur Lee was the first Black captain of the Richmond Police Department and, after retirement, became active on the board of directors of the Richmond Police Activities League (RPAL), a nonprofit corporation founded in 1981. Currently, youth participating in RPAL have access to training classes, after-school tutoring, and field trips, and crime-prevention programs embedded in a One-Stop Youth Center and gymnasium provide access to a wide variety of activities for youth in West Contra Costa County.

In 2009 the Richmond Police Department celebrated a century of service. Although not perfect, I believe that the Richmond

Police Department has made significant progress against crime and has improved its relationship with the community. In 2015, US Attorney General Loretta Lynch visited Richmond, ending her national tour in a city starting to shake off its reputation as a crime capital.

Richmond was ranked among the ten most dangerous cities in the United States, the so-called murder capital of the Bay Area, as recently as 2007. But under Richmond Police Chief Chris Magnus, the city was beginning to attract recognition as a model of improved community and police relations. As of this writing, Magnus has been nominated by President Joe Biden to be the Commissioner of US Customs and Border Protection. At the time of this writing, the Richmond Police Department is led by Bisa French, the department's first Black woman chief, who is targeting the work that needs to be done to continue to improve community-police relations.

Annex Child Development Center, circa 1985

Fallon, Roman, Gloria, and Kim at Annex Child Development Center

GAME CHANGER 27

DAY CARE CENTER

In 1971, I was a senior majoring in Child Development at California State University, Hayward, working part-time at Wells Fargo in Oakland. I decided that I wanted to open up a child care center.

I shared my goal with my mother, and she quickly suggested that her property on San Pablo Dam Road in El Sobrante was the perfect location. And it truly was: a small three-bedroom house sitting on an extraordinarily large parcel of land near a public elementary school and on a major street. I was excited and eager to dive more deeply into the possibilities.

First order of business was to find out the Contra Costa County restrictions and requirements to convert the existing house into a day care center. Without skipping a beat, Mother talked to the county planning department and scheduled a meeting for me at the proposed site.

The following Friday, I arrived early at San Pablo Dam Road and sat in my car, evaluating the possibilities and thinking that this could really become the location for my day care center. I would soon have a BS degree in Child Development and the knowledge and skills to be successful in the day care business.

I was thinking how lucky I was that my mother had offered me this location. I was in total bliss, full of excitement and joy.

The Contra Costa County representative, a White man who looked to be in his early sixties, pulled up and parked behind me. We greeted each other respectfully. He began asking questions about my plans while we walked the perimeter of the lot and the interior of the vacant house. He wrote notes on his pad while saying this and that will have to be done and telling me whom I needed to contact to move things forward.

He handed me his card and said, "We can make this happen. I don't see any major obstacles that would prevent you from moving forward with your plans for a day care center."

I looked up and smiled at the man. This was exactly what I was hoping he would say.

He smiled back and said, "But you are going to have to do something for me."

I looked at his card as he continued, "My wife and I are not getting along, and I need for you to do something for me."

I was stunned, and my excitement about the possibilities turned to anger. My men of choice were Black, young, and handsome and drove nice cars. Not old White men in power.

He stood there smiling as I walked away, saying, "This is my mother's property, and I will have to talk with her about that."

He looked puzzled, the smile fading from his face. I walked swiftly to my car and drove off while he was still standing in front of the house. This was one of those "what the hell just happened?" moments. All the way down San Pablo Dam Road, I processed what this old White man was suggesting. I remembered my grandfather's saying, "This is the way of the world." But like Baldie, I didn't accept that as my world.

My father was handsome, my mother beautiful, and I had the best of both of their physical features. I was dating a gorgeous

Black man whom I admired, respected, and loved. I remember thinking, "So the only way I can open a child care center at this location is on this White man's terms?" But my biggest concern was how I would respond to Mother's questions about the meeting. She was happy that I was coming into adulthood and graduating from college, with a hustle in my plans. She was ready to move forward to help me achieve my goal of owning a day care center. I began to wonder if she had ever encountered the same type of negotiating to pursue her goals.

Later, I shared the incident with my boyfriend. We were going out to dinner, and while he was driving, I related my experience with the county man. He never took his eyes off the road, but after getting a flavor of what I was telling him, he turned the radio down and directed his full attention to my words. He didn't ask any questions but listened to everything I had to say about how I felt and my fear of telling my mother.

We pulled into Albany Bowl. My boyfriend parked and said, "I love you. I can't tell you whether to tell your mom or not. But I do know, although that is definitely the way of the world for some folks, it's not ours. You will get a teaching job and be a dynamic teacher!"

We walked inside hand in hand, had dinner, and enjoyed each other's company. Leaving the bowling alley, he kissed me on the cheek and placed his arm around my shoulder as we walked through the parking lot. My world, for the moment, was perfect. I was so happy to have a young, strong, intelligent Black man walking by my side.

Being an only child, I was always the center of Mother's attention and always by her side. I heard stories of people who had wronged her and unfair situations she encountered. But she never did share a story reflecting anything like what I had experienced with the county official. Nor did I ever discuss with her what the man had proposed. I didn't know how she would react—probably she would have erupted like a volcano. And I had already made up my mind: I was no longer interested in opening up a day care center on San Pablo Dam Road.

My disgust for the proposal was something I wanted to put behind me. The rage and retaliation Mother would have unleashed was something I didn't want to go through. Avoiding the storm for me and for her meant putting the day care venture on pause.

After meeting with that man from the county, I focused my energy on becoming a teacher in Oakland.

* * *

During my first year as a teacher, I remember sitting in North Richmond Missionary Baptist Church with my grandmother, listening to Reverend Newsome preach about King Solomon: "Children are a gift of the Lord."

Grandmother leaned close to me and said, "You need to create an environment in your classroom that encourages children and provides them with a quality education. That is following God's words and your Ministry."

Grandmother, who knew every page of her tattered Bible, quickly found a relevant Scripture. Pointing at it, she whispered, "Read this, Gloria: 'Direct your children onto the right path, and when they are older, they will not leave it.'"

She focused on the choir singing, popped a peppermint into her mouth, and scooted closer to me. "That's what I tried to do with your momma and what I want for you. As a teacher, you must do the same for all children who cross your path."

After church, we stopped at the Pancake House. In the car, Grandmother continued to emphasize that it wasn't by luck that I had a career in teaching. After we ordered, she pulled out her Bible and began softly reading the Scriptures preached in church. She then quizzed me, as I did with my second-grade students to check their comprehension. She reminded me that the pastor's wife, Alice, was a teacher in Oakland, and that teaching was one of her many ministries. Grandmother continued reading, but my mind drifted to the piano lessons I took with Alice before she was the pastor's wife.

Her family lived a few blocks from our store, and I walked to her house every week. She was a young woman but very disciplined. Like Mr. Hill, my sixth-grade teacher, she made it known to me that her job was to teach me how to play the piano, and my job was to practice, practice, practice. She always knew from my weekly lesson performance when I was not taking my lessons seriously. She voiced her expectations in a crystal-clear tone before each piano lesson was over.

For some reason, I never did learn to play the piano. I wish I had! Playing the piano and singing gospel songs brought inner peace to Mother and Baldie. When they began playing and singing, everyone in the house seemed more peaceful and calm.

At the Pancake House, musing about my piano, my mind raced to the piano bench, which was the hiding place for the hammer. I couldn't help thinking about how Mother used that hammer for our protection.

The waitress brought our food and Grandmother tucked her Bible away. We sat and talked about teaching, learning, and ministry. No, not luck, not opportunity, but God's blessing to me and my chosen ministry. I was a teacher; it was a blessing from God. Obey his words and do the hard work.

• • •

Ten years after listening to the county official tell me his idea of how to open a child care center, and with nine years of elementary school teaching experience, I opened the Richmond Annex Child Development Center. On my own terms, in a house I owned, with a beautiful daughter and the new love of my life—a tall, strong, intelligent Black man who, my mother always said, looked like Smokey Robinson. Life was good.

Not long after our marriage, we bought a yellow Ford 1970, nine-passenger van, from a public auction. The exact color of the school district's bus. Some of the students enrolled in our center came through Greater Richmond Social Services, and lived in communities excluded from boundaries for attending El Cerrito schools. We transported Black, White, Asian, and Latino children to and from several El Cerrito elementary schools.

Parents like myself were seeking the best education possible for children. As my children Kim and Roman got older, they voiced displeasure of having to ride what they called "the yellow school bus" to school. That old yellow van served us well for many years, transporting students to and from school.

I often wondered why mother didn't push back when I told her my decision not to pursue opening a child care center on San Pablo Dam Road. In most situations, her reactions to my decisions changed my direction and thinking. But she was fine, believing my focus was on becoming a teacher in Oakland. She was proud of my accomplishments.

While I was doing my jobs for the Oakland Unified School District, and my husband, Al Scoggins, was working in San Francisco, mother dealt with emergency situations at Annex Child Development Center. Either she or one of her maintenance crew would arrive at the center to check out the problem. Frequently she would visit the center before going to work and spend time with Fallon. The staff and most of my clients knew her, and through brief conversations she knew some history of their past. She knew more than I did about where they worked, where they lived, where their family was from. And of course, she knew if they were interested in buying property.

Brokers fete set tonight

RICHMOND — The Associated Real Property Brokers of the Bay Area is holding its 12th annual banquet at the Hilton Hotel on Hegenberger Road, Oakland, tonight at 7 o'clock.

Ermestine Petgrave Martin, a local broker and member, urges interested individuals from Contra Costa County to attend the banquet and to join the organization "which is in need of representation for this area."

MRS. MARTIN
local broker

Mrs. Martin, who has been a member for 15 years, says she has found the organization "to be beneficial to minorities."

The association was organized in 1957 by black real estate brokers in a nationwide effort to improve professional standards of minorities and to better serve the public.

Ms. C. Delores Tucker, secretary of state for Pennsylvania, will be guest speaker at the banquet. Oakland Mayor John Reading will serve as banquet chairman, and Mrs. Terea Hall Pittman will serve as mistress of ceremonies.

Memberships in the association are available through Mrs. W. D. Martin at Petgrave Realty Co., Richmond.

In the late 1950s, Black real estate brokers were seeking greater representation in Contra Costa County

Realty Bd. Must Admit 1st Negro

MARTINEZ — The West Contra Costa Board of Realtors will get its first Negro member.

The Board of 401 members was ordered today by Superior Judge Richard Arnason to admit El Cerrito real estate broker William D. Martin, 45.

Referring to a hearing held earlier this month, Arnason decreed:

"The evidence establishes that the plaintiff has been denied membership arbitrarily and unreasonably and without just cause. . . .

"The defendants are commanded to forthwith admit him to membership with all the rights and privileges attendant thereto."

Martin had contended at the hearing that he was denied membership solely because he was a Negro.

William Martin vs. the West Contra Costa Board of Realtors

GAME CHANGER 28

NEW LOVE INTEREST

During my participation in the Links Cotillion activities, Mother was always networking and passing out her business cards. The debutante activities forever altered our lives—and led to Mother constructing and developing large HUD housing developments in both Northern and Southern California. "Access denied" was not an option—she had the knowledge, connections, and financial means to make it happen.

At one cotillion event, she met a smooth, polished, old-school, and well-established real estate broker, William Daniel Martin. He drove a new Cadillac, was well connected with the families of the debutantes, and a professed professional bridge player. He was childless and had an unforgettable style and presence of his own, with one glass eye that would initially capture one's attention. He owned Martin Realtors, a first-class real estate office located on San Pablo Avenue in El Cerrito. As a broker, he supervised local Black real estate agents. His office was bustling with activity, with handsome Black agents coming and going, charting the course and creating opportunities for Blacks to purchase property in El Cerrito and throughout the Bay Area.

Mr. Martin was originally from McGehee, Arkansas. He had dropped out of school at fifteen and worked on the Alaska pipeline before migrating to Oakland and starting work at Hunters Point Naval Shipyard in San Francisco in 1942. He continued his education to become a real estate broker in Oakland. Like my mother, he realized that minorities were being redlined to sell and buy homes only in economically depressed areas.

Mr. Martin was denied membership in the West Contra Costa Board of Realtors and, as a result, found it difficult to compete in the real estate profession. After a lengthy court battle, a superior judge decreed that "the evidence established for denying Mr. Martin membership was arbitrary and unreasonable, and without just cause."

In 1967, at the age of forty-five, Mr. Martin became the first Black person admitted to the West Contra Costa Board of Realtors. The case was a landmark decision for Black real estate agents in the county.

Soon after meeting my mother, Mr. Martin began to stop by her store and real estate office frequently. He would chat with Mother and her customers about real estate opportunities. He would buy his favorite alcohol (Jack Daniels) and a pack of cigarettes and share deals with Mother he was currently working on.

Within a few years, Mr. Martin and my mother were frequently together, chatting about real estate, driving through communities, and looking at investment possibilities. I went everywhere Mother went and consequently spent hours listening to them share and compare real estate experiences they had either dealt with firsthand or heard about.

Mother felt that Whites had isolated Blacks in North Richmond, the Canal Projects, and designated neighborhoods, trapping them into trumped-up housing contracts to siphon money from them. She believed that some White realtors made money by exploiting the hopes of Black migrants. Ways would be found to kick Blacks out of their houses and find another Black family excited to become homeowners, in order to start the process all over again.

She would hear horror stories of Blacks being lied to about properties' compliance with building codes or being swindled by White folks who presented themselves as real-estate brokers but guided clients to lawyers who were in cahoots with them. Blacks were hit from every direction by unscrupulous lenders, deviant behavior, discriminatory practices, and "self-fulfilling prophecies." Mother took all this in, and used it as fuel.

Mr. Martin also talked often about how Whites were able to cheat and swindle Blacks. He revealed to us that the National Association of Real Estate Board's code of ethics warned that "a Realtor should never be instrumental in introducing into a neighborhood . . . any race or nationality, or any individual whose presence will clearly be detrimental to property values." He kept that handwritten passage in his wallet and would refer to it when talking to friends or family members.

He became knowledgeable about the National Association of Real Estate Board's policies while suing the West Contra Costa Board of Realtors; he had done his homework in preparation for the case. This knowledge empowered him to find the best ways to help Blacks find and buy their dream homes. He understood special financing for homebuyers and had learned how to present offers in a clever way in order to ensure his clients were not at risk of losing their homes.

Mr. Martin brought my mother's real estate game to a new level. Mother was purchasing properties herself; acting as an agent for clients in her community to buy and sell property; providing jobs and services to Blacks; and becoming established and well known in her expanded social horizon.

Together, Mother and Mr. Martin were a formidable team—they were excited and committed, busy hatching plans, fighting for the rights of Blacks to achieve their goals.

* * *

Over time, Mother and Mr. Martin grew closer.

Mr. Martin was always accessorized from top to bottom, with hat, handkerchief, coordinated tie, and wingtip shoes. Shoeshine chairs were plentiful, and he would stop during his workday to get his shoes shined. He would keep an extra Panama hat in the back of his car. He often wore a conservative sports coat outfit or a suit. If he and Mother were going somewhere special for a casual occasion, he would be perfectly dressed in the newest trend.

He would join Mother and me for dinner at the bowling alley after work. He was quite charming, and he had a presence that captured your attention while demanding respect. Sitting in the booth across from Mr. Martin, eating my hamburger and fries, listening to the two of them talk business, I was always examining his glass eye, its movement and color, and listening to his life stories. His cufflinks would glimmer as he took a drag of his cigarette.

He shared the experiences and challenges of his day with humor and a determination to conquer. My mother and I would laugh with him and relate to his experiences and his fights to accomplish his goals.

He credited his current confidence and fortitude to his childhood and his life's many struggles.

During dinner encounters with Mr. Martin, listening to him share his real, vulnerable moments with my mother allowed me to see his passionate side and his caring attitude as well as his methods of attack.

He often talked about his mother and siblings. He was the oldest child and expressed his sincere love for his family. Not long after getting married to my mother, his mother and brother moved to California and lived with us. His oldest sister Doris would visit from Arkansas frequently and shared with me how he ended up with a glass eye. She said that was the incident that inspired him to leave Arkansas and never return to live. To anyone who got to really know Pop, his glass eye became invisible. The man he was is what we saw.

From the outside, Mr. Martin had it all together, but the stress and emotions he often encountered were sometimes overwhelming. He carried an expensive, engraved stainless-steel flask that he would pull out at a moment's notice to pour Jack Daniels into a glass with ice. He had a habit of shaking the glass between sips of Jack Daniels, clicking the ice cubes.

He often said that when he looked in the mirror, he was fine with his reflection, and he was proud that his real estate business was flourishing.

He was strongly opposed to the Vietnam War and was faith-based in the execution of his daily activities to create a better path. His actions were focused on taking steps to overcome the discrimination Blacks encountered on the way to becoming property owners. Mr. Martin was brutally honest in his attempts to push the reset button for change and would often say, "We deserve better than this."

Civil rights issues motivated him to become more politically aware and engaged in the Republican Party. Mr. Martin was a very relatable man who dealt with what he perceived as racism and discrimination with fury and fire; he soon became a powerful mentor for my mother. She began to get more involved in politics and with the Republican Party.

• • •

What I recognized most clearly was that I was slowly becoming less the center of Mother's attention than I had been. She was no longer asking me to put on a dress and patent-leather shoes to accompany her to meetings or affairs because she now had Mr. Martin by her side.

I was thankful for Mr. Martin—I loved his style and the way he treated my mother. She was still in charge of her own destiny, making her own decisions, purchasing her own property, attending fabulous events—but now Mr. Martin supported her efforts.

I was in college, dating young men and hanging out with girlfriends who, for the most part, Mother approved of. *The Jeffersons* TV show was popular then, and Mother confirmed that unlike *The Amos 'n' Andy Show,* it was okay for me to watch. Mr. Martin had the same characteristics as George Jefferson, a businessman with a flair for telling it how it is. He shared his opinions freely and openly, with a focus on helping other Blacks move on up.

But I was not completely independent yet—at least in Mother's eyes. One evening after work, Mother and I met Mr. Martin at the Albany Bowl for dinner. He loved his cocktails, and I was an adult, so when Mother went to the bathroom to wash her hands, Mr. Martin and I ordered a drink. He said, "I know that you're old enough to drink, but I'm not sure if that is a good idea."

Mother returned to the table before the drinks arrived and started looking at the menu. The waitress brought the drinks and announced what they were as she placed them on the table. Mother's eyes were no longer reading the menu; they were directed at me. "What did the waitress say that is?"

I glanced at Mr. Martin. He picked up his cocktail and began clicking the ice against the glass, then took a sip and looked away.

Before I responded to her question, Mother said, "Glo, don't you dare wrap your lips around that drink!"

When we left the restaurant, the drink remained untouched.

Drinking alcohol was not Mother's cup of tea. She didn't want to see it and didn't choose to be around it. For years, I had known that her conscience bothered her because she owned a liquor store. She took that same stance with everyone but Mr. Martin. She acted as if the no-drinking rule didn't apply to him.

• • •

Life was good! Mr. Martin and Mother were absolutely unstoppable. They had a deep connection and a commitment to achieve the impossible.

Mother, by nature, always spoke the unvarnished truth unapologetically and stood up for her beliefs and for those she loved. She had the guts and the courage to get out there and do her thing, refusing to be left out. In my eyes, Mr. Martin seemed to mirror her in so many ways. He was determined to fight for equity and reform opportunities for Blacks to become landowners within the Bay Area.

During the 1960s and 1970s, the civil rights movement allowed us to see a way forward—how much we needed to right all the wrongs and work to transform the world around us. Civil rights were center stage, and Bay Area Blacks were actively engaged in the struggle.

Both young and old Blacks sought to support and rely on one another for survival as they created a path to break down barriers and move forward. Mother used her connections to learn more about advocating for racial and economic equity for Blacks in Richmond and beyond.

She never wavered in her belief that what she learned from growing up on the Forty Acres and a Mule property empowered her self-determination and optimism, her civic engagement, and hard work.

She was proud that Mr. Martin had fought to join the West Contra Costa Board of Realtors and worked to create more opportunities for Blacks. She loved his company and she admired his social circle. She was content with the Richmond Annex fourplex she'd built, the new Cadillac in her garage, and the full-length mink coat hanging in her closet. The store was a thriving business and she was ready to sell; her real estate office was serving clients beyond her expectations; and her daughter was in college and working at Wells Fargo Bank. But she always stated that those Forty Acres and a Mule were at the root of her prosperity and her family's well-being. Those fundamental, childhood-learned principles were the guiding force of everything she did.

Ermestine, defining herself as an "Okie" on her own terms

Five years after my meeting with Superintendent Marcus Foster. I loved teaching at Dag Hammarskjold School and had full control of classroom management, with specific strategies and procedures in place.

Gloria escorted down the aisle by Isaac and William

Wedding day, William and Ermestine Martin

GAME CHANGER 29

MOVERS AND SHAKERS

On July 16, 1971, Reverend H. W. Watson presided over the wedding of William D. Martin (fifty years old) and Ermestine Petgrave (forty-five years old).

High-powered movers and shakers in the Bay Area attended, including Mother's first mentors, Viola Taylor and Ruby Bims. Mother was escorted down the aisle and given away by her father, who was dressed in a tuxedo, and Tressie beamed with pride, wearing a beautiful sky-blue formal selected by her daughter.

Shortly after their marriage, I asked my mother what I should call Mr. Martin. She looked me straight in the eye and said, "Mr. Martin." I said okay, and that was the end of that conversation.

• • •

In 1976, Mother sold the liquor store building and moved Petgrave Real Estate into her husband's El Cerrito office. Mr. Martin had several agents working in his office, serving mostly Black clients in the Bay Area. The office was always busy, with clients coming and going, agents chatting to each other, or family and friends stopping by with potential buyers.

Baldie had acquired her real estate license and also began working in the El Cerrito office. In 1969, Baldie had surprised her husband with keys to a beautiful five-bedroom, three-bathroom house in the El Cerrito hills, complete with a brick fire pit, kitchen island, beautiful beamed ceiling in the living room, and a large outside deck overlooking the Canyon Trail.

Moving to the El Cerrito hills gave Larry and Yvonne a passport to attend John F. Kennedy High School. Built in 1967, with a terrarium in the entrance and no windows in the classrooms, in its early years this public school gained acclaim for its innovative academic and vocational programs and was considered one of the top schools in California.

Baldie's husband was still operating his own trucking business, and she took classes at Contra Costa College. After her husband passed in 1972, she worked less frequently as an agent in Martin Realty, and focused on running her family trucking company with her son, Larry.

Baldie wasn't a flashy dresser but always wore clothes that accented her curvy shape. She had a beautiful smile, an unforgettable laugh, and a unique swagger in her walk. Baldie was a classy lady with her own style. She was confident in herself and happy with her life.

I loved Baldie. She was easy to talk to and fun to be around. She was my mother's younger sister but didn't take any mess from her. Their relationship was complex, with differences of opinion, values, and personalities.

Mother's resentment went back to her belief that her parents favored Baldie and had not demanded she do chores on the farm. Baldie resented her sister for trying to change who she was. Their sibling rivalry intensified as time passed. Baldie would respond to Mother with a straight-up attitude. Baldie had no shame in her game when it came to dealing with my mother

—she didn't hold back her thoughts or her actions.

Even during these sibling conflicts, my father and Baldie talked frequently on the phone. They had some experiences in common, through relationships with my mother, and enjoyed each other's company. They would laugh and chat for hours. Both loved to play dominoes, smoke cigarettes, and drink coffee.

When my mother and I were going through our own conflicts, both Baldie's and my father's house were my escape homes. At one point while I was in college, I moved in with Baldie for a few months. Baldie's house was a gathering place for young and old, and everyone enjoyed spending time with her. She was always sitting at the kitchen table, either studying, watching TV, or talking to visitors. A set of dominoes was always visible, waiting for someone who wanted to play.

Baldie also enjoyed attending classes at Contra Costa College. A straight-A student, she always shared what she was learning in her classes in an effort to make her friends and family more aware of the world around them. Baldie spent hours playing the piano and singing gospel songs. Although she wasn't one to attend church, she did love gospel. It was her way of praising God, something she did every day.

When I visited the real estate office, Baldie would be sitting at her desk, negotiating contracts with clients, talking on the phone, or rushing out to show property to potential buyers. She purchased several income properties and, as a real estate agent, sold numerous properties. Baldie didn't work in the real estate office long, though. Sibling conflicts came, including some that were never resolved, but sisterly love was always there.

• • •

Some women never know their fathers or the powerful influence they contribute to a daughter's life. It was truly a blessing in my life to have as my fathers two strong and loving Black men, different in profound ways, who both overcame obstacles to achieve their goals.

My father and Mr. Martin were the two men who, throughout their lives, served as pillars of strength and encouragement for me. Both men eliminated my fears at critical times by the words they spoke, their actions, and the love they provided. They were men who trusted God to guide the paths they ventured on and the actions they took. Most of all, my fathers loved Mother, and both supported her efforts to achieve her goals. I know she loved both of them in her own special way and always wanted them to do their best and achieve their goals.

* * *

On my winter wonderland wedding day in December 1974, my father, in his wheelchair, and I were in the church lobby waiting for him to escort me down the aisle. Just as the music began and the ushers opened the doors, Mr. Martin unexpectedly appeared and began pushing my father's wheelchair. The two men had never met in person before, and I still don't know whose idea it was, though I suspect my mother had a hand in it.

Both these men were businessmen, with visible physical limitations, but as different as night and day. My wedding day was the first time I had seen my father in a tuxedo. He was a gentle, quiet, calm man by nature, conservative in his taste in cars, clothes, living quarters.

My mother often told me that it brought so much joy to her when he would return home from work, put his lunch pail down, then pick me up and dance around the room. When Mother was angry with me about something, he was always there in a supportive, peaceful manner. And he had a way of making horrific-feeling things seem somehow not so bad.

Mr. Martin, on the other hand, was more flamboyant. He could be very aggressive when it came to business. When it came to family, he was loving, kind, giving, patient, and supportive.

On one of the most important days of my life, I realized how blessed I was to be loved by these two strong men. I admired and adored both and was so proud they were by my side. When the preacher asked, "Who gives . . . ," they both said, "I do." I had two fathers escorting me down the aisle to my new husband!

I am sure my father was just as surprised as I was when Mr. Martin suddenly appeared and began pushing his wheelchair. He never asked me why I didn't tell him in advance, or whether I knew he was going to participate in the wedding. I hope he was just as proud as I was, and happy it all turned out the way it did.

From that day on, I started calling Mr. Martin "Pop." In the coming years, Pop would be actively engaged in my life and my daughters' lives. He devoted time to being a grandfather, attending school events, taking the girls to church, and including them on vacation trips.

Both my father and Pop were by my side with support, encouragement, and love through my journey of being a wife and mother. What none of us knew was that they had escorted me to a marriage that would be over within a few years.

William Martin, talking with the St. John apartments construction crew

Pastor Robert Louis Johnson,
St. John Missionary Baptist Church, circa 1969

Pastor Robert Louis Johnson and construction crew at the St. Johns Apartment site, Richmond

GAME CHANGER 30

THE POWERHOUSE COMBINATION

As a husband-and-wife team, Mother and Pop began to dive deeper and venture out into owning property in Orinda, Martinez, Lafayette, and El Cerrito. They faced discriminatory practices and policy injustice head-on, fighting obstinate racism alongside fellow Black brokers and agents.

Another powerhouse in the Bay Area was Thomas L. Berkley. After World War II, he and friends had formed the Thomas Berkley & Associates law firm in the City of Berkeley. The firm was distinguished as the largest racially integrated, bilingual law firm in the United States. Berkley was known for working to ensure that legal services were provided to those who needed representation.

Berkley's vision of expanding opportunities for Blacks led him to the construction industry, finance, politics, publishing, and printing. Berkley founded and owned the Post Newspaper Group. The *Oakland Post* did not focus on crime, scandal, and sensationalism. It was a newspaper Blacks were proud of; they read it to learn about Bay Area Black communities' success and opportunities. Employment, education, civil rights, the fight against racism: stories that spoke to the ordinary affairs affecting our day-to-day lives.

Improving opportunities offered to Blacks was in alignment with the path my parents were walking. Berkley became a frequent visitor of the Martins. I remember observing Berkley with my parents. He appeared to be a complex thinker in discussions and very precise with words. Pop and Berkley would laugh and talk, always discussing their perspectives on worldwide issues. Pop listened attentively to every word. Mother, of course, took every opportunity to bombard Berkley with back-to-back questions. I remember hearing Berkley share stories of being a guest at the White House and at that moment realizing that beyond his humor stood a powerful man.

Berkley was a few years older than my parents, and in a natural way became their mentors. Like my parents, Berkley was a builder and developer of housing tracts and apartment complexes in northern California. My parents were always happy for the opportunity to spend time with him, working together to achieve their goals. Mother began researching and investigating to secure additional knowledge and learning opportunities so they could move forward as a team.

This accomplished man was also the cofounder and the first president of Beneficial Savings & Loan Association in Oakland. Beneficial Savings & Loan was organized to develop a funding source for people of limited means. Berkley was influential in opening doors at other banks and financial institutions in the Bay Area to make their resources available to Blacks. He was a board member or member of numerous business, public, private, and civic organizations that Mother and Pop were actively engaged in.

Mother and Pop knew that they were targets for denial of property purchases in certain locations, and they did not accept the "take whatever you got" mindset of Whites in positions of power.

As a team, they dealt with venomous retaliation, discriminatory practices, and housing inequality. They had personally experienced business transactions where the Federal Housing Administration had refused to back loans in areas that were predominantly occupied by Blacks. They had fought decades of deceptive financial schemes; they themselves had been offered predatory loans. These deep-rooted policies of segregation reminded them of injustices and prejudices they and their relatives had encountered throughout their entire lives.

While they cranked up efforts to provide better housing for Blacks, they also worked to improve the labor market. My parents were licensed contractors through the state of California. Their goal was to hire Blacks within the community and to provide residences to Blacks who were, in some cases, living in neglected housing projects. William and Ermestine Martin were always searching for classes and workshops to attend, seeking to learn more about the 1968 Fair Housing Act. Hand in hand, they began their journey to build low-rent housing for the Richmond community.

After many episodes of responding to 911 calls from my mother, and having the opportunity to talk with my parents over the years, Arthur Lee Johnson bought his first home from Pop. Not long after that, Arthur Lee's brother also purchased a home through Martin Realty. This sparked the beginning of a relationship and partnership with Arthur Lee's father, Pastor Robert Louis Johnson of St. John Missionary Baptist Church in Richmond. Pastor Johnson was a pillar of the community who spearheaded the construction of low-income apartments.

Pastor Johnson also had a vision of establishing more upscale housing opportunities for the Richmond community. Combining efforts to achieve their goals, he and my parents connected with retired congressman George Miller Jr., the US Representative from California's Seventh and Eleventh Districts, who told them about an opportunity through HUD.

My parents and Pastor Johnson then attended a conference in Washington, DC, to present their proposal. They were stepping out on pure faith. Not long after this, and with much surprise, they received notification that their proposal had been funded. The affordable-housing complexes they would build in Richmond and Los Angeles provided poor people with a decent place to live.

• • •

When my parents joined forces with St. John Missionary Baptist Church under the leadership of Pastor Johnson, they created St. Johns Apartments. This complex contained 158 HUD-subsidized apartments ranging from studios up to three bedrooms; these units were more upscale than most rental apartments available for Blacks.

When the first apartments became available for rent, my Saturday job was to put on my patent-leather shoes, white blouse, and black skirt and act as an open-house hostess to potential clients. Visitors marveled at the brand-new development, and many completed applications at the open house for subsidized rents based on income.

St. Johns Apartments is located in the Iron Triangle, once known as the highest-crime area in Richmond. With a bold demonstration of leadership, Pastor Johnson himself moved into a unit there in order to eliminate the fear some Blacks expressed about moving into the development.

Directly across the street from the St. Johns Apartments is Atchison Village, originally built to house defense workers at the Kaiser Shipyard. It was constructed by the Richmond Housing Authority in 1941. The grounds are landscaped, and within the complex there is a park as well as soccer and baseball fields. Atchison Village residents have become more diverse through the years. During the 1950s, Blacks were not the tenants of choice.

Soon after the construction of St. Johns Apartments was finished, my parents began to focus on other HUD developments in Northern and Southern California. They wanted to create more opportunities for Blacks to purchase homes as well as improve overall living conditions. They understood that homeowners would be able to tap into home equity to start a business, pay for their children's college expenses, or survive a medical emergency.

Past experiences had taught Mother that her success would be based on having the resourcefulness, knowledge, and determination to disagree with lenders and people in power. Plain and simple, she recognized that things were wrong in the housing market. No longer believing in her father's statement "this is the way of the world," she challenged it at every step.

• • •

In 1995, twenty-five years after St. Johns Apartments was constructed, St. John Missionary Baptist Church sold its interest in the complex. I remember my mother's frustration after hearing about the challenges the church was facing, some of which included tenants not paying rent, destroying units, removing heaters off the walls, and removing all carpet from units when moving out. I could relate to the church's frustration because I grew up witnessing Mother's preaching and teaching tenants how to respect her property; accompanying her frequent visits to tenants inquiring about past-due rents; and seeing evidence of mistreatment of her property. These would send her over the edge.

Sometimes she would be called by tenants in the middle of the night to referee disagreements stemming from someone not following her clearly articulated good-neighbor policy. After angrily restating her expectations for tenants, she would often end with, "I like you. I want the best for you. Do you like me as a landlord? Well, you are going to have to do better, and we will get along just fine. Clean up your house."

Mother consistently restated her belief that the cycle of Blacks' lack of property wealth had to be broken. The housing and economic policies designed to exclude Black buyers were her targets. Teaching tenants how to respect the property and live in harmony was her personal goal.

Listening to my mother express her opinions about rentals and purchases, financing and insurance over the years, I learned so much about the racist structures that were in place to block homeownership. When I started thinking about purchasing my own home, I engaged in serious Sunday conversations with my parents about home equity, and how to tap into that equity to acquire wealth. During the 1960s, Blacks who were able to purchase homes considered themselves lucky. In a system stacked against them, working hard to establish a good credit score and acquire a higher income simply wasn't enough. My mother and Pop devoted their lives to trying to change that.

Ermestine and William expanding their business to Southern California

Training Student Conflict Managers how to resolve conflicts

GAME CHANGER 31

REPUBLICAN PARTY POLITICS

During the 1970s my mother moved more and more into the world of politics. Mr. Martin had been a politician in his own way for a while, and he had no shame about the fact that he was a Republican. Conversations with him about politics had the potential to get nasty, but he wouldn't back down in disputes or attempt to de-escalate the conversation. He believed he had the right to affiliate with either Republicans or Democrats. His choice mattered, not others' thoughts. And he chose to be Republican.

Over time, my mother reinvented herself to become a Republican as well. Her ideological sense was based on the climate, her environment, and her right to make her own decisions in addition to her knowledge and awareness of both parties. She embraced some Democratic and some Republican policies and beliefs.

When I was a senior in college, at my mother's request I asked my friends if they would be willing to serve as hostesses at a fundraising event for the Republican Party. Mother articulated clear expectations of what she wanted us to wear, and we did our best to accommodate her wishes.

For the event I had my hair done professionally, applied more makeup than usual, and wore a floor-length formal gown purchased just for the occasion. That evening the Georgian Room East at HS Lordships restaurant in Berkeley (we always called it "His Lordship") was beautifully decorated. Seated together at the head table facing the audience were the guest speaker—assistant HUD secretary Samuel C. Jackson—along with my parents and other leaders of the Black Committee of the Contra Costa County Committee to Re-elect the President.

We handled our hostess duties as specified by Mother, and we did look elegant, fluttering around the room, registering and greeting guests, collecting tickets or donations from attendees, showing them to their table, escorting special guests to the head table. Whatever other request was directed our way, we performed in style for the occasion.

My friends and I observed the women attendees in their floor-length formals and mink jackets, walking beside their husbands, who were attired in formal suits, greeting and talking with one another. There were some unattached young Black men at the event as well, and one of my friends became giddy when she was approached by a handsome young man in a flirty way.

I sat at the registration table beside Maria, who had also made her debut in the Links Cotillion. We chatted about how much we enjoyed the activities we had attended and how happy she was with her boyfriend, whom she had met at a party. She asked when we could leave; she wanted us to join her boyfriend at a party that night.

Mother didn't want the hostesses volunteering—she wanted my friends to commit early on to perform designated tasks, and she was paying them for their time, with the expectation they would remain until the event ended. So my response to Maria was, "When this is over." Clearly, however, our minds were on leaving for that party as soon as possible.

Mother opened the reception standing behind the podium, elegantly dressed, with glittery accessories, her hair professionally done. My friends and I sat down at the hostesses' table in the back of the room, closest to the entry door in order to get up and greet late attendees. I was proud of my mother. She spoke well, with confidence, and for the first time, I saw the leadership side of her.

My grandparents were seated at the table in front of me, dressed in formal attire Mother had purchased for this event. (Baldie and Cousin Gladys were not in the audience; I believe the Republican Party was not their cup of tea.) My cousin Larry was seated at a table near the front of the head table with other young men and women; the goal of this fundraiser was to send them to the 1972 Republican National Convention in Miami.

My mother's welcome speech and introduction to individuals at the head table concluded with a prayer, then dinner was served. I enjoyed the food with my six hostess friends, sneaking peeks at the clock. A pianist was playing soft music, servers were floating from table to table, and we were chatting about the dilemma one of our friends was facing, an unwanted pregnancy. Her conversation was focused on the negative rather than the positive aspects of becoming a mother. I was happy I wasn't dealing with that problem in my life.

After dinner, while servers presented ice cream and a cookie to each guest, Mother returned to the podium and introduced the guest speaker. I could see that everyone was focused on him. Everyone, that is, except the women at our table and a couple of young men seated at Larry's table. My friend Flora noticed their glances and smiles toward our table; they had our full attention.

I looked at my grandparents, who seemed mesmerized by their daughter as she finished her introduction. From a granddaughter's view, they seemed proud of her. Mother was truly captivating, with her beauty and style, as she returned to her seat. I really didn't pay much attention to what the guest speaker was saying, since our table was still conversing about our friend missing her period and what that might mean for her. As she shared her thoughts about being pregnant, tears filled her eyes, and we tried to comfort her by painting an optimistic ending to her drama. Another hostess friend talked about plans for her wedding and honeymoon. She would be the first of our group to get married, and we were excited, because we were all going to be her bridesmaids.

Guest speaker Samuel Jackson's words faded in and out, but it appeared to me his overall message was about inspiring young Black voters to get involved and become aware of what was going on in the world, especially in the Bay Area.

While everyone was eating dessert, I noticed two Black men standing in the doorway, their faces divided vertically with paint—half black and half white. I thought *wow, that is strange,* and I noticed they both carried paper bags. Then they began walking toward the head table, yelling comments about President Nixon. The words I remember them repeating were *murderers* and *Vietnam*. Everyone's eyes were on the men, who were tossing dog feces out of the paper bags as they slowly moved forward.

Flora, who was sitting next to me, said, "Gloria, what the hell?" I didn't respond, as I was captured by the moment, watching my parents' expression of fear. I remember being fearful for my mother, and when I glanced at my grandmother, I saw tears rolling down her face. What was going to happen next? At that moment, I realized my mother was taking some serious risks by assuming leadership roles in the Republican Party. These two men were just a tiny example of the conflict raging throughout the country. Many people, especially young people, were angry at the Republican establishment. These two men, like many others, wanted Republicans to hear their voices, and they got their message across in an alarming way. The entire room froze in perfect silence, except for the voices of these men ranting and raging about sponsoring Blacks to go see Nixon. After throwing the feces at the head table, they called out, "Uppity Black folks."

As the two men made their way to the exit door, I noticed that Larry and the young men at his table were out of their seats in defense-attack mode. Larry could see the fear on the faces of the adults at the head table; his aunt's facial expression showed that she was dealing with an uncomfortable, threatening situation.

These young men made their way to the door, following the two intruders, and several older gentlemen quickly followed them to try to calm them down. The older men's voices echoed through the room: "Let them go!"

After a long stretch of silence, the speaker at the podium said, "They are entitled to their opinions, and we are entitled to ours. Thanks to all of you, we will be able to send ten Bay Area young voters to the Republican National Convention. Everyone has the right to gather information about this election, and vote. Thank you for coming, and have a good night."

My friends were speechless, but their facial expressions showed the horrific experience we had just witnessed. I remember searching for my purse under the table and realizing that ice cream had dripped all over my dress during the moments I had frozen. As I was busy wiping the ice cream off with a napkin, my friends said, "Let's get out of here and go have some fun. This is drama."

I went to the head table to chat with my mother, who at this point was surrounded by other members of the Black Committee of the Contra Costa County Committee to Re-elect the President. Larry was by her side.

I got her attention, waved good-bye, and walked back toward my friends. Pop was at the bar, sipping whiskey, surrounded by several men. I walked my grandparents to their car. My grandfather comforted his wife and stated, "That's the way of the world. Sister will be all right."

When I got to my car, my friends were waiting for me to unlock the doors. I heard one of them say, "That was a trip. Man, I knew I shouldn't have agreed to be a hostess."

I was silent, replaying the whole experience. I didn't know what to think or how to respond. I sat in the car quietly before putting the key into the ignition, watching couples walk to their cars in fur coats, tuxedos, and formal gowns. Flora, who was sitting in the front seat, shouted, "Gloria, let's go. This is too much drama. We need to party hard tonight."

I started the car and we were on our way to a party in Oakland, listening to Marvin Gaye sing "What's Going On?"

My parents never spoke about the incident to me, and I didn't bring it up to them. What was there to say? My friends, on the other hand, brought it up for months after the event and shared the experience with the broader array of friends we socialized with. I was consumed with embarrassment as I tried to find my way in life.

• • •

What happened at the fundraiser helped me realize that I didn't know enough about the guiding principles of the Republican Party and Democratic Party. What were they each advocating for?

My mother and the rest of my family had always identified as Democrats and voted accordingly. I know that my friends were not Republicans and were challenged by the idea of hostessing at a Republican event. I am convinced that all attendees were surprised by the men's actions and statements at the fundraiser, but I am not sure if anyone's way of thinking was changed by their intrusion. As for me, that incident still replays in my mind, even after fifty years. Recent events in our political history have brought it to the surface again. The anger and hostility between political parties and the trauma it brings are clearly present today.

Mother's sister, Baldie, who did not attend the fundraiser, heard about the affair from her son, Larry, and her father. She grilled me for a detailed account from beginning to end, exploding with laughter. She thought the whole thing was hilarious and said, "Now *that* was one of your mother's affairs I wish I had attended. I would have loved to have been there."

I, on the other hand, felt the embarrassment I believed my mother must have felt, and her fear of moving forward.

The following August, the group Republican Youth for the President sponsored ten Black young men and women to attend the Republican National Convention.

Mother tried to encourage me to go, but I was working at Wells Fargo Bank and had just accepted a teaching position in the Oakland Unified School District, and I felt quite cheerful to have legitimate reasons for not attending. After witnessing the aggression I felt at the HS Lordships restaurant fundraiser, I wasn't sure what to expect at a national convention, and I had safety concerns for my family.

Larry had a special relationship with his Aunt Ermestine, throughout adulthood, circa 1970s

GAME CHANGER 32

THE TEN STRONG

Mother had held several meetings to recruit Black youth to attend the national convention, most from families that were Democrats. During the meetings she explained that the purpose for attending was exposure and information gathering that might change their political minds. A once-in-a-lifetime opportunity to see politics in action. During the ten-day trip to the convention, participating Black youth would have the opportunity to take part in workshops and learn about the Republican Party.

Mother persuaded her nephew, Larry, who had just graduated from high school; several teenagers who attended North Richmond Missionary Baptist Church; and a few children of members of the Black Committee of the Contra Costa County Committee to Re-elect the President. These ten young Black men and women would be targets for anger, hostility, and direct racial slurs from White youth attending the convention. Fearing separation from one another, they formed a bond to become the Ten Strong.

Initially, Larry had thought of Miami Beach as a party and tourism city, home of the Super Bowl and other fun events. He was looking forward to having fun with nine of his peers.

He was eighteen, excited to be eligible to vote, with a new interest in politics. Attending the Republican Convention turned out to be an experience he would never forget. By the end of their ten-day trip, they had lifelong memories and a new understanding of politics. All the activities for young voters subjected them to racial tension, souring their view of politics.

From many conversations with Larry over the years, I pieced together the following depiction.

When these Black youth boarded a plane with a President Nixon banner, they thought they were going to the Republican Convention to learn about the Republican Party. Their education began immediately; even on the plane they quickly found themselves surrounded by White youth, the overwhelming majority of whom were Youth for Nixon. The plane stopped in several states picking up youth, but no other Blacks boarded. The Ten Strong, excited to be on their first adult experience with their peers, anticipating expanding their knowledge base of politics, soared coast to coast in an airplane filled with intimidation, hatred, and fear. This was a Nixon rally flying through the air, chanting Nixon slogans, such as "Nixon's the one!" "Our pick is Dick!" "I'm for Dick Nixon!" and "Youth for Nixon!"

The Ten Strong refused to participate in the chants because they were not there to show support for Nixon but rather to broaden their knowledge of the Republican Party perspective. Because of this refusal, they became instant enemies of the White youth, who felt they should not be on the plane. The adult supervisors soon became hostile as well and openly displayed anger at the Ten Strong for refusing to stand front and center for publicity pictures while chanting and holding Nixon signs.

Florida was Larry's first experience of feeling in-your-face racism firsthand. Growing up during the civil rights movement in the Bay Area gave his generation a sense of Black pride and strength.

The Black Panthers, Dr. Martin Luther King Jr., and Malcolm X presented a different perspective. Young Black men were proud of who they were, what they stood for, and what they demanded from the world.

The Ten Strong were segregated at a hotel quite a distance away from the convention center and given daily instructions of their itinerary: what time to meet each morning, where a van would pick them up for the day's activities, when they would return to the hotel at the end of the day.

Larry noticed that their hotel was directly across the street from the police department. When the Ten Strong entered the hotel to register, Larry felt a strong negative attitude toward them. The racial intensity was obvious. After going to their assigned rooms, the Ten Strong noticed holes in the wall where air conditioning units used to be. Their rooms were exceptionally hot.

They reported the problem to the main desk and were told to wait in a step-down lobby until repairs had been made. So the young Blacks sat in the lobby by themselves. There didn't appear to be signs of other hotel guests—just the Ten Strong puzzled by the room accommodations they were offered.

Suddenly, water started pouring all around them. A major pipe had broken, and everyone was scrambling to get away. Larry called my mother and informed her of their concerns and living situation. She immediately called and talked to the hotel manager, who made arrangements for the Ten Strong to be transported to a Holiday Inn across from the Orange Bowl, an even further distance from the convention center. Strangely, it appeared to Larry that the youths were the only occupants of the new hotel, which they were told was the only option available for them to stay in while attending the convention.

The Ten Strong learned right away that the daily itinerary was to be picked up in their private van, go to a particular location, be marched to the front, and hold up a "Nixon for president" sign for the media. The White youth traveled in a separate bus, and they were excited and eager to hold up signs and chant for Nixon. But after returning to the hotel the first day, the Ten Strong met and decided to refuse to hold the Nixon signs. They hoped they would be left alone to explore the convention on their own—and they wouldn't have to suffer the indignity of cheering for a segregationist organization.

The next day, the van arrived at the hotel and took the Ten Strong from location to location for the same media exposure, but now the Ten Strong refused to show support for Nixon. Seeing the adult supervisors upset with the Ten Strong for their resistance only fueled the aggression of the White youths, who hurled racial slurs at the Ten Strong when their paths crossed at these publicity events. All in all, the trip was a huge disappointment. There were no workshops, no opportunities to understand the Republican Party better.

The highlight of the convention for the Ten Strong was watching Sammy Davis Jr. introduce President Nixon and give him an awkward hug at a Young Voters for the President rally at the Miami Marine Stadium.

The Ten Strong spent every day riding through the city of Miami. Soon, looking out the van's windows, they began to feel a little bit safer among themselves. They were growing accustomed to riding through streets filled with violent mobs, threatening and intimidating voices, sides clearly defined—all made up of people fighting for what they believed was right for America.

Various types of political activists and counterculture groups were attracted to the convention, and many had traveled long distances to protest. There were hippies, gay rights activists, Vietnam veterans, members of the Black Panther Party, and many other groups. Some residents were horrified and angered by the presence of the protestors and the changes they were creating in their communities.

Police and city officials worked hard to avoid bloodshed. They tried to keep the protest groups apart, creating and enforcing separate demonstration routes to avoid conflicts between residents, protestors, and delegates. The police force was backed by the Secret Service, FBI, and the United States Army.

The day Nixon was nominated for reelection, August 22, there were thousands of protestors demonstrating in the streets of Miami. Some of them clashed with police and delegates, burned an American flag, smashed windows, chanted anti-Vietnam War slogans, and terrorized Republican delegates. Approximately two hundred demonstrators were jailed and several protestors were injured—rumors circulated that they had been clubbed by police.

The police department had assembled buses from across the state to park in front of the convention center to shield the delegates. A massive chain-link fence was constructed across the street to hold back protestors. The smell of pepper spray filled the air and burned peoples' eyes. While all of this anger and hostility permeated the area, the Ten Strong from Richmond were dealing with their own battles. Racial battles here were very different from what they were accustomed to experiencing in the Bay Area.

That day the Ten Strong were standing in front of the convention center, waiting to be let in. They could see a group of Whites with tanks and military equipment gathering not far away; then the Whites began throwing tear gas in their direction.

Soon everyone was in panic mode. The police quickly rushed the Ten Strong toward a nearby bus with other young adults already on board. The police ordered the bus driver to open the doors, and the Ten Strong scrambled in, the doors closing swiftly behind them. They were safe from the street violence, but now racial slurs and hostility came from inside the bus. A White youth jumped in front of one of the Ten Strong and screamed, "What are you niggers doing getting on this bus?"

A quick punch knocked the guy down, and the entire bus froze in fear. What was going to happen next? The Ten Strong, male and female, were caught in a dangerous situation and ready to put up their dukes if necessary. The White guy struggled to get off the floor of the bus and returned to his seat with, "You guys must be from California."

Larry had not seen many other Black young adults among the attendees, and if he had, it was usually one Black in a group of Whites. During those rare occasions, the other Black youth made it known that they did not want to associate with the Ten Strong. Now, Larry noticed in the back of the bus a young Black girl who averted her eyes and stared out the window. Later Larry ran into her again, and she explained, "I could not get involved when you guys were attacked. I have to return to North Carolina on that bus, and I am scared."

* * *

One of the convention events, the Presidential Dinner, was held at the Blue Dolphin Restaurant. Everyone had badges around their necks to identify who they were. Outside, there was chaos all around, but inside the Blue Dolphin, there was an atmosphere of excitement and energy.

Larry, who was happy to be in the mix, was caught up in the excitement, unaware that his badge was covered by his shirt. As he walked around, taking in what was happening around him, Secret Service men approached and, without a word, knocked him down and held him down until they could see his badge.

After discovering he was a guest, they released him, saying, "Make sure your badge can be seen at all times, young man, or this will happen to you again!" Then they disappeared as quickly as they had approached.

• • •

While my mother's paths and activities at the Republican National Convention were far different than that of the Ten Strong Black youths, her experience was just as dramatic and horrific. The political scene was turbulent on all fronts, the nation torn by the Vietnam War. The 1968 violence that erupted in Chicago at the Democratic Convention was still fresh in Mother's mind. She talked about how fearful she was in Miami surrounded by conflict, witnessing the terrifying behavior exhibited by protestors or residents. She saw Vietnam War protestors face off against police and the Secret Service and then get swept up in the mayhem. She recalled walking to a restaurant and hearing residents express how upset they were because protests had erupted, shutting down traffic, and because tear gas had been deployed. These residents of Miami were forcefully angry, and they articulated their hostility toward her.

There were some good moments at the convention. At a public rally at the Miami Marine Stadium, Sammy Davis Jr. introduced President Nixon and gave him a hug, to a standing ovation. The crowd went wild: Mr. Bojangles onstage with President Nixon. Mother was proud to see Sammy Davis in that role, but thought it was funny when he hugged the president. When Mother met Davis personally, she was astonished he was so short. She shared details about meeting other superstars, Ronald Reagan and Frank Sinatra. Mother also mentioned that she was impressed with Pat Nixon's speech at the National Convention and the manner in which she presented herself.

When the president announced his acceptance of the 1972 Republican Party nomination, the room was filled with festivity, balloons dropped from the ceiling, and the noise level rose with excitement. After the convention was adjourned, Mother talked about going through the reception line and greeting the president and first lady. She was especially elated to meet Mamie Eisenhower in person.

I imagine that during those moments she was caught up in the excitement and glamour of meeting celebrities and being able to attend the affair with a fearless husband by her side. But after she returned to Richmond, things looked very different.

Steven Bates (far left), City Councilman Nathaniel Bates, unknown jockey, and Ermestine in the winner's circle at an annual fundraising event at Golden Gate Fields racetrack, 1981.

Ron Brown (left), Ermestine, and Ron Dellums

GAME CHANGER 33

THE ULTIMATE MEASURE

When the Ten Strong returned to California and shared their experiences at the convention, Mother was livid. She felt that the Republican Party had bamboozled her by leading her to believe the Ten Strong would be provided opportunities to learn more about politics, giving them a broader knowledge base for voting. She expressed anger after realizing they were being used for media purposes and had been exposed to relentless intimidation and hostility. She had also dealt with fear at all the anger aimed in her direction.

Mother was always searching for knowledge for herself. She had known very little about the Republican Party before marrying her husband. She returned to California with a different perspective, a new truth, a feeling of being taken advantage of, and an awareness of the vulnerable position she had placed the Ten Strong in.

In 1968, Shirley Chisholm became the first Black woman elected to the United States Congress, representing New York in the House of Representatives. This was a woman Mother admired and respected, one whose words she listened to carefully. Shirley Chisholm spoke at the Democratic National Convention in 1972 and announced her presidential candidacy. She fought for educational opportunities and social justice, the same battles Mother was fighting in Richmond with her boxing gloves on. Anne Armstrong of Texas, about the same age as Mother and the first woman to present a keynote address at a major national convention, was also inspiring to Mother. These two women were my mother's political role models, shining examples of women standing up for what they believed. Their success guided my mother's decision making and influenced her thoughts to achieve her goals.

A Democrat with a new Republican husband, Mother had believed attending the Republican National Convention was truly a once-in-a-lifetime opportunity to dive deep into Republican politics and expand her understanding of why her husband was a Republican. But her desire to learn more about the Republican Party died quickly after returning from the convention. Soon afterward, she removed Pop's autographed pictures of Lyndon B. Johnson and Richard Nixon from the office walls and placed them in a closet. I overheard Mother tell her office staff, "From now on, all Republican political calls go to Mr. Martin."

Pop couldn't miss her anger—she expressed her feelings straight up. One day he had a beautiful bouquet of roses delivered to her at the office. She read the card, glanced in his direction, and tossed them in the garbage. In a loud voice in front of office staff and clients, she said, "Martin, the Republican Party made a fool of me, but you won't. Take those flowers and put them on *your* desk." She returned to her desk and answered the phone, "Hello, this is Mrs. Martin, may I help you?"

I observed the situation, smiled to myself, and thought, *my beautiful mother has such class.* Pop grabbed his straw boater hat and left the office. And my mother seldom attended Republican activities or events. She still supported her husband's efforts but was finished with Republican politics.

• • •

Everyone in the family breathed a sigh of relief when Mother shared how she felt about the Republican Party's deceitfulness. I was happy because it helped make sense of the nightmare at the HS Lordships fundraiser event. Now I no longer had to worry about Mother asking me to participate in Republican affairs.

When Baldie heard that Mother was no longer interested in learning about the Republican Party, she teasingly but sincerely said, "Well, I am happy you came to your senses. That was among the stupidest things you have come up with, besides being determined to give birth to Glo in San Francisco."

Mother quickly responded, "Shut up and take care of your business."

Grandmother simply stated, "Ermestine, I am praying for God to order your steps."

This period was one of those Game Changers our family never talked about again. But it was an experience that shook up my life for a long time. I remember Mother telling me, "Everything that comes in a box with a beautiful bow is not a gift." I think she opened a box without a bow from the Republican Party, looked inside, tossed it aside, and never seriously looked back. And for that I was grateful and happy. Peace and harmony was restored to the Williams family.

Pop remained a Republican and Mother a born-again Democrat. Throughout their marriage each traveled a different political path without infringing on the other's beliefs. Just like she never understood why that cross placed in her front yard didn't seem to bother my father, she felt that the Republican Party taking advantage of her should have bothered Pop. Especially because she was trying to learn more about the Republican Party to please him. In the end, they were still a strong team with the same objectives and goals, but they identified with different affiliations.

• • •

A decade later, I was sitting in the teachers' lunchroom at Brookfield School. A Black male substitute teacher on a long-term assignment sat next to me. The majority of the teaching staff had nicknamed him "The Professor" because, upon his arrival to the school, he boasted that he had a doctorate in Black Studies. Word was that he taught his third-grade students as if they were in college, so he was having difficulty with classroom management.

He didn't engage much with the regular staff, would often eat by himself, and did not engage in chitchat during lunch. An interesting character who didn't seem to connect with faculty or students. Whenever I saw him walking around school, he had a cinnamon stick in his hand or mouth, manipulating it like a cigarette. One of my colleagues asked him about it, and he told her the stick was for health reasons. His choice of attire reminded me of college professors. Tall, slender, a studious man who projected the appearance of being a scholarly, critical thinker.

He sat down next to me, said hello, and began taking out his lunch. The Republican Party controversy frequently resurfacing in my mind, I wondered what his thoughts were about the matter. I quickly surveyed the lunchroom to ensure we had privacy, then shared with him the disturbing incident that had occurred when my mother hosted the Republican fundraiser. He listened attentively while eating his sandwich, glancing at me a few times, asking one or two clarifying questions as I painted a picture of the affair.

Other teachers were trickling into the lunchroom and sat around us, talking together. I ended our conversation about the incident abruptly because I didn't want my other colleagues to know my mother was a Republican.

After school, the Professor came into my classroom and handed me a handwritten piece of paper. He looked me straight in the eyes and said, "In Dr. King's 'Strength to Love' speech, he said, 'The ultimate measure of a man is not where he stands in moments of comfort and convenience, but where he stands at times of challenge and controversy.'"

He took the cinnamon stick out of his mouth and started twirling it with his fingers. "So whether your mother is right or wrong in your eyes, or in the eyes of others, you have to respect her for standing up for what she believes in." He turned toward the door, said, "Think about it!" and left my classroom.

I sat at my desk, read Dr. King's quote, and reflected on his message. I reviewed my lesson plan book, gathered materials I needed to copy for the next day's class, and headed to the teachers' workroom.

As I passed by the main office, the Professor was walking out, the cinnamon stick dangling from his mouth. He said, "Keep thinking about it." He turned to exit the building, and I continued to the teacher's workroom to make my copies. When I returned to my classroom, I cut the handwritten quote small enough to Scotch-tape it on top of my desk.

At the end of the school year, the quote was torn and tattered from books and school supplies. But I reread the quote so many times and repeated it in my mind when dealing with challenging decisions in life.

Yes, the Professor was a little weird. But he had given me something to think about that I could relate to and that cleared my mind. I respected and was proud of my mother's standing up for what she believed.

• • •

President Nixon won the election, carrying forty-nine states and nearly 61 percent of the popular vote; he was the first Republican to sweep the South. In 1972, the voting age was lowered to eighteen, promoting more interest by youth. Nixon's campaign emphasized a strong economy and success in foreign affairs. Democratic candidate George McGovern ran on a platform calling for an immediate end to the Vietnam War and a guaranteed minimum income. Among the Democratic candidates McGovern defeated was Congresswoman Shirley Chisholm, the first Black person to run for a major party's presidential nomination.

• • •

Forty years later, Cousin Gladys stopped driving to monthly chapter meetings; she was picked up by a rotating cast of sorors—including me—who were delighted to help. During our rides together, Gladys humorously shared stories about Mother, and like Baldie, she sprinkled her tales with compassion, love, and showers of laughter.

I learned that Gladys did not receive an allocation of land from the Five Civilized Tribes because she was born in 1910, which disqualified her from the opportunity. She was proud of being Creek Freedmen and talked frequently of her father, who was a lawyer. Spending time with Gladys provided opportunities for me to gain a deeper understanding of our family history.

During one of our rides, she began reminiscing and mentioned the Republican fundraising affair at HS Lordships, which she had heard bits and pieces about.

"Gloria, I told your mom she doesn't need to follow any man. Your mother was doing good before she met and married her husband. She didn't need to follow in his footsteps. He should be following in hers." She laughed and asked curiously, "What did your Grandma Tressie say about that?"

I could see why my mother respected and admired Gladys so much. She was vivacious, articulate, and purposeful, and she was elegantly dressed even in casual attire, her hair a golden blond, nails always freshly manicured. There were two women in Mother's life who could tell it like it was, without hesitation and no fear of retaliation: my grandmother and Cousin Gladys.

"My grandmother told my mother that she was going to pray that God orders her steps."

With a big grin, Gladys replied, "You know, 'Order My Steps' is my favorite song."

I slid my gospel DVD into the radio, and we listened to the song more than one time.

With a good hearty chuckle as she got out of my car, she said, "I think Tressie also prayed for God to order her son-in-law's steps."

Mr. Martin was a smart, hardworking, and fun guy, making his way, determined to build a better life, and he had no shame in his game. Gladys felt that someone was certainly praying for him to find the right path to success. I believed Cousin Gladys was right.

Driving home, I remembered reading that Shirley Chisholm survived three assassination attempts during her campaign for the Democratic presidential nomination. Growing up and living above the store, I had experienced years of fear. I was happy that I hadn't been one of the Ten Strong, soaring coast to coast on an airplane, attacked with racial slurs by White youth, facing uncertainty and terror. The political fundraising event was enough for me.

Political party divisions run deep and can be scary. I was proud of the Ten Strong. They agreed to attend the convention to gain understanding of the conservative principles of the Republican Party, not for recruitment and mobilizing, not for the media. I applauded the strength and courage of those ten male and female young adults. Their faith in God brought them home stronger, smarter, and—yes—more knowledgeable voters.

William Martin talking with President Gerald Ford

Ermestine posing with her Rolls Royce in front of her office building

Gloria, Principal (second row) – a reflection of the times, circa 1998

GAME CHANGER 34

NEW AND EXPANDING HORIZONS

Fifty years ago, my generation began searching for greater opportunities for our children. Like our parents, we sought pathways to our dreams and goals.

In the 1960s, affirmative action at certain employers and higher-education institutions expanded equal opportunity. Affirmative action opened the doors for members of my generation in historically underrepresented communities. Our parents owned businesses and homes, and they were making a decent income. They wanted their children to break out of the constraints imposed on Blacks and have the opportunity to achieve their career aspirations.

We walked through the doors of opportunity, determined to be successful and excel academically. We dealt with attitudes such as, "If not for affirmative action, you would not be here."

We did not believe we were given special preference because we were Black, but rather, that racist, discriminatory practices against Blacks had blocked our way. Boundary lines prevented our attending schools with adequate AP classes for college-level math and reading ability. Few Black students occupied seats in college-prep high school classes; success in higher education arose from our sheer determination to become academically competitive. We worked hard to achieve on our own merit—through self-confidence, a strong work ethic, and a desire to learn and prosper.

We wanted to attend quality schools and acquire jobs with better wages. We rejected the racial stereotypes of substandard work ethics and performance that we encountered in the workforce. We wanted opportunities to invest wealth back into our communities. We were like fish contained in a large tank; when the glass broke, we swam with every skill we possessed in order to arrive at our destination, transcending the limits imposed on our parents.

In most cases, my generation did not choose to pursue a career in the family business. We attended college, found our passions, and put in the hard work to achieve personal success. We purchased homes near good school districts where we believed our children would be able to have equal opportunities for academic success and be in a position to compete for jobs. We fought against systemic racism and voiced our support for change in the organizations we belonged to. We took action to prevent discrimination and ensure equal opportunity in the jobs, colleges, and careers of our choice.

Today the Black family businesses my generation worked in, side by side with our parents, in order to prosper and to serve our communities, are rare and treasured. We redefine who we are and what we can do to maintain a sense of self-worth, struggling to hold on to hope and remembering the despair in our parents' hearts.

• • •

In the 1970s, Black educators—teachers, principals, and administrators—were advocating for Black children to have the necessary educational support, eliminating the inequities that had become common practice in schools. With the force of my family's pride and inspiration supporting me, I began my first teaching assignment in 1972 at Dag Hammarskjold Elementary School in East Oakland, less than four miles from the Oakland International Airport.

Within four months I was sitting in the superintendent's office. Dr. Marcus Foster had been appointed superintendent of the Oakland Unified School District in 1970, becoming the nation's first Black superintendent of a school district in a large city. Responding to a phone call from his secretary, who had not explained why he was requesting a meeting, I drove nervously to the district office.

Dr. Foster appeared, saying, "Hello Miss Petgrave. Please come in and have a seat."

I watched him close his office door and return to his desk. His presence and mannerisms reminded me of my sixth-grade teacher, Mr. Hill. The similarities with my memories of Mr. Hill were profound.

"How are you enjoying your first teaching assignment, Miss Petgrave?"

I was struggling with classroom management issues, so much so that tears of frustration would flow while driving home after a really bad day with my students. There were moments when the students were in control of the classroom.

I responded with, "Things are going good."

Dr. Foster was thumbing through a stack of folders on his neatly organized desk. There was a moment of silence as he focused his attention on items in one of the folders.

He resumed the conversation with, "You are working at Dag Hammarskjold?" and provided some background history of Mr. Hammarskjold. Behind his desk, bookshelves held award plaques, certificates, and honors, neatly displayed. He closed the file folder and focused his complete attention squarely on me.

I thought to myself, "Maybe he is meeting with all new teachers, checking in and introducing himself personally."

"Miss Petgrave, the reason I have asked to meet with you is that one of your parents filed a complaint. Apparently recently there was a fight in your classroom. Tell me what happened." He returned his glance to the folder, waiting for me to respond.

"Yes, Dr. Foster, there was a fight in my classroom. The students were returning from recess, and I was writing information on the chalkboard. In an instant there was chaos, and the class was in an uproar. I turned around to witness a fight between a female and male student. Both students were sent to the principal's office with a referral for fighting."

Dr. Foster's disposition was calming, although I was thinking, "Oh my goodness, I am getting ready to be fired!"

However, I connected with his concern and why I was sitting in his office and listened as he began advocating for alternative classroom-management strategies. He articulated his vision of creating safe classrooms immersed in learning. His words provided coaching for emerging teachers like me, offering strategies to spark growth and build relationships with my students.

Before ending the meeting, Dr. Foster said, "Next week, winter recess begins. Create some strategies to implement when you return in January and focus on having control of your class. I have visions of social reform and believe that classroom management is your key to success."

I scurried out of the District Administrative Office, completely oblivious to people around me. Then I heard a car horn, followed by a voice, "Hey Gloria, where is your car? I can't find a parking space."

I approached the car; it was another new teacher I had just met.

"Girl, I am running late and have an appointment with the superintendent."

I pointed to my car parked across the street. She made a U-turn and pulled up behind my car as I drove away. I wondered what her meeting was about, grateful that I still had a job. I thought about the similarities between Dr. Foster and Mr. Hill. It was uncanny how much they resembled each other in appearance and in the spirit they created to motivate success.

In November 1973, while leaving a school board meeting, Dr. Foster was assassinated by members of the Symbionese Liberation Army because of his support for implementing a student identification card system within the school district. His efforts to make schools safe environments for students became the catalyst for his death.

My one and only personal encounter with Dr. Foster motivated me to create a classroom environment where all students felt safe and had the opportunity to learn. I strived to ensure that any consequences I issued fit the behavior. I spent the entire winter recess developing new classroom management strategies that would enable me to be in total control of my class. From that day forth I never turned my back to the class until all students were in their seats with their attention totally on me.

• • •

Throughout my forty-three years in the field of education, I observed firsthand the inequities and biases that Black students encountered because of systemically racist policies and practices.

After a few years as a classroom teacher I recognized that Special Needs classes continued to be filled with a disproportionate number of Black males. Teachers who could not relate to a Black male child and had difficulty controlling that student in class generally preferred that the student be tested and placed in Special Needs classes. Black students were subjected to suspensions from school more often than students of other races.

When students are not in school, they are not learning, and Black girls and boys were being put out of school at an alarming rate.

Throughout our history flows a generational concern of Black families trying to ensure that all students get an education that will prepare them to become competitive in the career they desire. But research has shown that predominantly Black/low-income schools do not get the necessary support and high-quality teachers that can help create a school climate where students feel safe and can grow.

In a 2014 report, the Civil Rights Project found that segregation in California schools had increased over the past several decades, especially for Latinos. Black and Latino students were relegated to inferior schools, while White and Asian students received better college preparation in highly rated schools. As of that report, Blacks had become a minority in schools: "The typical black student in California today attends a school with more than 2.5 times as many Latinos as blacks, thus making them a minority within a school dominated by another disadvantaged group."[9]

One of the many things I learned after years of work in the field of education is that school segregation in racially and socioeconomically isolated schools is related to opportunity gaps that limit educational opportunities and outcomes. I am not currently aware of a California initiative to deal with issues of resegregation in California.

* * *

In the hope of finding better schools, many Blacks from my generation moved from historically Black neighborhoods in Richmond and other Bay Area cities to suburban cities like Antioch, Stockton, Tracy, Fairfield, and Vacaville as well as to San Joaquin County. These Blacks moved to the suburbs by choice, but others were pushed out by government agencies under the guise of "urban renewal" or by developers pressuring them to sell their property.

One thing I have noticed since I retired in 2004 from West Contra Costa School District is that the Black population in traditionally Black neighborhoods in Richmond has continued to decline, while the Latinx population has increased steadily. There are no longer predominantly Black communities within the city of Richmond but, rather, Black neighbors here and there within Latinx neighborhoods.

In a 2018 report, the Othering & Belonging Institute affirmed "Richmond's neighborhoods are highly segregated by race, especially for Latinos and African Americans. Although the Black population has declined in numbers substantially in recent years, partly as a result of displacement and gentrification, Richmond is currently 18 percent African American, 17 percent White, 13 percent Asian, and 48 percent Latino."[10]

Immigration from Mexico rose during and after World War II, with many Mexicans moving from farms to cities, searching for jobs in factories. Many came to Richmond. This fact is reflected in the ethnicity of Mother's tenants. When my mother started her work in Richmond in the 1950s, all of her clients were Black; today, most of our housing units are rented by Latinx tenants. The Latinx communities in Richmond are thriving, with healthy businesses and recently remodeled schools. With pride and determination they have created their own communities in their search for generational wealth.

Blacks in California have strong traditions of owning and operating small businesses. In the 1940s, Richmond had all-Black neighborhoods, with Black-owned businesses circulating money within the community. When I was growing up, Black families in Richmond owned not only their business, but their building and the land it was built on. Some of the most prominent Black-owned businesses in Richmond were insurance companies, funeral parlors, barber and beauty salons, restaurants, retail clothing stores, grocery and liquor stores, gas stations, candy shops, real estate offices, and dentists' and doctors' offices. Blacks also have a history of ownership in music-related businesses, including record stores and nightclubs. My question is, where did they go? Today in Richmond, only a few Black businesses own their own land. It makes me wonder where are the Black businesses today? Where is the Black generational wealth?

* * *

In 1978, Mother and Mr. Martin built their new home in El Cerrito, on top of the hill. The entryway had a gorgeous crystal chandelier, and a bedroom deck overlooked the living room. There was a sauna in the bedroom and a bidet in the bathroom. It was a premium home in so many ways. The views were dynamic, and their personal touches were lavish.

Pop identified one room as the Prayer Room. Grandmother's living room couch and coffee table were there, spiritual pictures decorated the walls, and Bibles and Christian books filled the room. There Pop had his favorite chair to sit in and think, write sermons, have alone time with God, and surround himself with prayer in God's room, in his own house. He would spend hours there reading his Bible, praising God, and—a few years down the line—preparing his weekly inspirational religious hours to be broadcast on the San Francisco radio station KEST. Family members knew that the Prayer Room was sacred and respected it as such.

When they were in the Bay Area together, my parents regularly attended North Richmond Missionary Baptist Church, and many Sundays they also visited other Bay Area churches. They became active members of North Richmond Missionary Baptist, leading to Pop's becoming an ordained minister in 1982, sitting in the pulpit and even delivering the message some Sundays.

They had God in their lives, each other, family, and that's all they needed. Their lives were unified, and both brought to that unity past experiences of defeat through racial discrimination. Their new home represented the hard, unending work of overcoming illegal practices that put restraints on where Blacks could live. They were witnessing and making it possible for Blacks to move into areas beyond the limitations they were accustomed to, if they so desired. They were branching out to develop housing projects as far as Los Angeles. They were connecting with the people in power to be successful.

In 1977 my parents purchased the historic landmark American Trust / Wells Fargo Building in Downtown Richmond, and made it the formal headquarters of Martin Realty. Mother often laughed about how her husband had given up on pursuing the purchase because the White man was trying to exclude them from the opportunity to buy, while she on the other hand was persistent and demanded equal treatment. She said, "I didn't know how the mop was going to flop, but I wasn't giving up as easy as Martin, without a fight."

Pop would always add, "Yes, but the next time we met with the bank officials together, it was on. We didn't hold back on what we knew were unfair, discriminatory practices, and they backed down and started presenting options that made sense."

That's the way they rolled. When one would become defeated and overwhelmed with the struggle, the other would rise to the occasion, put on boxing gloves, and come out fighting. They supported each other in confrontational situations dealing with tenants, employees, City of Richmond and county officials, financial institutions, contractors, lawyers. It didn't matter who they felt was doing wrong, White or Black, young or old, they responded as a husband-and-wife team, bringing force and fury.

The real estate agents working in Martin Realty during the 1970s had gradually left to open their own real estate offices, and my parents embraced the idea of a team effort, working together as independent brokers. This team was not without conflict. Throughout college, I worked in the Martin Realty office at various times and saw firsthand many of the confrontational discussions that occurred there. Sometimes they would become intense with anger; sometimes there would be gifts given or received.

On one of my working days, a friend of Pop's visited the office. Pop excitedly greeted him at the counter, as they had not seen each other for a while. After a brief conversation, catching up on things going on in their world, the man asked Pop to loan him some money.

Pop took a few steps back, and in a highly agitated voice, he responded, "Man, I like you, you are my friend and I want to remain friends. So in order to remain friends, I can't grant your request. If you want us to sit down over a drink and discuss how you won't get in this situation again, we can do that right now, or anytime you want."

Pop reached out to offer a handshake, which the man accepted, and Pop said, "I like you, and you seem to like me as your friend, and that I am."

Pop and his friend left the office, walked down the block to CJ Lounge, had a few drinks, and talked about financial management. A couple of hours later they returned to the office. Pop gave the man some phone numbers and they continued to talk for a while.

Pop's friend left with another handshake and said, "Thanks, friend. I'll stop by to see you next week."

Pop sat at his desk for a while, thinking and watching the cars passing by the office. Speaking out loud to himself, with anger in his tone, he said, "Man, I hate for friends to come in and ask me for money. I can help them work for money, I can help them save their money, but I can't give them money."

I responded with, "I understand."

He looked away from the window, somewhat unsettled. His facial expression made it clear that he had forgotten I was in the office.

"Glo, let me tell you this. Past experiences have taught me that if you want to keep a friend, don't give them money. If you give friends money you will look around and not have any friends."

His words truly expressed what I had already begun to realize in my own personal relationships.

My mother and grandparents functioned on that same flow of thinking. My cousins and I learned early in life not to ask for money from our parents. Working for Mother was always available for us as a way to make money, but asking for money otherwise was a challenge. We already knew her response would be "NO," followed by the words "Your grandmother always says *N* comes before *Y* for a reason."

Mother's demeanor with tenants and employees ranged all the way from confrontational to encouraging and praising. Her expectations were high, and she never lowered her standards. On the other hand, she had a heart for those going through hard times and was supportive and unwavering with efforts to help. She liked to say, "You never know how the mop is going to flop. It depends on who is holding the mop."

It was clear to me that my parents didn't pick and choose how to respond to individuals, whether they be tenants, employees, city or county officials, contractors, family members, or friends. My parents' responses were not based on who the person was but rather came from a place of morality, of right or wrong.

There was no shame in their game, just pure determination to improve living situations for Blacks and fight unjust discriminatory practices.

• • •

During a vacation to London, England, in 1978, Mother and Pop stayed at the Hilton on Park Lane. The hotel was located in the center of London, minutes away from Buckingham Palace. Their vacation consisted of sightseeing, checking out real estate, and pampering themselves. They scurried around London with their granddaughter, using town car services. On one outing Mother saw Queen Elizabeth, who was the same age as she was, riding in an older-model Rolls Royce.

On her return to the hotel, she stopped and asked a doorman, "Why does the Queen ride around in an old Rolls?"

The doorman responded, "The Queen is quite thrifty with her money. She knows that a well-kept old Rolls is just as valuable as the newer ones. She loves her old Rolls but has many other cars."

A short time after their vacation, my mother called and said excitedly, "I just purchased a new Rolls Royce. I love it and will never sell it. The Queen's birthright entitled her to a Rolls Royce; she can buy property wherever she wants to. She is my age, but I got my Rolls Royce through struggle and hardship. I've worked hard to fight racial discrimination and limitations Blacks had to overcome, and I fought for legal rights."

At the end of the conversation she stated, "I just decided what I am going to have on its license plate: *Mrs. WDM.* Because that's who I am. Mr. William D. Martin's wife and Mrs. Tressie Williams's daughter. Do you know who you are?"

Quite blindsided by her question, I was speechless, and it took time to process how to respond.

She paused, waiting for a reply, and then started singing "Precious Lord." After a verse or two she ended with, "Your grandfather always said, 'This is just the way of the world.' Well, this is my world, and I hope it's yours as well. See you at church tomorrow. We'll go to San Francisco for lunch afterward."

• • •

In 1986 Mother established Grace Center, remodeling the real estate office basement in the Wells Fargo building into a small chapel. She purchased a beautiful piano, drums, and organ at an auction, and then bought a podium, microphone, stereo equipment, and recording devices. Religious pictures and artifacts were beautifully displayed. Chairs were neatly positioned, and artificial flowers graced the room. During working hours, it was not unusual to find Pop in Grace Center, reading the Bible and practicing sermons. Or Mother listening to gospel music, playing the piano, and singing religious songs.

Pop began to teach and preach the gospel to a small congregation that met weekly in Grace Center. These church services were broadcast on a Bay Area gospel radio show, aired on KEST, every Sunday evening, with Mother's voice sprinkled throughout. Every Sunday after attending church services, we would drive to San Francisco, drop off the tape at the radio station, and have lunch in the city. Sunday evenings, we would listen to the radio broadcast.

Mother would invite clients, tenants, business associates, city officials, church members, friends, and family members to go down into the basement, where she would play the piano and sing to or with them. Grace Center became their place at work to escape their daily struggles and praise and worship God. Grandmother's frequent visits to the office included going into Grace Center and singing and praying with her daughter. Before everyone returned to the office area, her prayers always asked God to order family steps in every path taken, every direction turned. At home and at work, Mother and Pop had created a special place to honor God and all his blessings, and they devoted time every day to spend time reflecting on His glory. Grace Center and the Prayer Room were off-limits to do anything but honor God.

• • •

Mother and Pop became well known as a power couple and were highly respected throughout Richmond and the greater Bay Area. They employed and trained Blacks looking for work, helped local families buy real estate, and provided housing in low-income and predominantly Black neighborhoods throughout the city. They built HUD-funded housing projects and financed loans for homeownership. They provided loans to Black churches throughout Richmond.

As a couple, they fought racial discrimination head-on and continued to challenge the status quo, focused on how to combat racism and the discriminatory practices perpetrated against Blacks—simply because of their minority status in the world of real estate. Landlords were still denying Blacks with good credit, good jobs, and excellent references the opportunity to rent in certain locations—based solely on their race.

In 1972, during a New York trip she referred to as their honeymoon, they were relaxing in the hotel room and watching TV. Mother noticed that her husband had picked up the phone, but she wasn't paying much attention until he said, "I'm calling Donald Trump."

"Donald Trump?" she repeated, quite surprised, but now totally focused and listening.

"Hello, Mr. Trump, this is William Martin from the Bay Area."

Mother was shocked that Donald Trump had personally answered his phone, and she moved closer to her husband so she could hear the conversation. They talked about real estate in New York and the Bay Area for a brief time. He learned that Trump had recently taken charge of his family's real estate business and was working on expanding into Manhattan.

Later that evening, Mother and Pop spent time riding around New York City in a cab, looking at some of the available real estate opportunities, and they had dinner at a restaurant that Donald Trump had recommended. She often reflected on that phone call and was impressed with her new husband's desire to expand his knowledge of real estate beyond the Bay Area. In their journey to grow and learn, they aspired to talk with those in the business who were movers and shakers, who made things happen and took risks.

Preaching in Grace Center, William's greatest joy

Alpha Nu Omega Chapter of Alpha Kappa Alpha Sorority, Inc.
hosted an annual birthday celebrations for Gladys.
Ermestine, Gloria, Gladys, Loretta, and Betty
at a celebration of Gladys's 106th birthday.

Gloria and Gladys, circa 2000

GAME CHANGER 35

SISTERHOOD

In 1981, after going through a divorce with my first husband, I began once again spending more time with family and friends, especially my cousin Gladys Meriwether Jordan.

Gladys was born in 1910 in Oklahoma. She was the eleventh of twelve children born to A. J. Meriwether, an attorney, and Susie Brown Meriwether, an educator. Gladys spoke highly and consistently about AKA. She was initiated into Alpha Kappa Alpha Sorority, Inc., in Okmulgee, Oklahoma, in 1942. She was a former president of Alpha Nu Omega Chapter and held many positions on the executive board. Gladys kept encouraging me to become a member of the sorority.

At that time, I had no interest in joining a sorority. I lacked the background knowledge about sisterhood and the experience of how sororities functioned. My focus was on being a mother to my young daughter, Kim, and on finding out how to make additional income to pay the mortgage on a house I had purchased while my first husband and I were separated (we were officially divorced in 1977). But Cousin Gladys spoke of the sisterhood, support, and unity of women in the Alpha Nu Omega chapter. She shared literature with me about the history and historical meaning of AKA.

In March 2021 Alpha Kappa Alpha Sorority, Inc., released *Twenty Pearls,* a documentary that chronicles the history Gladys shared with me: "Only 40 years past the emancipation of enslaved African Americans, nine Black college women enrolled at Howard University where they organized and built a sisterhood in 1908 . . . Alpha Kappa Alpha impacted the Harlem Renaissance, World War II, NASA, Civil Rights, Women's Rights, Historically Black Colleges and Universities (HBCUs), all culminating in the election of the first woman, African American and Asian American Vice President of the United States of America."[11]

The more I read and the more I listened to Gladys, the more interested I became. I was inspired by the determination and power of Black women sharing their history and their vision.

So at thirty-two years old, I became a member of Alpha Nu Omega Chapter, Berkeley, California, along with ten other members.

Being a debutante in the Links Cotillion at age seventeen had provided me a new way of thinking about myself and polished me for success in life. AKA provided me opportunities to effectively carry out its mission and purpose with sisters who were committed and determined to grow and serve their communities. They had achieved accolades in the educational, medical, legal, and business fields. Not to mention the government—both my mother and Gladys would have been ecstatic over the 2021 election of the first Black and Asian woman vice president of the United States. Vice President Kamala Harris exemplifies Alpha Kappa Alpha's accomplishments of changing American Black history.

I believe that if Mother had stayed at Langston University as her parents initially requested, she would have become a member of AKA. Living in Oklahoma, she was aware of and surrounded by sororities and fraternities. She valued and understood their missions and purposes. Those hopes and dreams she envisioned for her life came true, but through me.

One of my last classroom assignments at Brookfield, 1987

Gloria and Al on their wedding day in 1984

Kim, Roman, and Fallon (center) at Annex Child Development Center

GAME CHANGER 36

LAUNDROMAT LOVE

One day I was experiencing problems with the washing machine in my home, and I decided to go to the laundromat. I went into a nearby grocery store to buy some detergent, and in line, I noticed a fine-looking man behind me engaged in conversation with a little boy. The man glanced at me and smiled.

We started talking, about what I don't remember; the little boy was busily checking out candy displayed at the checkout counter. I thought to myself, *Now this is a handsome man. I wonder what kind of car he drives?* He had a beautiful smile, was dressed nicely, and had a presence that captured my attention.

I left the grocery store and walked to the laundromat. Soon after I arrived, I noticed the little boy sitting on a chair while the man was putting his clothes in a washer. I couldn't stop looking at him; there was something about him I liked and that intrigued me. I was paying so much attention to this man and was so fascinated by his style that I poured too much detergent in the washing machine. I put my coins in, sat down, and waited for it to start.

The little boy was happily enjoying a candy bar, sitting in front of me within view of the man. I wondered if that was his father.

The boy appeared to be a little younger than my daughter, Kim, who was at her preschool. I glanced at my watch and began strategizing a plan to make sure I picked her up on time. I looked at the little boy and smiled. He smiled back and then looked in the man's direction.

Within a few minutes, bubbles started pouring out of the washing machine and onto the floor. I was totally tripping out. The man came over to my assistance. I was embarrassed, but he was cool and calm.

He smiled and said, "What did you do? Put too much soap in there?"

I wanted to say, "I think so, because I couldn't stop looking at you."

But now I had to be cool and so I said, "I guess so."

While he helped me deal with the big mess I had created, we introduced ourselves. I found out that the little boy, Roman, was his son, and that he also had three daughters, Ursula, Stacy, and Tamiza. Before I left the laundromat, he asked for my phone number. That was the beginning of my falling in love with my husband.

• • •

Al Scoggins and his son lived a few blocks from my house. We were always either at my house or his, surrounded by our children. Courting involved fun weekend outings and getting to know each other's family and friends. In my mind, we were perfect for each other. He was my dream come true. The man I had been searching for, the man I wanted to marry.

On one memorable date, Al and I attended a political fund-raising event with my parents at the Sheraton Hotel in Concord. I was at Mother's house when Al arrived, and we were all dressed up. I was upstairs when I heard the doorbell chime. I quickly put on some lipstick, checked my hair, and left the bedroom.

From the top of the staircase I saw Pop open the door. Al entered, truly looking like Smokey Robinson, his swagger and stance exemplifying my definition of beauty.

This was the first time my parents had met Al; so far, they had only heard me mention his name. After brief introductions, we left for the event.

My mother spent the evening asking Al question upon question. Other family members sat at our table. Pop was floating in and out of listening to our conversations and being his regular people-person self, acknowledging people he knew at the event.

After we returned to my mother's house, Al left. It was late, and I started getting ready to go home. I still had to go by Baldie's house and pick up Kim. While I was getting my car keys out of my purse, Mother began to ask detailed questions about our relationship and specific questions about Al. I knew she already had the answers, since I had heard her ask Al these same questions during dinner. I had also heard his responses and learned some things I hadn't known.

Pop shared that he really liked Al, and stated, "He could be the one for you." Mother, on the other hand, expressed concern about my marrying a man with children. She shared sad stories about her mother dealing with her stepchildren and talked about watching her mother being physically attacked by my grandfather's ex-wife. Pop and I listened. Neither of us had a comment.

Mother looked at me in her "this is serious" business look, and in a soft voice said, "Glo, you do what you want to do, but I know from what your grandmother encountered dealing with ex-wives, it's not easy; you may face some unexpected problems you won't know how to handle. Al has children with not one but two exes. He may or may not be the one for you."

Pop, quick as a wink, said, "Ermestine, you said that right. Glo, you do what you want to do."

I smiled and said good night. I was thirty-two years old, happy that Al was in my life, and determined to live my own life, regardless of what my mother believed was best for me.

* * *

More important than anything else, I was in love. Before meeting Al, I opened Annex Child Development Center in my house. Initially I was licensed for six children, then expanded to twelve, and, eventually, twenty-four.

By the time Al and I met, I was licensed for twelve children; sections of my house resembled a day care center. When you entered my home, there were clear indications that children were the focus. Baby beds, play pens, cots, cubbies, thematic bulletin boards, chalkboards, learning centers, curriculum posters, books, toys, a parent attendance clipboard—all organized and defined in designated areas. I was a kindergarten teacher in Oakland Unified School District during the day and provided child care from 6:00 p.m. to 7:00 a.m. to nurses, doctors, toll bridge workers, and correction officers at San Quentin. My clients primarily worked swing shifts and weekends. I hired an employee who worked five days a week.

On one of those rare occasions when our children were off spending time with family members, Al and I were watching television in my bedroom. Something caught my eye on the ledge of the headboard. Reaching for the small box, I said, "What is this?"

Al didn't answer, but had a grin from ear to ear. I opened the box, and it was the most beautiful engagement ring! I was mesmerized, and overwhelmed with joy and happiness. I couldn't wait to show my mother.

We made plans for a small outside wedding at Lake Tahoe. My mother, perhaps too dubious about my relationship, decided not to attend the wedding. Baldie was especially excited about going to Lake Tahoe, and the day before the wedding, she drove out with her daughter, Yvonne. Yvonne was my maid of honor, and Al's good friend Ron was his best man.

Shortly before the ceremony, I asked Yvonne, "Where is your mother?"

With a twinkle in her eye, she chuckled, "You know where she is. In the casino, sitting in front of a slot machine. She wasn't ready to leave, so I left her happily dropping coins into the machine. She said that she would catch a cab to the Chapel." Yvonne quickly looked around at the guests and said, "I hope she arrives in time." I adjusted the flower arrangement in her hair and giggled, "Well, I am so happy that you are standing by my side."

Al and his best man took their places, music began playing, and Yvonne started walking slowly toward the decorated wedding arches. Yvonne was seven years younger than I, the baby in our family, and I never forgot that as a toddler she would catch me off guard and bite me if she didn't get her way. I remember thinking that my little cousin, the biter, looked glorious as she swayed elegantly to her spot. I glanced toward the entrance, hoping to see Baldie strutting in.

During the ceremony, tears were continuously dripping down my face, and to this day I don't know why. Then, shortly after we were pronounced man and wife, Al almost fainted. Family members scrambled to make sure he was okay. He was sitting on a bench, surrounded by family members, his head down, staring at the ground while his sister ran into the chapel searching for some water for him. A few seconds after being announced as Mr. and Mrs. Scoggins, the wedding party was in crisis mode, with Al the center of attention.

Like a flip of a light switch he had become weak and sweaty, apparently dealing with a medical issue that came out of nowhere. Once again, tears began flowing down my cheeks as I watched

Al sitting there and heard voices in alarm saying, "Are you okay?" "Do we need to call an ambulance?" Speechless, I didn't know if he was suffering from a heart attack or was overwhelmed by committing to our marriage vows.

After a few minutes Al was able to recover. He smiled and told everyone, "I am okay." His brother teased him with, "Man that must have been hard for you to do." Everyone got a good laugh, including Al, and the worst was over. Nothing like that ever happened again.

* * *

I don't recall when I finally saw Baldie in Tahoe. But I do remember sitting next to her while she played a slot machine and listening to her say, "Your mother said, 'I'll pass on attending Glo's wedding and wait for the next one.'"

I watched her take a drag on her cigarette and pull the slot machine handle.

"But I'm here, Glo."

I looked at her curiously and quickly responded, "But you didn't show up for the wedding."

She focused on the slot machine for a few seconds, looked at me, puffed on her cigarette, and laughed. "I know. I was winning at the casino and lost track of time. But I'm here now," she chuckled again. Her focus returned to the slot machine. "Glo, the main thing is that you have to live your own life. That's what I'm going to do."

In a defeated voice, she stated softly, "What a shame; I lost all my money." She puffed on her cigarette, looked at the slot machine, and started frantically searching in her purse. "Glo, don't feel sorry for me, just loan me some money until the next time I see you."

As I handed her the money, she smiled and said, "When Ermestine and I have a little fight, and I walk away, it doesn't mean we don't love one another. What else can I say? Mothers worry about their child. Ermestine is never going to stop asking what have you been doing and where have you been."

Then cherries rolled across her screen, and she became attentive to her machine. My eyes moved from her to the machine.

"Glo, if that other cherry had popped up, I would have won big!"

There were crowds of people in the casino, a constant flow of movement through the aisles and around us.

"Your mother really works my nerves, but I love her and know she will always have my back." She resumed playing the machine, sighing, "I understand Ermestine gets mad at us, but we are trying to do the best we can. Live your life." She put her cigarette out and returned to dropping money into the slot machine.

I was happy Baldie was in Tahoe. Her presence made me feel better. As I left to find Al, she said, "Glo, you have any more money you can spare?"

• • •

The next morning I woke up earlier than usual. Al slept on, undisturbed by my movements. I made some coffee and sat outside on the deck with a picture-perfect view of sparkling crystal water with little wave movement. Savoring the moment of nature's beauty, my mind zigzagged back to Al sitting on that bench having his own personal, challenging moment and then to my mother's absence from my wedding. I wondered if she was thinking of me as I was of her.

I returned my focus to the water's tranquility and calmness, which created a sense of peace and joyfulness. I was deep in thought when Al appeared with a cup of coffee and sat next to me. We sat enjoying the scenery and sipping coffee. The blissfulness of summer was drawing to an end. In three weeks, after our honeymoon cruise, I would return to work and begin a new school year.

Driving home, we heard on the radio that Marvin Gaye had been shot and killed by his father. My day became misty blue. That was sorrowful news, but I was still feeling blessed, contented, and happy to be Mrs. Scoggins. I listened to the radio play songs in tribute to Marvin Gaye, watched Al drive, and thought—this time we have a good love, something special. I was hoping that this time we would both put our minds to getting it right. A serenade of Marvin Gaye songs added a different atmosphere to the ride home and painted the sky gloomier, with the reality that life can be taken away in an instant by someone you love deeply.

Baldie called me after she returned home and said, "Glo, come get the money you loaned me."

She was especially elated because she had finally won big. I was happy for her, and she was happy for me.

Before we ended the conversation, she said, "Seriously, you can let Ermestine control your life, but I'm not going to. No one is going to control my life but me. I think Al is a great guy."

Al frequently dropped by her house to visit and check on how she was doing. They enjoyed each other's company.

Shortly after this talk with Baldie, Mother called, excitedly sharing news of a new real estate venture she was pursuing. She never asked about the wedding, and I didn't volunteer any information related to my special day.

• • •

Six months after meeting Al in the laundromat, we were married, and his little boy Roman was calling me mom. We became a family of his, mine, and ours. We had a daughter together, Fallon, and my life was complete. I had a cute son, two amazing daughters, three teenage stepdaughters — Ursula, Stacy, and Tamiza — who were very much a part of our lives, and the man of my dreams. Although my mother did not attend our wedding, through the years she realized that our relationship was solid and began to respect our marriage.

Within seven years of our marriage Al was working at the Office for Civil Rights in San Francisco. I was no longer a classroom teacher but the chairperson for the Discipline Hearing Panel in Oakland Unified.

I was learning more about the discrepancies among Black children and other races in suspension rates and expulsion procedures. Al and I were both working in roles dealing with education, learning and expanding our knowledge of students' educational experiences.

• • •

February 25, 1984, was one of the saddest days of my life. My parents were out of town on a real estate business trip, and my grandmother's caregiver called my home. I was out and about with our kids. Al answered the phone and heard the caregiver's frantic voice saying that my grandmother was having problems. Al rushed to Mother's house and watched my grandmother take her last breath. That he was present meant so much to my mother. Her mother, Tressie Williams, who received that allocation of Forty Acres and a Mule, and whose life is the foundation of this book, left this earth with Al by her side. Whenever Mother needed help of any kind, Al was right there.

• • •

When I was seventy years old, while researching family history for this memoir and asking my cousin Larry questions, he spoke words that disturbed my thinking.

"You know your mother was pregnant with you, and that's why your parents got married."

I was blindsided and dumbfounded at hearing his words. I couldn't process what Larry was saying, and I sat in complete silence, my mind racing. How would Larry know this? Aunt Lillian had never shared this information with me, even during conversations when she was truly upset at my mother.

I connected the dots in my mind and remembered that my father's best friend, who was the best man at my parents' wedding, was a close acquaintance of Larry's. Larry had kept this secret from me for years. My probing of his brain brought this secret to light. My parents eloped to Reno, Nevada, and returned as Mr. and Mrs. Petgrave. A big surprise to family members.

I started thinking back to Mother's words during the divorce proceedings, "God and you brought us together, and now a judge is going to separate us." Those words suddenly had more meaning. I quickly found my parents' marriage certificate and realized that Larry's words were true.

Never before had that possibility entered my mind. I struggled to internalize that reality. I don't know why this knowledge affected me so profoundly. My mind raced back to when I found out that Al and I were pregnant a few months before our planned wedding. In the grand scheme of things, Al and I were falling in love, and that should have been all that mattered. But I was a teacher. I felt I had to be a role model for my students. I did not want to bring shame to myself or my family. I'd believed Mother's teachings that I had to be married before getting pregnant. I remember walking into Kaiser for an abortion, with those messages ingrained in my brain. That it would be an indictment on my character and bring shame to me.

I grew up with the belief that marriage should be a commitment separate from pregnancy. You should get married without outside forces or feelings, or because one is "supposed to be married." My mindset is so different now.

Cultural and religious views of marriage before pregnancy were my norm, the explicitly communicated expectation. How did Mother shake the guilt or shame, dealing with the ugliness some people associated with being pregnant before marriage—the thoughts of generations past? I can imagine the judgment my mother might have felt from family members, or even just herself, because she believed she had failed her own standards and her mother's standards. Today, I believe no fear or shame should be in the equation.

In their marriage vows, my parents decided to be there for each other and to raise a child. That promise makes me feel that their love for me brought them together. Forty years ago, it was easy to get an abortion. Planning and scheduling the procedure meant a phone call to the medical facility. Having the abortion was a mental roller-coaster ride, but one could easily go through with it without missing a step in daily routines. This would circumvent the shame associated with being pregnant before marriage—family and friends wouldn't know that the abortion had even occurred. No public shame associated, perhaps, but an uncertainty that could last a lifetime, wondering if the right decision had been made.

Baldie was my confidante, my connection with family history, offering a clear picture of the dysfunctional parts of our family. Yet neither she nor my father ever shared that Mother was pregnant before marriage. A well-kept secret. The three of us spent endless moments together, sharing family jokes with laughter and recalling memorable incidents, good and bad. But never that one.

More often than not, after I graduated from high school, Baldie would greet me with, "Hey, Glo, how is your love life?"

She asked questions about the really personal aspects of my life. The emotional side of what I was experiencing. Topics that Mother and I had never discussed. But when I found out that I was pregnant, I, too, kept that a secret from everyone. Baldie's sisterly relationship with Mother was, strikingly, a reflection of my experiences as her daughter.

Ermestine and Baldie's bedroom window, first one on the left, in Checotah

PART FIVE:
A TRAIL OF TEARS

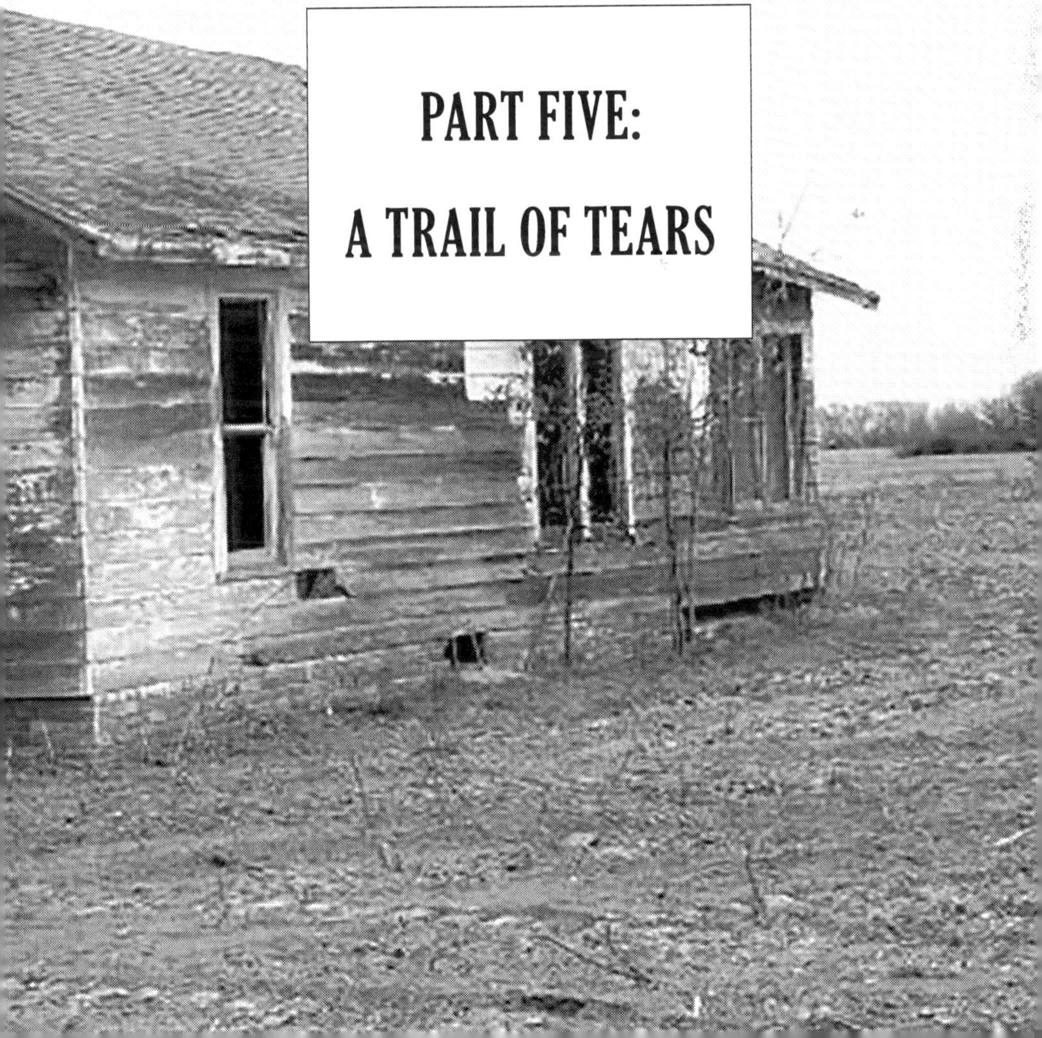

Ermestine and Reverend C. W. Newsome, Pop's homegoing services, North Richmond Missionary Baptist Church

GAME CHANGER 37

UNEXPECTED CHALLENGES

One evening in 1992, Mother was playing her piano and singing. Pop came into the living room and stood behind her. Suddenly he fell to the floor, his eyes blank and his body still. Mother called 911 and returned to his side, calling "Martin, Martin!" She ran to her next-door neighbors' house for help, crying. The husband and wife were both doctors. They rushed back to her house. Pop was still lying in the same position, unresponsive.

The couple began CPR, and Mother called me. Her voice was panicked. "Glo, come quick. Martin passed out." She hung up the phone.

Kim and Fallon were sitting at the kitchen table; Al and I were in the family room. I repeated Mother's words and said, "We have to go."

Within a few minutes, we were on the freeway. Al was putting the pedal to the metal, and no one said a word. Fallon, who by nature was always asking questions, was speechless.

Al pulled into the driveway; an ambulance was parked in front of the house. He jumped out of the car and told the girls to remain in the car. As we entered the house, the paramedics had Pop on a gurney and were approaching the door. The next-door neighbors were comforting my mother. She said, "Glo, find my purse and keys. I have to go with Martin."

When Kim and Fallon saw their grandmother appear on the porch, they scrambled out of the car and ran to her.

The following day, after dropping my children off at school to be picked up for day care, I went to the hospital to visit Pop. My mother was in the room, sitting next to the hospital bed. Pop was sleeping, and she was scanning through some work folders. She said that Pop had had a heart attack.

"I don't know what to do. We are in the middle of this big project and need to pay millions of dollars to close the deal. We have other projects already started, and I'm not sure if now is a good time to move forward with this one."

A deacon from the church entered the room and began talking with my mother. I stood there staring at Pop, who was motionless, unaware of the three of us in the room. The deacon glanced over at Pop frequently while engaged in conversation with my mother. After about twenty minutes, he left.

My mother stood by Pop, looking down at him, and said, "Martin, I will be back. Glo and I are going to get something to eat."

When we returned, his food was on the hospital table, untouched. She woke him up and tried to feed him, but he went back to sleep without eating. When I left at 5:30 p.m. to pick up my daughters from day care, she was sitting in the chair next to the bed, looking through her briefcase, pulling out folders and starting to work.

* * *

After a brief stay in the hospital, Pop returned home with a new attitude about life as a seventy-two-year-old. The frequent trips to Baskin Robbins Ice Cream became a special-treat occasion. My parents no longer went to restaurants on a regular basis for lunch or dinner. My mother cooked foods that Pop's doctor recommended and did not deviate from the menu. She started preparing lunches for them to take to work. They went to Europe and attended a two-week health retreat. When they returned from the retreat, they began walking together, and Pop joined the YMCA. He was faithful in attending early morning exercise classes before going to work.

He returned to working in the office, but made a conscious effort to leave at 5:00 p.m. He was actively engaged with supervising his maintenance crew, delegating work to office staff, meeting with consultants, managing tenants, and interacting with city and county officials. It was now rare for him, however, to function in the role of a broker or get involved with selling property. He remained active in NAACP, community, and social events as well as family affairs. More often than not, he would be in Grace Center, the office basement, reading his Bible or talking with friends who stopped by the office to visit. He spent more time at home in the Prayer Room, preparing sermons, rather than talking about work.

One ritual that my parents engaged in frequently involved shopping trips to San Francisco with their grandchildren. My mother would spend hours and hours strolling through Macy's, floor by floor, trying on clothes. Pop would visit the men's department and, within thirty minutes, had purchased his selections.

While waiting for Mother he would entertain the grandchildren, buying ice cream and people-watching. On one memorable weekend, while on their shopping trip, Pop and my mother separated. Seven-year-old Fallon ended up shopping with Pop, and Kim was with her grandmother. After a couple of hours, Fallon and Pop wandered around Macy's looking for her grandmother. Pop told Fallon, "Your grandmother left us and went home."

Fallon knew her grandmother would not have left, and she started getting a little frightened. As they were walking out of Macy's to the parking lot, Fallon kept telling Pop not to leave.

She knew her grandmother and sister wouldn't have left Macy's. Pop was persistent and continued on to the parking lot. Fallon knew there was something wrong with this picture, but Pop was convinced they had left the store and gone home.

He paid the parking lot ticket, and they headed back to El Cerrito. She tried to persuade him not to leave San Francisco. The thirty-minute drive home was made in dead silence. About this same time, Kim and my mother were actively searching in Macy's for Pop and Fallon. Macy's announced on the store speaker, "Mr. Martin, please meet your wife in the shoe department." They stood there while the request was announced several times. After an hour of waiting, they called home. Pop answered the phone and said, "I thought you had left."

My mother was confused and upset that Pop had left her in San Francisco. She couldn't understand why he had decided that she had left Macy's. She decided to catch BART to El Cerrito, and she told him she would call him once they got to the station, which was less than five minutes away from their house. When they called him, he said, "I'm on my way."

As Mother and Kim were standing at the BART pickup area, they could see Pop and Fallon ride by several times. They were confused by his behavior and actions! After waiting and watching his car pass by several times, they caught a cab home. When my mother asked him why he left them in San Francisco, and why he didn't turn in to the BART Station, where he knew they would be standing . . . he had no response.

Kim and Fallon didn't understand what had happened, but they clearly recognized something was not right with Pop. This incident was the beginning of family members recognizing a big difference in Pop.

In 1991, another strong indication occurred when Pop officiated a wedding for my friends, George and Priscilla, to renew their vows after twenty years of marriage. The wedding was in a beautiful church with a large wedding party. I was the maid of honor, standing close to the bride. When it was time to ask the bride to repeat her vows, Pop turned and looked directly at me and asked, "Do you take . . ."

My mother had positioned herself behind him in the pulpit. I didn't know why she was standing there, but in hindsight, I understood that she wanted to help him through the ceremony. It was at that time I knew something was happening to Pop, and that Mother was aware of his challenges.

• • •

Pop's slow decline had a definite impact on my mother. They had been a strong husband-and-wife team. Mr. and Mrs. Martin never stopped asking each other, "Where have you been, where are you going?"

Their love for each other was always present. They complemented each other when responding to situations, either in a professional manner, with facts based on research, or with street talk, when they felt the receiver was not getting their message. They refused to back down after taking a stance on what they believed was right or wrong.

But now Mother's husband was growing quieter, talking less. His thinking and processing skills were in steady decline. As she became his caregiver, she faced the challenge of running the business they had worked so hard to build plus meeting his everyday needs. They were in the midst of several projects, and she wasn't sure how to move forward.

They were a power couple. They had an unbreakable love and supported one another against any and all odds. But Mother no longer had her partner to strategize and make decisions with, or to fight the battles ahead for achieving their goals. She was scared and sad, and she found herself struggling to put the puzzle pieces of her life together.

This was the beginning of a new chapter in their lives.

Pop's weekly Sunday religious broadcast continued with tapes of sermons he had prepared in the past, until Mother decided to end the contract with the radio station. She believed for months that he would once again pick up his Bible and spend hours in the Prayer Room preparing a sermon, but that was not to be.

She was now the lead communicator for completing both old and new business deals. She was the negotiator, the decision maker, the risk taker. She continued to function in the spirit of a husband-and-wife team, but Pop was now the silent partner. The Ermestine Petgrave who was determined to move forward after her first husband's tragic accident once again found herself the captain of the ship. She was, however, confident in her abilities to navigate on her own terms.

She was now on a different journey, a new path, walking alone. She challenged herself to forge ahead.

• • •

In 1994 father's health issues began to surface and after much persuasion he moved into my home. A male caregiver provided father companionship during our working hours. I was working in Stockton Unified and driving home on a daily basis, and Al was spending more time with his father-in-law.

Father adjusted to giving up the independence of living in his own home and being surrounded by family. In 1996 Hospice service were in place. Father passed with his nephew, Richard, by his side, reading the Bible. I awaken to the sound of Richard's voice, "Gloria! Gloria! Your father passed." I ran with Al in motion behind me to father's room. The three of us stared in silence. Hospice was the signal that this day would come but it arrived much sooner than I was ready to accept. He looked so peaceful.

Family gathering: Ermestine, William, Larry by his side

Ermestine doing what she loved, spending time in Grace Center

GAME CHANGER 38

LIFE CHANGE

In 1998, a newly widowed Ermestine Martin focused her energy on going to church activities and family get-togethers, overseeing her business and buying and selling property. It was common to see Ermestine in the toughest of neighborhoods, wearing a hard hat and a suit, orchestrating projects. Communities slowly but steadily transitioned to predominantly Spanish speakers, and she began trying to talk to her tenants in Spanish, asking their assistance in pronouncing words correctly, always in charge, always seeking to improve things and to give more.

She played a more active and consistent role in her grandchildren's lives, attending events, graduations, and football games. Strong-minded, she never believed in sugarcoating her words, and she delivered powerful messages filled with her beliefs and values to her grandchildren.

Every summer, Kim, my daughter, worked in the real estate office. One day her boyfriend entered the office with a beautiful bouquet of flowers. He happily strolled in, smiling and pleased. Kim was surprised by his gesture and was caught in the sunshine that comes with receiving flowers. Mother overheard their conversation and stepped out of her private office to see what was going on. She stood at the counter observing Kim and Altonio's interactions.

She returned to her private office until Altonio left and then quickly reappeared at the counter. Kim was still in awe, admiring the flowers, when her grandmother said, "Don't get too happy! He either has done something wrong or is fixing to do something."

Mother chuckled as she returned to her office, "Yep, he has either done or is going to do something you may not be too happy about."

Later, Kim shared with me her mindset holding those flowers and reflecting on her grandmother's words. As she started to second-guess her boyfriend's motives and intentions, her sunshine drifted into black clouds.

Listening to Kim, I reflected on my teenage years, when Mother had said to me, "Glo, everything you receive in a box with a pretty bow is not a gift. Just keep on living." I remembered receiving gifts from boys with some suspicion of their motive and intentions. The joy of receiving gifts was diminished and demoralized within the gloom activated by internalizing Mother's words—words left for me to ponder for years with a multitude of different emotions.

And now Mother herself felt heartache. She had felt safe, secure, and cherished with Pop by her side, and no one could break their bond. Their love for each other had allowed her to experience life's blessings more fully. She often would tell me, "Every good and perfect gift comes from the Lord." Pop had an inner light that people gravitated to, a light that intrigued your mind. Although Pop's light was still shining through her, it was dimming. She was in the midst of struggles ahead—alone.

The chemistry she'd had with her husband had sparked a force of business-related energy, a team effort. Now that Pop was gone, Mother was embattled in her day-to-day business activities. She told me that she was broken-hearted but still determined to run her business on her own terms. If she believed that she was being taken advantage of, she reacted with hostility and anger. During our daily telephone conversations, more often than not she would share with me her negative interactions with tenants, employees, family members, contractors, and city and county officials.

* * *

Mother woke up every morning in a rush to get to her office: the battlefield. Battle after battle created a hostile office environment. Mother was not one to go along to get along. Rather, she would take the bull by its horns and hang on until the end. When the combat zone within the office was too rough, she would retreat down to Grace Center in the basement to praise God.

Often, when tensions were high, she would invite the tenant or colleague she was in conflict with to join her in Grace Center. She would play one of Pop's recorded sermons, then play the piano and sing gospel songs while giving praise and love to the Lord. God was her mental doctor, the spiritual power to take away negative forces, the feelings that she was being taken advantage of. She would return to the office uplifted; the battle was over.

Then she would smile and say, "I need you, and you need me if we're going to make it. Let's stay with God; we can make this work." As the person she was in battle with said good-bye, she would always look back and say, "Well, you have a good day, but remember what we talked about: I need you to pay your rent," or, "I need you to keep the outside around your unit clean," or, "You can't have parties every day in your apartment; respect your neighbors." Her faith in God was unwavering.

However, in the next instant an employee, a visitor, or a caller could start the rage boiling again. An office environment of less productivity and more dysfunction continued to grow. Mother began to say that she was honestly enjoying spending time in Grace Center with her clients, office visitors, family members, and friends more than sitting behind her desk.

* * *

Mother won more battles than she lost with the City of Richmond, and she took advantage of her connections with people on the inside. For example, Chuck was her best friend's ex-husband, one of her tenants, and an employee at the City of Richmond. When their paths crossed, Mother shared projects that she was proposing to the City of Richmond. Chuck enlightened Mother of the real deal, the right, the wrong, his perspective of the situation, and she planned accordingly.

The battles she did lose were fair, and she accepted those losses. She would soon have another new project in motion with even more knowledge and determination to achieve her goals.

Throughout fifty-five years of ongoing visits to the City of Richmond, employees knew Mrs. Petgrave and then Mrs. Martin well, and they were familiar with her approach. Quick with questions, she had a way of gaining a perspective on whomever she was dealing with. She interrogated individuals with a friendly persona, finding out where they lived, who their family was, what schools their children attended.

But when Mother met resistance to her efforts to receive a building permit or approval from the Planning Department, her words became less friendly. Taking off her gloves, no longer smiling, she would begin, her voice elevated and strong: "Listen. You live where my family can't live, even if we choose to. You don't want us on your block. Your kids go to a school I wish my daughter could attend. But I own this property, and you won't stop me."

Everyone within the sound of her raised voice knew she was speaking the uncomfortable truth. The person she was addressing had unwittingly provided her with the needed ammunition during previous friendly chitchat. Even as a child, listening to her words, I knew she was speaking truth. Those who received her message often went quiet, a sign that her truth had landed.

"You can't stop me" was my mother's mantra, repeated project after project.

• • •

Throughout the years, Mother's trust in the City of Richmond dwindled. She truly believed discrimination was the root of the painful battles she fought every step of the way. She would remove her gloves and flip into a Muhammad Ali saying, "Float like a butterfly, sting like a bee." She never wavered in her beliefs or put down her guard, and she fought resistance with resistance. No shame in her game, no regrets to her methods.

Business-related matters rarely brought Mother to tears, but the City of Richmond could push her to the limit when she perceived unfair treatment. In 2000, Mother met Janet L. Johnson of the Richmond Redevelopment Agency. Initially, Mother painted Janet Johnson with the same brush of distrust she felt for most Richmond officials. Over the years she gained respect for Johnson, and they developed a relationship of trust and admiration, but her distrust sometimes prevented her from moving forward on projects that were to her advantage.

For example, in the early 2000s Johnson was managing the Façade Improvement Program, and she offered Mother a grant for the historic Wells Fargo building. Mother refused the grant for several years; she believed that White folks were getting more money for their buildings and she was being discriminated against again. Then, after years of distrusting city and county officials, she finally came to believe that Johnson shared her vision and goals for the community, and she decided to accept the grant.

But by that time, Johnson was no longer managing the program, and funds were no longer available. Once she was told it was too late, Mother once again felt that discriminatory practices were in place. Over the years, she would tear up every time she told me this story.

After Pop passed, I began to sense that Mother was becoming more distrustful, exhibiting more anger while reflecting about past experiences, and having difficulty flipping the switch to push projects forward. I noticed a difference in her critical thinking and follow-up skills but attributed it to Pop's passing, the loss of her soulmate. Never did I consider the possibility that she was dealing with the onset of Alzheimer's disease affecting her cognitive abilities. Many opportunities were lost, but Mother's determination remained strong.

Ermestine and Gloria attending a social event

Tressie Williams

GAME CHANGER 39

BECAUSE YOU LOVED ME

In 2006, nine years after Pop passed, I wanted to bring some sunshine into my mother's life, so I decided to have a surprise birthday celebration for her. I shared my idea with my daughters, Al, and Larry, a date was set, and planning began. And somewhere along the way, the surprise birthday party exploded into the "Because You Loved Me" event.

The party was to be held in Mother's office building, on the fourth floor, with a panoramic view of the old shipyard. I envisioned our guests surrounded by family and friends, eating an elegant meal in a Black-owned historic building in the center of Downtown Richmond, much as they might have done in the 1940s. A decision was made to transform the first floor into the lounge and entertainment stage. Unbeknownst to Al, Larry, and our children, they all had significant roles in my plans.

This wasn't going to be any old surprise birthday party. The Because You Loved Me event would be for everyone. I wanted our generation of friends and family members to have an opportunity to honor our parents' or grandparents' contributions to creating the environment we grew up in Richmond. Mother's surprise birthday party became the foundation of an event celebrating parents who settled in Richmond after migrating from the South.

Some twenty individuals were selected, and we began contacting their family members to fill them in on the event and obtain historical information about their relatives. I defined the tasks each family member was to complete, while keeping our work secret from Mother.

My first task was to ensure we could use Mother's office space. I stopped by her office and told her that I needed space to host a sorority event.

She sprung off with, "Your sorority! When do you plan on having it? Well, you take the fourth floor; I love that view. It needs a little work, but I have enough time to get it done." A member of her maintenance crew was standing at the counter, glancing at the work orders. She glanced in his direction and said, "Take Glo to the fourth floor and see what she needs done, then let me know."

We rode the elevator to the fourth floor and walked through the rooms, jotting down work that needed to be completed. For several moments I stood looking out the window—the view held so much history, so many memories of my past.

I returned to Mother's office. She was on the phone, and I picked up my belongings while chatting with a client who was inquiring about apartments for rent. I remember this client so vividly because I admired her hairstyle—it had a lot of flow and bounce—and at that moment, I decided on that style for the Because You Loved Me event. The client informed me who her hairstylist was, and I handed her the apartment availability list and told her, "Mrs. Martin will be with you shortly."

Walking to my car, I thought, "Wow, that was easy." And plans for Because You Loved Me zoomed swiftly ahead.

• • •

One Sunday evening, I was visiting Mother's house, secretly searching for pictures of Pop. Gladys called, and Mother began proudly reporting progress being made on the fourth floor in preparation for what in her mind was the AKΛ event. I was so relieved that I had already discussed my plans for Mother's surprise birthday celebration with Gladys. Unfortunately, Gladys wasn't going to be able to attend, but she kept my secret.

My mind was free to focus on how to transform the first floor to a totally different environment and atmosphere for the event. Moving forward with plans for the menu, decorations, entertainment, and programs was a much bigger task than I anticipated.

One day I was in Point Richmond contracting with a company to deliver white tablecloths, tables, chairs, china, and silverware. Things were going so smoothly. I returned to the office and snuck peeks at my mother, thinking how happy and surprised she would be.

Then came the explosion. A couple of hours before the event was to start, I was in my bedroom examining what I planned to wear. My mind was moving in slow motion, reviewing details of the plans we had put in place. Al was doing last-minute things at the office, and I was thinking that he should be returning home soon to dress for the affair when the phone rang.

It was Mother, and she was yelling. "You can't plan a party for me! You don't know what I like! Why do you think you can plan something for me? This is the stupidest thing you have ever done!"

She was out of control with anger. Her voice was strong, her words were stronger, and she continued to tell me off—probably for less than five minutes, but it seemed to take forever. "I don't want any alcohol drinking, and no one playing the blues!" She hung up on me.

I held the phone to my ear in shock, my mind and body reeling. A few minutes later Al called and said, "Your mother is upset.

You need to talk with her. She needs to go home and get dressed."

I could hear Mother in the background, still yelling. Unable to bear it, I said, "I will call you back," and hung up.

For a long moment I was unable to function, to move—I was just crying and sobbing. My daughter Fallon, who was in her old bedroom getting dressed, overheard the conversation and rushed to my side. She listened and tried to move me into a better zone. My sobbing stopped, but I couldn't shake off that phone call. Stunned with disbelief, I sat looking at the clothes I needed to put on, unable to make any move to get ready.

The phone rang again; it was Larry. Again my emotions exploded into sobbing and tears. He listened for a few moments and then said, "Glo, get yourself together. We don't have much time before the event starts. We are already on our way to your mom's office."

I later learned that Fallon had slipped out of my room to call Larry and let him know what was happening. She then left for the event to make herself available, as needed.

I called Al back and found out that Mother had left the office and headed home. I couldn't get her words out of my head; they repeated themselves over and over. Tears still streaming down my face, I drove to the office. When I arrived, I headed straight to the lady's room to check my makeup and found my face was a mess. I cleaned up, put on some more makeup, and stared at myself in the mirror for a long while. I was still not in control of my emotions. I didn't feel like greeting, smiling, talking with folks. I wanted to be alone.

Finally, I went into the main office, where I found that guests had already started arriving. The office was totally transformed into a lounge area. Food and drinks were displayed and arranged attractively, and guests helped themselves to refreshments while soft music was playing. Everywhere in the room, honorees were surrounded by family members and friends.

My daughter Kim approached and said, "Are you all right?"

My grandchildren were standing with serious faces, waiting for me to respond.

"Yes, I am okay. I just have to get through the program." I wanted to change the subject, to push on, so I asked, "Are you guys prepared to sing?"

I walked further into the room and noticed Al by the door, looking worn and tattered in his work clothes. He was the only man in the room not dressed in formal attire.

I walked over and said, "You still have time to go home and change."

He replied, "No, I may be needed here in case something goes wrong. Are you okay?"

Al had overheard Mother's phone conversation with me, he had witnessed her anger, and he knew at that moment that things had gone terribly wrong. I nodded my head and glanced at the happy people who had come together to celebrate the lives of our parents and family members. As I moved away to check on other things, I glanced back, capturing in my mind the image of Al standing near the entrance door in the lobby.

Then I saw my friend Flo. Like everyone, she was dressed to the nines, smiling and happy. The event was honoring one of her relatives. Flo had been one of my best friends when I lived above the store, as well as one of the members of the junior high school dance group that performed with me in the talent show. We had not seen each other for at least forty years. I was shocked and joyful to see her. Given all the drama of the day so far, seeing her was a delightful surprise.

Then I took a moment to truly look around. The environment was no longer an office—it was a top-notch social affair with all the requisite glitter and gold. The scent of food floated through the air, and strategically placed candles lit up the room, creating an absolutely divine atmosphere. People sat on bar stools at the office counter and in rows of chairs facing the stage. Large posters, each focused on one honoree, were displayed around the room.

All of the honorees had migrated to Richmond from Southern states and endured the hardships, discrimination, cruelty, and unfairness of racism while creating a nurturing environment where we, their children, developed and grew into adults. We were honoring doctors, judges, educators, pharmacists, business-people, politicians, and most importantly, our parents.

We were in a historic Downtown Richmond building now owned by a Black woman, where billions of dollars throughout history may have been swindled away, denied through discriminatory policies and practices put in place to prevent our parents from being successful.

It was truly a remarkable event, and one that was complimented for years after by those in attendance. As the mistress of ceremonies, I was supposed to take the audience through the schedule of activities on the program. Feeling frazzled, I looked out at all the beautiful young and old Black women in party dresses and the handsome young and old Black men in formal suits. My children and grandchildren were in the audience, cheering me on, helping me stay on point. Al remained standing in the same location pretty much all night, waiting to protect me from whatever could go wrong.

Finally, I looked at Mother sitting in the front row with one of her best friends. She was not smiling but looked absolutely gorgeous in a red St. John knit suit, her makeup in place, wearing her best wig and beautiful jewelry. I was struck by feelings of pride—this unpredictable, glorious woman, my mother.

We had an entire program of entertainment and speeches ahead of us; I had to pull it together. Honorees and their family members, friends I had not seen since childhood, waited expectantly with smiling faces. I had to shake it off and celebrate why we were there.

After we'd honored about ten honorees, plus several performances, everyone went to the fourth floor for a sit-down dinner. Al helped elders get on the elevator for dinner on the fourth floor. I chatted with guests waiting for their turn instead of taking the stairs.

The dining room had been transformed with first-class decorations: the white tablecloths glowed, and an individual menu sat by each table setting. My male family members were the servers—dressed in classy black and white, with bow ties and cummerbunds, they professionally served our guests. We were eating, talking, laughing... young and old, with an on-point view of the city we loved, the streets we grew up in, living a good life. I took a deep breath.

As we ate we looked out over the bay, not too far distant, which had been the epicenter for the shipyards and the military support facilities. Hotel Carquinez, which is now on the National Register of Historic Places, was a block away. Below, Macdonald Avenue represented the most prestigious location in Downtown Richmond in 1930. That street, and the streets beyond, we all knew so well—streets that were the hustle and bustle of the community during our youth. Our parents and grandparents had migrated here to take advantage of the wartime boom, and women's involvement as shipyard and factory workers in the war effort opened up new opportunities nationwide. But once the war was over, basic needs of housing and employment were harder to come by. Our honorees then worked more fiercely than ever to make things better for the whole community.

In the 1950s some of the honorees had medical and business offices in this same American Trust building, the center of culture and business in Richmond during our youth. As I looked around at people socializing and enjoying themselves, what we were accomplishing finally struck me: The Because You Loved Me event was hosted in my mother's office, in this historic building, giving testimony to our parents' and our community's achievements.

The heart and soul of the event were the people we were honoring.

After eating, we all returned to the main floor and continued the program. To keep my head clear, I avoided any interactions with Mother during the affair. All evening she was engaged in greeting the other Richmond pioneers, all of whom had fought, were fighting, for future generations. I tried to keep that in mind whenever I glimpsed her and whenever her angry voice threatened to return to my mind.

Finally, after the last attendees left, Kim took Mother home. I stayed to help clean up and then drove alone to my house, delighted that the event had been a huge success, but still rattled. Growing up, I had witnessed my mother's reactions to folks she felt had disrespected her, but this time the rage was targeted at me, and with such anger and force. I couldn't shake it off, and her words lingered in my brain all through the night.

The next day, I answered the phone to Mother's excited voice, sharing details of the event, conversations she'd had with old friends, her joy at seeing honorees and their family members. She commented on what she could have done to make the building more beautiful if she had known. I listened attentively for at least an hour without interrupting.

I should have asked the questions foremost in my mind: "Why did you react in such a negative way when you found out it was an event to honor you?" And "Who told you about it?" I knew it had to have been a family member, and I couldn't help but wonder why that person had felt a need to tell her an hour before the event began. But listening to her words and the tone of her voice, I came to realize she was pleased and appreciative.

A few days later, the front page of the *Richmond Post* showcased the event, with pictures of my mother surrounded by other Richmond pioneers, dressed elegantly in after-five attire and being honored by family, friends, and associates. Once the paper had been distributed within the community, Mother obtained several copies and called me with excitement and pride, again expressing how much she enjoyed the event.

Thinking about her vastly different reactions, I came to the conclusion that Mother simply did not like surprises. And she didn't like deception, either. After all, I had lied to her for months, pretending the party was a sorority event all through my secret planning. Once she realized the event was *not* what I had told her it was, she exploded with unfiltered anger—and I knew well she could unleash that anger in a heartbeat to anyone, except her mother and father. I should have thought of that.

My goal had been to bring some sunshine into her life. To spread some joy and happiness with expressions of love from a generation appreciating the Richmond pioneers' efforts and accomplishments. I achieved that goal for my mother, but for the sunshine to enter my life, I had to go through a personal storm.

With the passing of time, now that I'm running her business and understanding all the things she had to deal with, I, too, hate surprises. Surprises from employees, tenants, contractors, city officials, family members—no matter the source, surprises can send me over the edge and into zones of unsettling anxiety and frustration. My mother knew that surprises are not always good and emotionally healthy.

After the party, we continued our mother-and-daughter relationship and resumed our rituals of spending time together, and gradually peace was restored. Mother talked about the Because You Loved Me event for years in a loving way, and I was so happy the storm had passed! I was happy my generation had come together to honor those who paved the way to our success. I was happy Mother was in a good mind and able to understand that she was being honored because of the things she had accomplished in life, demonstrating her love for me.

Gloria and Yvonne, celebrating Yvonne's birthday

Yvonne's senior portrait, from Kennedy High School, 1974

Clarice's senior portrait, from Harry Ellis High School, 1966

GAME CHANGER 40

LIFE AFTER DEATH

Both aunts, Baldie and Lillian, were diagnosed with breast cancer within the same month and year. They took different approaches to treatment, traditional and holistic. The health challenges both dealt with, and the disheartening changes in their bodies, were unforgettable, and their faith in survival was unwavering.

Each believed that if the right actions were taken, her cancer would be defeated. Baldie chose chemotherapy and radiation therapy. Lillian's journey for treatment was a trip to Tijuana, Mexico, where she remained in a specialized cancer facility for one month. Within two years the cancer had spread and began to pinch her spinal cord. Suddenly, Lillian was paralyzed from the navel down. Traditional techniques were once again an option offered. Lillian chose radiation and in time was able to walk again. Lillian passed in 1986 and Baldie in 1988, leaving memories and heartfelt pain for my mother and father, their only siblings. My cousins Yvonne and Clarice both left generational wealth to their sons, who are holding on and taking care of the land.

• • •

Then I was diagnosed with breast cancer in 1997. After internalizing the fact that the disease was within my body, I reflected on the journey both of my aunts had endured in their fight for life. I remember their ups and downs of hope, remission and reoccurrence of cancer in their bodies, to profound pain and then death. I recalled observing my parents and listening to each of them express their feelings while their younger sisters were challenged with serious health issues.

I was forty-eight when I first felt a lump in my breast. I recall the day so clearly. I felt something that I hadn't felt before. I secretly sought medical advice, anxious and scared. I was told by a nurse practitioner after she examined my breast, "It's probably just dense tissue. You're young. No mammogram scheduled, no plans to return."

I was happy and content with her words. I told Al about the lump in my breast and the good news shared by the nurse practitioner. He smiled, then in a firm voice said, "Next time you are going through something like that, let me know."

A couple of months later, I shared with Al that I had noticed that whatever I was feeling inside my breast was growing. In a concerning way, he said, "You need to schedule another medical appointment."

I didn't want to worry about it. I let the nurse practitioner's comforting words penetrate my mind, allowing me to believe there was nothing wrong with me. For two months, Al was persistent, insisting I make a doctor's appointment. I could tell he was worried and concerned about my health. He, too, had witnessed firsthand my aunts' struggle with breast cancer.

I returned to Kaiser; the physician examined my breast and gave me a referral for a mammogram. A few days later, while I was sitting in my office in the Staff Development Department in Stockton Unified School District, my phone rang. A voice said, "I am calling from Kaiser. I'm sorry to inform you, but you have breast cancer." I was devastated.

My mind instantly zoomed to memories of Baldie's and Lillian's experiences. They both went through crying spells after being diagnosed with breast cancer. Each chose and undertook an aggressive treatment plan. I knew that women with a family history of breast cancer have an elevated risk. I read that Black women are more likely than White women to die from breast cancer in the United States.

I got up, closed my office door, and sat there, staring into space for a long time. Al was so far the only person I had shared the change in my breast with. Now, sitting motionless, my mind racing in fear, I called Mother. She was at work and, after being told I was calling, she picked up the phone, upbeat and happy. I heard her tell a client, "Hold on, I will be with you in a moment. My daughter is on the line. Hey, Glo, what's up?" We talked daily, but always after working hours, unless it was an emergency.

Before I could find the words I wanted to say, she cheerfully repeated, "Glo, what's up?"

"Mom, I have breast cancer."

There was a long, silent pause on both ends of the phone. I started crying and couldn't stop. She was at a loss to know what to say. Silence prevailed.

The next words from her were "I love you."

Her words were comforting because I was consumed with uncertainty. My life had changed in an instant. Positive thoughts were crumbling, and dreadful possibilities invaded my mind. I had a 4:00 meeting at a school site to attend, and I needed to get myself together.

Before we ended the call, she said in a soft and soothing voice, "God is our refuge and strength, an ever-present help in trouble: Psalms 46:1." She quoted the Scripture as if she had anticipated my phone call. Like she had searched the Bible for the right words to say. She ended with, "God will get us through this news. We are fighters. We will get through this together. You may go through deep waters, and fall into the deepest hole, and I will be with you."

I fought back tears. All I could do was listen to her words, which were comforting. Mother's solace and uplifting message brought strength to my soul. I got the mirror and makeup pouch I kept in my desk drawer and did a touch-up. I gathered my belongings and shot out of the office without saying good-bye to anyone.

The first couple of weeks after being diagnosed, I hid my disease from my children. I was planning for the worst, praying for the best, and struggling to get through each day for many months to come. I felt anxious, afraid, and overwhelmed, struggling to get through working days and maintain a normal lifestyle.

Gradually, with my mother, family, and friends cheering me on, I began facing my journey with optimism and courage. My aunts were dealt the breast-cancer card, and now that same card was staring me in the face. I remember thinking how my aunts had endured treatment without complaint. I knew that both of them never gave up hope.

I shared my feelings honestly with Mother, who was a spiritual adviser and a source of support. We expressed our emotions honestly and gained strength from each other. She wanted to take me to each doctor's appointment and know all the facts and details, accepting that my decisions regarding a treatment plan were mine and mine alone. Mother was standing by my side, grounded in prayer. Her support came in doing and helping out with practical things, when I was going through a horrible and fearful storm. She put her world on hold for me. She supported me with gifts more precious than gold: compassion, strength, and love. When I was weak, she stood by my side and took care of me, inspiring courage and hope.

Now, I have been cancer free for more than twenty-three years. But still, every discomfort or bodily pain triggers the thought that the cancer may be returning, and I can't help but fear the suffering, pain, and anguish my aunts endured during their fights with this same disease.

And today Mother is consumed with battling Alzheimer's. Remembering how gratifying her words and actions were to me, I speak the sweet words she spoke, read the Scriptures she read, and express my love in the same manner she did for me. I don't believe my messages and actions bring her much comfort, but I stay by her side.

Mother taught me many things, but there is one thing she could never teach me. How to live without her.

• • •

One morning in November 2003, I was standing at my bedroom window, looking at a Japanese maple tree recently planted in my backyard. I answered the phone and heard a familiar voice say, "My mother passed."

I couldn't comprehend the message. "Chip?"

He responded with, "Yes, my mother passed."

I continued staring at the tree in disbelief.

"No, Chip! No, Chip! No! No!"

"Yes," he said, his voice trembling, "my mother passed."

"Oh, my God! Chip, I am on my way," I told him.

Yvonne, his mother, was my forty-seven-year-old cousin. She was seven years younger than I. Larry, Yvonne, and I were always together at our grandparents' house while our parents worked. With the difference in our ages, I viewed her as the baby girl in our family. Early on, Yvonne learned to defend herself—or to get her way—by biting. Oh, the pain she could bring!

When Yvonne started kindergarten, I was in the seventh grade, dealing with adolescent issues and spending less time at my grandparents' house. I still loved spending time at Baldie's house, and Larry and Yvonne were constants in my life. After Yvonne returned home from college, and I moved back to Richmond from Union City after divorcing my first husband, we bonded in a special, loving way. The seven-year age difference didn't matter anymore. She was my confidante and I was hers. Yvonne was my maid of honor in both of my weddings. We shared the same family life experiences and the same values and beliefs our grandparents inspired in us as children.

Death had knocked at our door in the past. We as a family had experienced the deaths of our senior citizen grandparents, and our parents, but this was an unexpected and heartbreaking death, caused by a seizure in her sleep. Losing Yvonne felt very much out of order, and we all needed time to heal.

About a month after Yvonne passed, I was talking to Mother on the phone about work-related issues, meetings she had to attend, places she needed to go. After sharing her plans, she asked me, "What are you doing today?"

I was trying to suppress my emotions, but now I was on a roller coaster. My response was, "I am still grieving, and depressed about Yvonne's passing. I feel a big loss in my life. Yvonne's death is a test of my faith; I just can't believe she is gone. I would call her in the middle of the night, and we would talk and laugh. I miss her so much. Her love meant so much to me!"

My mother adored Yvonne. As children, Yvonne and I would be playing together, and Mother would whisper in my ear, "Yvonne is fragile . . . be careful how you play with her."

Throughout Yvonne's life, Mother encouraged her to continue in school, to work hard, and to be the best. Yvonne heard of the harsh realities of life from my mother, and she understood the expectations Mother had for family members. Now she was gone, and all of my emotions were released, leaving a dead silence—except for my crying.

After a long pause, Mother said, "Well, I have to stay among the living, and so do you. We have to accept God's will. Glo, we have to keep busy and can't get stuck in not trusting God's work. Go clean yourself up, and put on one of your work suits and patent-leather shoes. I have a one o'clock meeting, and I need you to take me there. Be at my house in an hour."

Click; she hung up the phone. Leave it to Mother to get me moving again. Her words seemed harsh and confusing at that time. But now, the message in her words is clear in my mind. We do have to stay among the living, with pain in our hearts and ever-lingering memories of our loved one.

Chip was Yvonne's only child, and he was eighteen years old when Yvonne passed. I know he experienced grief, anger, and depression after her death. But he, too, was able to move on to accepting God's will.

Yvonne would be so proud of her son. She had left him property wealth, and he graduated from college and became a responsible, hardworking young man, exhibiting many of Yvonne's characteristics and personality traits. He is mature enough to handle his own finances, and he has enough knowledge and business ethics to hold on to his property and move forward to obtain his goals. He felt the loss of his mother intensely. But in time, he, too, was at peace.

• • •

In the summer months of 2017, my cousin Clarice began to talk more often about retiring. She shared plans of adding a deck to her upstairs loft, buying a new car, and working more in her yard. She bought the car, and one Saturday in September she stopped by my house and took me for a ride. In October, her conversations included being extremely fatigued, losing weight without trying, and scheduling a doctor appointment.

In November, I received a phone call from Clarice's brother, Richard, and his daughter, Sarita. I was happy to hear Sarita's voice, and I asked, "What you been up to?"

She hesitated and then informed me that Clarice had stage 4 cancer. Bam, her words knocked me to my knees.

I ended the call abruptly with, "Oh, my God, I can't talk right now. This is terrible news. I will call you back after I can get myself together."

I wondered how Clarice was feeling after receiving news that she had stage 4 cancer. I reflected on fond memories Clarice and I had shared, and my father's determination for us to be treated like sisters. I thought about how comforting my mother was at the time of my cancer diagnosis, and the spiritual strength she provided during my battle. I wanted to do the same for Clarice.

But time was not on our side. We never know when our lives will end, or what to expect, but a loved one is always gone too soon. Time seemed to freeze into an emotional experience of grieving. Clarice's illness was terminal, and her life ended the day after I visited her in the hospital.

Painful in so many ways, but I cherish the opportunity to visit Clarice in the hospital to say "I love you" and offer encouraging, hopeful words. With Yvonne's sudden passing I had regretted not having a chance to say "I love you" for the last time; I learned to be content that I had told her I loved her throughout her life.

Life is up or down, good and bad. Throughout life, I learned to worship, obey, and praise God. I believe he is our bridge over troubled waters. My grandmother and Mother instilled in me the importance of beginning each journey with God, building a personal relationship with God, and worshiping God. Their teachings made a lifetime difference in how I gather courage and strength through challenging times.

Ermestine and Novelean Harris, a businesswoman, politician, community activist, and a model of spiritual strength for Mother, circa 1980

Ermestine at the last event she attended independently, the quinceañera of a tenant's daughter

GAME CHANGER 41

"YOU SHOULD BE TALKING TO *ME*"

After retiring from West Contra Costa Unified in 2004, I began working as a university supervisor at California State University, Hayward (now California State University, East Bay) as well as Teach for America (TFA), Loyola Marymount University, in school districts throughout the Bay Area. Amazingly, I had come full circle at California State University, East Bay. Now I was walking in and out of the Teacher Education Department in the role of faculty member and lecturer rather than student. Most of my colleagues had life stories that were very different than mine, but we were all faculty members.

I was a liaison between the university and classroom setting, supervising interns and student teachers in developing competency through observation and feedback. I was responsible for mentoring, coaching, and evaluating teacher candidates working in diverse educational settings. I provided resources and guidance to candidates in the areas of curriculum development, instructional strategies, assessment techniques, and classroom management. I was trained to be an effective instructional leader by the universities, equipped with years of educational experience—

and I had a personal goal of effecting systemic change within the school buildings. Observing teaching and learning in the very classrooms I remembered so well from my childhood brought back elementary-school memories.

Teach for America's mission was to cultivate and support a diverse network of leaders, predominantly from Ivy League institutions, who were committed to expanding opportunities for children and creating an inclusive community of learners. Teach for America Bay Area had established itself in the educational landscape as a key partner in the movement to fight educational inequity.

I felt that a stereotype existed that Teach for America teachers would somehow be superior because of the elite Ivy League degrees they possessed. I knew that was not true in many classrooms. I sensed a strong commitment to social justice in the candidates' words but a lack of the preparation that a candidate with an undergraduate or graduate degree in teaching had. I quickly recognized that after two or three years, many TFA teachers left the most troubled schools, moving on to private, charter, or suburban schools—or new careers entirely. The students they left behind still needed the most highly trained and skilled teachers and continued to struggle to achieve academic growth.

Sitting in classrooms at Nystrom, Verde, Peres, I couldn't divert my eyes from the crisis right in front of me. I began to think it was better to have teaching candidates from local universities who wanted to make a more permanent impact on the community. I felt that districts partnering with a local university with a strong teaching program brought more success for student learning. I knew that it could take several years of solid instruction to make up for one year of ineffective teaching.

I came to the conclusion that candidates with a sincere passion to become teachers; positioned in classrooms supported by master teachers, university supervisors, and professors; and located in schools embracing a community approach to learning were more inclined to be effective teachers, translating into improved educational opportunities for students.

• • •

I was assigned to supervise interns working at several schools in locations surrounding my mother's office. Before or after conducting observations, my routine was to stop by the office and visit my mother. I located a small space with a private desk in Mother's real estate office for working on report visits between observations. It was secluded and private, yet within view and earshot of Mother's conversations and behavior.

I began to notice that she would repeat statements and questions. She began to express routinely that she had misplaced her keys, telephone book, cell phone, and other possessions.

• • •

One day, after visiting a local elementary school near the office, I stopped by to see Mother. She was sitting at her desk with a young woman and her two children. The children were running around the office while Mother engaged in conversation. Her employee (I'll call him Mr. Bob) was at his desk, completing a paper-and-pencil task.

Mr. Bob then approached her desk with a handful of checks requiring her signature. "Mrs. Martin, please sign these checks. I put a big X where you need to sign."

Check by check, he stood over her and pointed to where her signature was needed.

Back to the conversation with the tenant: "Look, I can't keep paying a plumber to unstop your toilet because of things you are flushing down the toilet."

"But Mrs. Martin, my children are the ones flushing stuff in the toilet."

Mother paused in signing a check, looked up over her glasses, and said, "Have you heard of training your children? You are going to have to do better. Instead of having all those folks in and out of your house, focus on training your children."

"Gloria, take her rent check and give her a receipt."

The children had resumed running around the office, screaming as they played with each other. The little girl fell and began crying loudly, and the mother yelled at both kids to stop playing. She handed me the check, walked toward her children fussing, picked up the little girl, and said, "Shut up!" The little boy was happily turning somersaults across the floor. She grabbed his arm and yelled, "Bring your ass over here!"

A maintenance crew employee entered the office, greeted everyone, and started looking through the work-order clipboard.

"Where are you working today? Have you already gone by Ninth Street to see what the problem is?" Mother began shooting back-to-back questions at him, inquiring about maintenance issues. "That makes no sense to me. We just worked on that problem last week. I can't keep paying people to fix and refix, and yet it is still not working. If you can't do it, say that. I'm paying you to fix problems, not make more problems for me."

At this point, her voice was raised, and Mother's employee tried to refocus her back to signing checks.

"Just hold your horses," she said to Mr. Bob. "What is this check for? How much is it? Where is the X? You need to calm your nerves." Then, on another topic, "I'm paying you to complete the taxes. Where are you with that?"

"Mrs. Martin, I plan to talk with you about taxes after you sign these checks," Mr. Bob responded.

"Yeah, okay, because I need to know what you are doing."

I had become distracted by all the activity. The children were once again running around the office; the tenant was talking to the maintenance crew while standing at the counter.

As I gave the tenant her rent receipt, my mother asked her, "How is your father? I heard he has been sick."

"He is good."

"Well, tell your parents I said hello. What school do your children go to? What grades are they in? How are they doing in school? Are you still working at the restaurant?"

Mother was a professional question-asker. She was good at finding out what was going on in her tenants' lives. Many of her current tenants were the children of parents who had been renting from her for years. She knew the family struggles and the history of all her tenants.

As the woman and her children headed toward the exit door, a man scurried past the lobby doors.

"Who was that?" I asked.

Mr. Bob's response was, "Either the T-Mobile or Sprint man."

My mother responded, "Why are they here? They are tearing up my building. We have birds entering the building because the workmen keep leaving the windows up. Go tell that man I want to talk with him now. I didn't give anyone permission to do work in the building."

Mother's employee got up from his chair and headed toward the lobby, passing a tenant entering to pay rent. He turned and said, "Gloria, can you take her rent and give her a receipt?"

The lady, who looked to be in her late seventies, wobbled into the office with a big smile. "Howdy, Mrs. Martin!" she hollered.

My mother rose from her chair, smiling and waving her hands. "Come on in here. I've been thinking about you. I wish our elevator was working so we could go into Grace Center. I've been practicing a new song."

"Well, Mrs. Martin, I can't walk down stairs, but you can sing it right now," she said as she continued walking very slowly toward the counter.

Mother smiled and took a deep breath, then began singing a new song. The older lady stopped, leaned her cane on the counter, put her purse down, and began clapping and praising the Lord.

The phone rang and I answered, while my mother and the lady continued to praise God. The call was from the City of Richmond, asking to speak to Mr. Bob.

"He is away from his desk right now. May I take a message?"

My mother overheard the conversation and said, "I need to speak with them. Tell them to hold on." She made her way to her desk.

The lady at the counter said, "You must be Mrs. Martin's daughter. Your mother has been my landlord for over fifty years. Last time I saw you was when you were working in your mother's store. You look just like your mom. Do you remember me?"

I smiled and nodded my head.

The truth was, I didn't remember her. So often I would meet folks and they would say, "Your mother gave me my first apartment. Your mother sold my parents their first house. Your parents sold me my first house."

I thought about Mother's decades-long, firsthand experience of hearing tenants' and homebuyers' dispiriting stories as they struggled to find housing. She had served several generations of Blacks and had dealt with a variety of institutions and White landlords, homeowners, realtors, government officials, and lenders who had demonstrated blatant and intentional housing discrimination. Through her tenants' eyes, through the eyes of clients trying to become homeowners, and through her own experience, she well understood the role of racism in housing, education, and employment.

I thought back to when my mother was attempting to purchase property in El Cerrito, searching for a house address that would give me the right to attend El Cerrito High School. After a few attempts to purchase a house, with a thriving business, good credit scores, and financial status affording her the opportunity to buy, she felt that she was encountering racial barriers. She persuaded Shirley, her White employee who worked in the store for years, to test out her theory and try to purchase a property.

So Shirley joined us in the car for this potential real estate deal. Sitting in the back seat, listening to their conversation, I surmised that Mother had wanted to make an offer on a particular property in El Cerrito, but after meeting with the agent was told the property had been sold.

When we arrived at the property, Mother parked out of sight. Shirley remained in the car for a moment to gather herself and listen to Mother's tips on questions to ask and how to respond. Then she set off. About half an hour later, Shirley returned to our car. Shirley got in and Mother drove past the agent's car, waving, as Shirley said, "Ermestine, you are right. The property is still on the market."

Through that test it became crystal clear to me, more than ever before, that Mother was dealing with racism in her attempts to purchasing property in El Cerrito. She had believed the wealth that she had acquired would shield her from lending institutions subjecting her to unreasonable fees, risky subprime mortgages, and unfavorable mortgage terms. She knew that some of her clients barely met the requirements for purchasing a home, but now it hit home that it wasn't about qualifying—it was about race.

However, Mother never put all of her eggs in one basket. There was always a plan B and C. Within a few days, her offer to purchase the Richmond Annex property was accepted with a solid purchase contract. Her main objective was to get an address that was within El Cerrito High School residence boundaries, and she achieved that goal.

Mr. Bob returned to his desk and resumed going through the checks Mother had signed, then engaged in chitchat with the tenant. The T-Mobile representative entered the office and misjudged who was in charge. He positioned himself in front of me, flipping through his work material.

He looked at me and said, "I'm from T-Mobile, and I'm here to work on the cell tower on the roof."

My heart sank. I knew this was not going to turn out well. I looked at my mother, whose voice level was at level ten. She was demanding that the City of Richmond talk with her instead of Mr. Bob regarding her properties. All conversations in the office stopped, and everyone was focused on the telephone conversation and Mother's behavior.

She told the City of Richmond caller to hold on and yelled to the T-Mobile employee, "Why are you speaking to her? You need to come down to this old lady's desk and talk to me. I run this business; you can't do anything without talking to me first. Why did you go to her?"

The older tenant shouted, "That's right, Mrs. Martin, you are in charge." I gave the tenant her rent receipt and she continued, "Mrs. Martin, I have to go, but I loved your song. I will come back and visit you soon."

Before the T-Mobile employee could respond, I said, "Mom, I have an observation scheduled at Nystrom and need to leave now. I will call you later tonight. Try to leave the office before it gets dark."

She smiled and said, "Okay, doll."

She picked up the phone and continued angrily talking to the City of Richmond. The T-Mobile man positioned himself at the counter in front of her desk. Mr. Bob never looked up from his desk and just continued shuffling the checks.

After completing my scheduled observation and returning home, I got a call from Mr. Bob. I could tell something was very wrong by the tone of his voice, and I could hear my mother yelling in the background. He said, "Gloria, your mother is having problems. She is out of control."

I asked to speak to her. She got on the phone and was crying. "I don't know why he called you. I am handling my business, and you handle yours." She yelled at him, "Did I ask you to call Gloria?" Click.

"Hello, hello, are you still there?"

I held the phone, trying to process what had just happened, and decided I needed to go back to the office. I called the office to inform Mr. Bob that I was on my way. In an unreassuring manner, he said, "She has calmed down, and there is no need for you to come to the office."

In the background I heard her screaming at me, "Just take care of your own business, as I am trying to take care of mine. Train the teachers, that's what you do. Do that well."

Then I heard someone else ask to speak with me. It was a City of Richmond employee who had rushed to Mother's office. He said that while he was talking to Mother on the phone, she had a mental breakdown. He was so concerned that he decided to come to the office to make sure she was okay.

I heard Mother's voice in the background, "Why are you telling her that? You need to talk with me, not with her. Get off my phone!"

• • •

In 2013, Mother was diagnosed with glaucoma and, with much resistance to the UC Berkeley doctors' diagnosis, she allowed herself more of a dependency on me. She continued to go to work by cab, or a family member would take her there and pick her up after work. She would sit at her desk, trying to manage the business. No longer able to read written communication and with no technology skills, she relied on employees to read documents and inform her of business matters.

She became increasingly frustrated with the business but was determined to remain in control and in charge. Getting her to leave the office at 5:00 p.m. to go home became a battle. She was fighting for her independence.

The family struggled to do what was necessary so she could continue to work. In May 2013, my daughters and I began working in the office with her. We then noticed that there had been a decline in her memory and other cognitive skills, and her mood swings were more irritable, hostile, and aggressive toward clients, employees, business associates, and family members in the office. She began to openly express distrust in others. Multitasking, a skill she had always been very good at, now appeared difficult for her. On a daily basis, problems that warranted immediate decisions were challenging for her to process and take action on. When I was driving her home from the office, I became aware of her getting lost in familiar places near her house.

Visitors to the office noticed the change in her behavior and began to take their business concerns to other family members. Mother would then burst into anger, believing they were overlooking her because she was seen as an old lady. My daughter and I learned quickly to immediately address visitors with, "Mrs. Martin will be with you in a moment," and return to our task at hand.

As some of her mental skills worsened, others were preserved, such as telling stories and reminiscing, talking about her business, singing, and listening to church music. She never exhibited signs of depression, apathy, or social withdrawal. Going to her office was the focus of her daily activities, and she was good at functioning on a social level. But it was challenging for visitors to get a straight answer from her about business matters.

During visits to her office, I noticed her total reliance on employees to manage finances, including balancing checkbooks and paying bills on time. It also was brought to my attention that her taxes had not been filed for several years, even though that was supposed to be Mr. Bob's primary task.

Then in July 2014, Larry and I received a phone call from extended family members stating that Mother was in Oklahoma attending a family reunion, and she seemed disoriented and confused. We were surprised to learn that she was in Oklahoma and immediately scheduled flight arrangements there.

By the end of that summer, Mother's impaired judgment and other cognitive changes caused by Alzheimer's made her office a hostile environment, and it was difficult to be there. Her verbal attacks on employees and family members began to create stress and emotional pain. My daughter found another job within the county, and I was happy to return to my full-time supervisor work at California State University and Loyola Marymount University, a job I loved and deeply enjoyed.

We were flying like geese, low enough to observe what was going on but high enough to stay out of direct aim of Mother's attack. We created our own V-formation of flight, and family members began visiting Mother's office more frequently and became concerned about observed interactions between employees, clients, and business associates.

Although Mother's ability to function independently kept declining, she continued to fight off family support. It became clear that employees and tenants were starting to take advantage of her health issues. Because Mother was determined to remain in control, her business began to suffer financially.

Her home became disorganized and cluttered. Ongoing family attempts to assist were met with resistance and anger. During visits, any actions by family members to clean up were rejected and frowned at.

"You just need to take care of your house. Why you worrying about mine? I bet your house is not perfect. When you get home, take a good look at your house and find something to do there." She would end the conversation by playing her piano and singing "Precious Lord." We would sit and sing with her. And she continued to go to work every day.

I didn't realize a train wreck was approaching. Arriving to pick mother up from work, I found the office locked and she was not inside. In panic mode I drove around looking for her and finally parked in the parking lot of the shopping center across the street. Parked facing the stores, surveying my view, I saw mother walking toward my car with shopping bags. She was focused straight ahead and didn't notice my car parked in front of Walgreens, as she walked past my car. I on the other hand was focused directly on her. Something about her was different. Her steps were not as deliberate as I've known. Her facial expression and especially her eyes displayed fear. As she passed, I called out, "Momma." She smiled and got in the car eagerly showing me what she had purchased. I was truly upset because she had not waited in the office for me. She was happy with her purchases and I was relieved that she was in my car. But something in the glare of her eyes was strangely different and for me exhibited her fear and created sorrow while thinking about her situation as I drove home.

Mr. Bob became weary of battles with mother trying to persuade her to leave when her cab arrived. When he realized that she was determined to stay at the office, he would lock the security door behind him. She had keys to unlock the door from the inside. She called me, her voice was frantic and she was crying. "Glo, come pick me up, I can't find my keys and Mr. Bob locked me in the office. I can't get out and I am ready to go home." She was experiencing tough and frightening experiences and I didn't know what to do.

The strategies she had used raising me to change my way of thinking didn't work with her. She pushed back with deliberate force anyone who expressed concern about her well-being. She was struggling for life as she knew it, independent and on her own terms, and detested being edited by me. I was lost in fog trying to help and beginning to realize something was terribly wrong. The fog was getting more intense for both of us.

Ermestine attending a womans Black History luncheon with Cora Ward, NAACP President of the El Cerrito Branch, 2017 - 2019

GAME CHANGER 42

THE BEGINNING OF THE LAST GAME

On Christmas Eve in 2014, when my mother was eighty-eight, my phone rang. It was the El Cerrito police: my mother's neighbors had called them because she was wandering around the neighborhood. She was having delusions about her immediate environment.

The El Cerrito police analyzed the situation and informed me that they were taking her by ambulance to Kaiser Emergency for a thorough assessment and diagnosis. That was the last night she stayed in her own house for a year.

My husband, daughters, and I rushed to Kaiser Emergency and were greeted by Mother stating, "There is nothing wrong with me. I want to go home. I am getting out of here. Let's go. I have to go to work tomorrow, I have things to do. These doctors don't know what they are talking about."

She was having problems organizing her thoughts to respond to her doctor's questions, but she communicated clearly that she was going home. After a few hours, she fell asleep and family members left for the night, planning to return early the next morning.

According to a Kaiser employee, during the night she awoke, hell-bent on going home, agitated and aggressive, and had to be physically restrained.

We arrived before she woke up. Once awake, she began talking about her business and her properties. A doctor arrived in her room and she said, "Hello, my name is Mrs. Martin, are you looking for a two- or three-bedroom unit?" She was more determined than ever to return to her house but calmed down after being told they were going to run a couple of tests before discharging her.

After the tests, a doctor visited Mother's room and informed her that she had been diagnosed with dementia/Alzheimer's.

Mother's response was, "Get out of here with that, there is nothing wrong with me. I am going home."

The doctor stood firmly with, "No, Mrs. Martin, you are not going home until you have 24/7 supervision. A social worker will visit you soon to discuss your living situation for discharge."

She left the room as Mother repeated, "You don't know what you are talking about. You're not God. I can think and do for myself. I've done that all my life. I have a business to run!"

After the doctor left the room, Mother's voice was the only one heard. My daughters and I were processing what the doctor had said, while Mother continued to rant and rave that she was being treated this way because she was an old lady. Meanwhile, we were fighting back tears. My mind was racing from the enormity of the situation: delinquent taxes, tenant lawsuits, employees not performing, vacancies, and a mom who wants to return home and do business as usual.

Later I often wondered what Mother's thoughts had been while listening to her doctor's Alzheimer's diagnosis. I remembered her eyes focused on the doctor, listening to his words, and my eyes focused on her face as she lay in the hospital bed in total disbelief, unable or unwilling to comprehend what the doctor was saying—and all the while, Alzheimer's was defining the person she was to become, the big abyss encompassing her world.

After lots of conversation and resistance, I was able to talk her into living with me after being discharged from the hospital, until we had time to work on cleaning and repairing her house. She reluctantly agreed. This was a Christmas Eve I will never forget, and a Christmas Day that was full of uncertainty—the beginning of a new chapter in our lives.

Fortunately, California State University was on winter break, and I filed for a family personal leave in order to devote time to my mother and her business.

My daughters and I arrived early the day after Christmas to pick up my mother from Kaiser. We were nervous and afraid of her mood and level of hostility toward our plans to bring her to my house. Entering her hospital room, we found her in good spirits and anxious to leave. Her social skills were at their best, and she was leaving on a good note with hospital staff.

As soon as we got into the car, however, she demanded to go by her office and to her home. With some hesitance and fear we granted her desires, but at each location, it was challenging to get her to leave.

The memory that will forever be etched in my brain was after arriving at my house. My mother was sitting on the couch, and my daughters and I were standing nearby, listening to her say once again, "There is nothing wrong with me. I am going home. I need to go to work. Those doctors don't know what they are talking about."

I said, "Mom, the doctors said you have Alzheimer's."

She slowly stood up, and tears began flowing. Kim rushed to her and started hugging her. We were all crying. No more words were said. Just silence, and tears.

After a few minutes, Mother returned to the couch and sat quietly. We were all caught in the moment of sorrow and pain, knowing what was lying ahead for my mother. That was the one and only time she acknowledged that she had a problem. After a few minutes, she said, "Well, I'm going to work tomorrow. I have a lot to do. I'm not thinking about that doctor and what she has to say."

* * *

We had prepared a bedroom for her arrival. She seemed to be pleased with her new living arrangements. A Jack-and-Jill bathroom was attached to her room, with a guest bedroom on the other side. Down the hall was my husband's man-cave. The master bedroom was on the other side of the house.

That first night she started getting ready for bed while talking out loud to herself about what she planned to do in the morning. I sat in the chair next to the bed as she put on her nightgown. I turned on the TV and started watching Jimmy Swaggart. She focused in and out on the sermon and would start singing with the choir. She went into the bathroom and started combing and putting rollers in her wig.

I left her room and returned to find her in bed, asleep. She woke up and said, "I am only staying here temporarily. I need to go to my own home."

I walked over to the lamp next to her bed and asked if she wanted the light on.

She replied, "Yes, but close my door."

I gave her a kiss and said good night.

She said, "Good night, doll," and closed her eyes.

About three o'clock in the morning, I woke up and went to check on Mother. She was in the bathroom combing her wig and singing.

She asked me what time it was. When I told her, she said, "The early bird catches the worm. I've got a lot to do today at the office."

She asked me if I had some more hair rollers. I went into my bedroom and found a few. I stood in her bathroom, watching as she got some toilet tissue and began wrapping the rollers before putting them on the wig.

She said, "I like this wig. Do you? You know, I cut and style my own wigs. I have one at my house I like a little better than this one."

I lay across her bed and watched her messing with her wig until I fell asleep. I woke up about 7:00 a.m. She had already showered and was brushing her teeth.

"Get on up, girl, I need to go to work."

I left her bedroom with the Kaiser doctor's words replaying in my brain: "Your mother lacks the mental capacity to manage her own affairs and the affairs of her real estate business." I also knew that she felt threatened by my presence in the office because clients were bypassing her to address their concerns with me. I was frightened to upset her, uncertain of how to intervene, and worried about the state of affairs of her business.

She followed behind me, asking, "Where is your makeup?"

While I was in the shower, I watched her putting on business attire and makeup. She kept telling me to hurry up; she had to go to the office. When I responded that we had plenty of time to get to the office, her answer was fiery: "This is my business, and we need to go. You can't tell me when we will go. Get out of the shower, put your clothes on, and let's go."

This back and forth went on and on, with Mother urging me to get going and my stalling for time. I convinced her we needed to eat breakfast to start the day, and she made oatmeal and toast. Al joined us in the kitchen, and we listened to Mother talk about her plans.

Al became my savior. Whenever he entered the equation, Mother's attitude changed to a business mindset, excitedly and proudly sharing projects she was working on instead of defending herself against a perceived attack and saying "There is nothing wrong with me." She always greeted Al with, "Hey, man, what's going on? Did you work today? What are you working on? Where you been?"

The conversation quickly moved to highlight her properties, her employees, the tenants, and problems within her business. Our time in her office seemed to bring comfort and joy to her life.

At that time, I knew little of the disease except that it would eventually take her cognitive skills. While she talked with tenants and employees, I Googled websites and read of the devastation of Alzheimer's and the destruction of physical and mental health. I was struggling to find the courage to do what I was advised to do: obtain conservatorship and take over her business.

• • •

Mother had a doctor's appointment on December 29. She was not reluctant to go to the appointment; she woke up preparing for the visit. She put on her business attire, makeup, and wig and was ready to leave several hours early. Kaiser Hospital was across the street from her office. She voiced her plans, which were to tell the doctor there was nothing wrong with her and that he was the crazy one. She also wanted to go by her office before the appointment to check on some things and talk with Mr. Bob.

When we arrived at Mother's office, Mr. Bob gathered some papers and checks needing her signature. All at once, she began exploding about problems that needed to be dealt with.

A prospective tenant was standing at the counter completing a rental application and asking Mr. Bob questions. Immediately, Mother snapped at her, "Young lady, you need to talk with me, he don't run nothing here. You need to ask me. I am Mrs. Martin, and this is my business, not his."

Mother turned to Mr. Bob: "How many times do I have to tell you; this is my business. Why are you trying to answer her questions? Your job is to finish my taxes, and you can't seem to do that. Just do your job!"

"Okay, Mrs. Martin, but can you finish signing these checks before you start talking with her?"

For the next two hours, before leaving for her doctor's appointment, she attacked him about what he should be doing, and what he was not doing, on his job. Before leaving the office, she informed him that she was going to a doctor's appointment and would return soon. She added, "I want an update on where you are with my taxes."

As we walked across the street, she kept rehearsing this message to say to the doctor: "There's nothing wrong with me. Maybe there's something wrong with you!"

After we registered and sat in the lobby waiting to be called, a man came and sat beside my mother.

"Hello, Mrs. Martin. How are you doing? I haven't seen you for a while."

She wasn't remembering him, so he added, "I'm your tenant on Ninth Street."

She smiled and responded, "I'm okay. How are things going?"

He complained that he had submitted several work orders, but no one had come to fix the problems.

"When I go back to the office, I'll talk to him," Mother said.

The tenant smiled, then leaned close to Mother and said, "I have a friend who is interested in renting out the vacant unit. How much is the rent?"

Just then, the nurse called out "Mrs. Martin." Mother picked up her briefcase and said to the tenant, "Have your friend come by my office. And tell your wife I said hello."

In the doctor's office, she pulled out the discharge papers she had been given when she was released from the hospital. Her doctor greeted Mother with a big smile, and said, "How are you today, Mrs. Martin?"

"How am I today? Just fine, except for you guys trying to say I'm crazy. I am not crazy! I have good sense and a business to run. My office is right across the street. I have tenants and employees. I need to work. You are at work doing your job, and I need to do mine!"

He listened while sitting at his computer, reviewing her recent hospitalization, then turned to me and asked, "How is your mother doing since she was released from the hospital?"

Mother said, "I am sitting right here, so why are you asking her? You doctors don't know what you are talking about. Talk to me. I am the one they say is going crazy. Don't direct any questions to my daughter; talk directly with me."

"Well, Mrs. Martin, tell me how things are going with your business."

For more than thirty minutes the doctor asked her questions about her business and listened patiently as she responded, inputting information on his screen.

"Mrs. Martin, you are going to need twenty-four-hour supervision. It's okay for you to go to your office periodically during the day, but you cannot live by yourself."

She was silent, processing his words.

I said, "Well, Mother, you will continue to live with me."

Her doctor then piped up with an excellent idea. "So, Mrs. Martin, you can continue to live with your daughter, or work out a plan to have twenty-four-hour supervision in your home."

At the end of the examination, I followed the doctor around the corner to his office, and he said, "Your mother is having periods of agitation and is displaying thought disturbances. Her judgment and reasoning skills are severely impacted by her dementia. Make an appointment to bring her in sometime next week. She is now incapable of carrying out her own affairs or managing her finances. You need to begin work on getting a power of attorney."

We could hear Mother's voice calling, "Hello? Hello?"

I quickly returned to her. "Okay, Mother, we've made your next appointment. Ready to go back to your office?"

Her doctor said, "Good-bye, Mrs. Martin. Don't work too hard."

"Doctor, I'm an Okie from Oklahoma. The only thing I know how to do is work, and that's what I am going to do. I have a business to run!"

It was always curious that in certain situations Mother would refer to herself as an Okie, a term she felt was demeaning when others used it. When she identified herself as such, the term expressed strength, determination, and perseverance. Depending on whom she was talking to, her definition of Okie changed back and forth like clockwork. I could get very confused between my mother's personality and her attitude. Her personality was who she was; her attitude depended on who you were.

As we exited Kaiser, we passed by an information station where one of Mother's long-term church members was working.

"Hello, sister Martin. How are you doing?"

For ten minutes I stood there, listening to chitchat regarding church activities and family.

Finally, Mother said, "Well, I have to get back to my office. See you at church on Sunday."

While walking back to her office, she was clearly irritated, talking about racist domination and oppression. She started recalling her meetings with bankers and loan officers.

"Glo, I don't know if you remember those meetings you attended with me. But I believe those White men in expensive suits, telling me what I can and can't do, subscribed to White supremacy, and viewed me as an Okie. I believe that's the same thing those Kaiser doctors are trying to do."

All of a sudden, she lost her footing and fell to the ground. Cars were stopped at the traffic light, and drivers noticed her fall.

One young man jumped out of his car and yelled, "Mrs. Martin! Are you okay?"

I tried to help her up, but she said, "Let me lie here for a moment."

The young man was there by my side, waiting to provide help.

After a few minutes, she said, "Okay, Glo, help me up."

After getting her on her feet, we noticed that her knee was bleeding. The young man said, "Stay there. I'll be right back."

The traffic light had turned green, and his car was blocking traffic. He returned to his car and drove it over to the curb, walked us to her office, and helped her sit down at her desk.

"Okay, Mrs. Martin, I hope you are okay."

She said, "Thank you for helping me; what is your name?"

"Mrs. Martin, you don't remember me. My mother was one of your tenants. I grew up living on Ninth Street."

• • •

When we returned to Mother's office, several folks were standing around the counter. As she entered, all eyes focused on her and everyone excitedly greeted her with, "Hello, Mrs. Martin, are you okay?" She remained seated at her desk, engaged in conversation with individual folks, answered the phone and talked for long periods of time about business, but mostly, general conversations about life.

At 5:00 p.m., Mr. Bob packed up his belongings and said goodbye. It was dark outside and time to go home.

I said, "Okay, Mother, tomorrow is another day. You can finish this tomorrow."

She became agitated and told me to shut up. She was not going to leave the office until she was finished. "Go over there and sit down. I have work to do. If you want to leave, go on, get out of here. I can call my cab."

"Okay, but can you finish within the next thirty minutes? We have a long commute."

I sat behind a desk, facing her, watching her pick up papers on her desk and eat food from her lunch bag. Finally, she said, "I am tired; let's go."

In the car she began fussing about her doctor and said she was going to drop Kaiser. They didn't know what the hell they were talking about.

"Hey Glo, swing by my house, I need to get some things."

My brain went into panic zone. What if she refuses to leave? Her house was still a mess, and we had not finished cleaning up in preparation for her to return home.

"We have a long commute to my house. Let's go by your house in the morning."

"No, I want to go by my house now."

I drove to her house, listening all the while to her nonstop complaints about Kaiser. As we pulled up in front of her house, she saw her next-door neighbor driving off.

"They are the ones who called the police on me. I should call an attorney and sue them for calling the police." She was searching frantically in her purse and briefcase for her door key. "Where are my house keys?" She began looking all around the car. "Glo, help me find my keys."

"Maybe you left them at my house or in the office. Let's go to my house and look for your keys. I know we'll find them."

She wasn't a happy camper, but agreed. Rummaging through her purse, she stated, "That Kaiser doctor is racist and is trying to dominate and oppress me."

I glanced at her. "Mom, how could that be, since your doctor is a Black man?"

"Glo, stop being naive. He sees me as an old lady, an Okie. He is discriminating against me. There is nothing wrong with me.

I don't need twenty-four-hour caregivers. I want to live in my own home, go to work, and take care of my business. I would be crazy not to want that. Don't you want that for your mom?"

"Yes, Mother, I do want that for you," and I put her favorite gospel CD in. She smiled and said, "It's not over until the Lord says it's over. Doctors can't tell me that it's over."

The remainder of the ride was pleasant, with the two of us singing gospel songs. The rest of the evening she spent talking to Al and fussing about Kaiser, until finally she was worn out.

"Well, I am tired and going upstairs. Al, I need to get to work early tomorrow morning, so can you drop me off at my office?"

Al agreed and said, "Yes, I will take you. We will leave at about ten."

"Okay," she smiled as she and I headed upstairs for the night. We had managed to make it through another day.

Ermestine hosting her last open house for selling property

Gloria and Ermestine at a family event

GAME CHANGER 43

THE LEAD BIRD'S DREAD

After Al and my mother left the next morning, I sat down with the packet of information Kaiser had given me when she was discharged. It contained information about Alzheimer's disease along with a list of support resources. The house was quiet, and this was the first time in several days I had been alone to think. The doctor's words surfaced in my mind, "Mrs. Martin's judgment and reasoning skills are severely impacted by the disease."

My mother was a very strong person and had accomplished so much in her life. She was always the "rock of the family"—a very strong and independent woman who fought for what she wanted. Some people had learned how to stand up to her. My father had stopped trying. Baldie, using choice words, would basically tell my mother to leave her alone: "You are you, and I am me, so leave me the hell alone." Baldie had learned to deal with her sister's strong and overpowering personality, something I had not mastered and had a fear of doing.

Throughout my life, I wanted to please my mother, and her desires became my goals. She wanted me to obtain my doctorate and encouraged me to enroll at the University of Southern California.

The program had a cohort of candidates residing and working in the field of education in Northern California, attending classes in Sacramento. During the summer, candidates were required to attend classes on the Los Angeles campus. Renting an apartment close to USC, with my husband and children continuing their daily routines in the Bay Area, I completed all the coursework and had nearly finished writing my dissertation when I discovered that I had breast cancer.

At that point, having a doctorate was not my priority. I had already earned two master's degrees and an administrative credential. I had achieved my career goal of being a school principal. I wanted to focus on being a wife, mother, and grandmother. I started focusing on my health and found a principalship closer to my home. After three surgeries, I was cancer-free. But my mother was insistent on my completing the dissertation. She consistently and forcefully suggested I start working on it again.

For the first time in my life, I told her, "No. I am happy with my life and accomplishments."

That was a big step. And now I had to take the even bigger step of interfering in her business. All those nights of staring at Mother long after she had fallen asleep, thinking and wondering, "what if?" long into the night—this worry had to end. I had to overcome my fear of her response or reaction to my involvement in her business. I would break into a sweat just thinking about it. But everything she'd worked so hard to build over an entire lifetime was floundering, with significant financial consequences. Lacking leadership, this train was coming to a wreck.

I had shared my fears with Al, Larry, and my daughters. All responded with empathy, acknowledging that Mother's business was suffering. In their eyes, seeking a conservatorship was my only choice, and I was the only one who could save the business.

One of my biggest joys is watching birds fly in V-formation, especially the visual of the lead bird floating to the back, letting another take the lead. This seemed so natural among the birds, but assuming the lead role in Mother's business felt anything but natural. I was terrified to hurt her. My deepest fear was that one morning she would wake up in her right mind, thinking that I was doing something underhanded instead of working on her behalf.

That morning was less and less likely to come. She continued to slowly lose her cognitive skills. Yet I felt frozen, unable to move forward with the conservatorship process. My daughter suggested that I should seek help from a psychiatrist, and I agreed wholeheartedly, but I couldn't seem to find the time. On my own, I kept trying to figure out how my thoughts and emotions could align with hers. If I couldn't bring myself to agree with what she wanted, then I wanted her to accept and appreciate my efforts to get involved with her business. I had to shift and find internal peace in believing that what I was doing was right, even though she didn't seem to believe in me or trust my decisions. I had to gather the spiritual strength to proceed.

• • •

I knew that Mother was always fussing and yelling at Mr. Bob about her taxes. Over the years, I'd learned about Mother's tax strategies while accompanying her on visits to her certified public accountant. I called the CPA to get some direction on how to manage her tax situation, scheduling an appointment for later in the day.

As I walked into the CPA's office, my mind was jumbled with thoughts and problems. I informed her of my mother's diagnosis and said I was seeking information about her delinquent taxes. I knew that Mr. Bob had neglected his responsibilities, but I didn't know whether the CPA firm had everything they needed to prepare her returns. I also worried that there might be loyalty concerns, since they had worked directly with my mother for so many years.

The CPA informed me that their office could not discuss my mother's taxes without authorization as her legal representative.

This was a real blow. I couldn't say a word in reply. I needed some time to process and think, so I got a cup of coffee and sat in the empty lobby area.

Mother believed the doctors didn't know what they were talking about. And apparently Mr. Bob was encouraging this belief, telling her "Nothing is wrong with you." There would have to be some sort of reckoning with Mr. Bob, but at this moment my anger was with the CPA firm. They knew I was Mrs. Martin's daughter and that I needed their help.

While I sat in the lobby, deep in thought, a CPA whom I had not met before emerged with a warm-hearted greeting and introduction. Alison had heard about my mother's condition, and she shared her experience with her own mother's decline from Alzheimer's and how her family coped. She told me about having to file for a conservatorship in order to handle her mother's affairs and enduring the emotional strain of the responsibility while helplessly watching her mother suffer.

Fighting back tears, I listened as Alison described the slow transformation of her mother as Alzheimer's consumed her physical body and mental abilities. I saw what was to come, and the surreal world of living with Alzheimer's ricocheted in my brain.

After Alison left the lobby, my tears flowed. Hearing about her empathy with her mother's suffering and her family's struggle to regain their footing was enlightening and helped me understand what was at stake. My mind confused and racing,

I was torn between feeling courage and fearing the unknown.

Sipping on cold coffee, staring out the lobby windows, unaware of people entering or exiting the building, I realized I had to seek conservatorship. I truly had no other option. I had to risk going against Mother's wishes, even if it harmed our relationship.

The very thought of what I had to do brought anxiety into my heart and soul. I kept thinking, what if my mother is right and her doctor's diagnosis is wrong? But as I walked to my car, I understood that I had to overcome my fears and assume the lead in the V-formation that had been floating aimlessly in various directions, with me at the end struggling to keep up. Retreat was no longer an option. I had to move forward.

Grandmother Tressie and Gloria,
"Be strong in your faith and lean on the Lord"

GAME CHANGER 44

BE STRONG, DOLL

The real estate office was my mother's Disneyland, an escape that let her stay in the hustle-and-bustle world. Throughout the day, a constant flow of people entered the office to visit and say hello or talk with her about housing and property. She was determined to go to her office daily and was resentful of my presence there.

My fear of this resentment could be sparked in subtle ways. My husband Al has a 1999 pickup truck with loud mufflers. I used to love to hear the sound of his truck, both leaving and coming home. It reminded me of my father's truck when I was a young girl, before he was paralyzed. But now I hated Al's truck.

My mother's bedroom faced the street, and Al always parked the truck directly in front of her window. He would leave at about five in the morning on Tuesdays and Thursdays to play golf. The sound of the truck revving up was loud and pronounced. It would wake her up, and immediately her mind would be set on going to work. She knew that Al was leaving, and she was determined to do the same. There were nights when she would be awake at three in the morning, messing with her wigs or playing the piano, but the sound of that truck was like an alarm and focused her on getting out and about.

I asked Al to park down the street, but he dismissed my request. Why should he be inconvenienced? I don't think he understood how that truck set the way the next few hours were going to play out.

A typical morning started early, with Mother preparing to leave for work. She loved to take a bath, listen to Jimmy Swaggart—seldom would she sit and watch TV, but rather she would listen to it as she did other things. I would come into her bedroom, lie across her bed, and listen to her talk about tenants, properties, employees, and what she needed to do.

At some point she began to show signs of being paranoid and began to close her bedroom door. I would knock before entering. She would respond with, "Yes, can I help you?"

One morning, she was deeply agitated when I entered her room. "I have to get rid of that tenant down the hall. He was in there fighting with someone. He has to go. I can't have tenants making that much noise."

She was standing in front of her bedroom door, looking in the direction of Al's man-cave. He had also begun to close his door.

"I can't handle this; that man has to go. He has too many people coming in and out, and he's probably not paying rent. Do you know how much rent he is paying me? Is he in there? I need to talk with him."

She walked down the hall and knocked on the door. "Hello, this is Mrs. Martin, are you at home? Hello! Hello! Are you in there?" She turned and walked back into her bedroom, fussing about. "That tenant has to go."

I started playing the piano and singing. She sat next to me, began playing the piano, and we enjoyed moments of praising the Lord. She was now in a good zone. This is how it went.

During periods of being in a good space, she would tell me, "Glo, you have to be strong. This is not an easy business. People will take advantage of your kindness. You may have to kick people out of your way when they don't mean you any good. Yeah, baby, you have to be strong like your momma."

• • •

One evening, a cab brought Mother back from work. She had a beautiful scarf draped around her neck and a hat stylishly cocked to the side of her head. She put her briefcase down, took off her hat, and told me, "Mr. Bob told me there is nothing wrong with me. He said I am doing a good job of managing my business. Why are you telling the doctors something is wrong with me? I love you! Don't you love me? Why are you trying to hurt me?"

She continued, "I would never do that to you. Tomorrow, we are going to Kaiser and you tell them that I am okay. I want to run my business and go back to my house. I can live by myself!"

We were already dealing with so much, and Mr. Bob had been on my radar for a while. He now had my full attention as I attempted to anticipate his motive and his next move. Mother always was one to seek knowledge; she wanted to be on the right side of truth. Mr. Bob's misleading words became her truth. He was fueling the fire, and the flames were now surrounding me with fear.

• • •

On June 13, 2015, a court investigator came to my house to interview Mother. She informed the investigator that her daughter was trying to do a "dirty trick" and should make her own money. She said that in her mind, she could do business better than her daughter, and she was still independent. She proudly stated that she went to work every day and conducted business as usual.

Throughout the interview, she spoke about how her mother had received Forty Acres and a Mule, and she learned about farming on that land. She restated repeatedly that her parents had imparted a strong work ethic to her. Mother made it clear that she was not happy with the prospect of a conservatorship and was convinced her daughter and "other women downstairs" were scheming to do something with her real estate. Toward the end of the interview, she became frustrated with the situation and confronted me about it. She didn't seem to recognize me as her daughter.

On June 17, the investigator visited Mother a second time. During the visit, Mother stated, "I knew I was having problems," and she acknowledged "shortcomings" that she was currently experiencing. Similar to the first meeting, Mother repeated stories about how much she accomplished in her life, claiming that her daughter had not done as much as she had. She stated, "Gloria has reasonable senses" and is an "okay kid." She reiterated that she did not believe she needed to be conserved and wanted to show the judge how much she had done.

I realized that real estate was her passion, going to work was her goal, and denial of the Alzheimer's diagnosis was her game.

Six months after my mother began living in my home, I attended a hearing for the Petition for Appointment of Temporary Conservator in Superior Court. For months, while searching for legal counsel, I was encouraged to seek a fiduciary agency to manage mother's estate because of the quantities of properties. But I held on to mother's voice, "Be strong, Doll" and her belief that "Gloria has reasonable senses." After listening to and asking clarifying questions of mother's court-appointed attorney and my attorney, Judge Sugiyama granted me conservatorship and stated, "You have a big job ahead of you, and I wish you success."

• • •

Now I was legally in a position to represent Mother in a lawsuit filed by clients claiming that their property had fallen into disrepair and alleging that my mother had yelled at them, as well as a case to evict a tenant who took advantage of my mother by neglecting to pay rent for five years. Bankers who would not talk to me about the status of her bank accounts now had to acknowledge me to resolve issues.

Mother's CPA scheduled meetings with me to discuss her delinquent taxes going back several years. I began to engage in conversations with multiple agencies involved in business interactions that needed a resolution.

Mr. Bob kept dealing me a cruel hand by sparking a flame of hope in Mother's mind that there was nothing wrong with her. I was so angry with this employee. So confused and emotionally drained by the sorrow I held about Mother's diagnosis, I became suspicious of Mr. Bob's motives and frightened by my mother's behavior. My world was crashing down.

One evening I heard Mother's voice, and I could tell by her tone that something was wrong. I walked into the kitchen while she was on the phone talking to the police. I listened as she said that she was fearful for her life and wanted to go home. Within a few minutes, Hercules police officers were walking through the house. They began asking her questions and calming her down. After about twenty minutes, they encouraged her to go to bed and get some rest.

"Okay, young man, thank you for coming to see about this old lady. You're right, I am tired, and I have to go to my office in the morning. You need a place to live? I have some nice houses for rent. I can't allow one tenant to create a thug-like environment or tear me down. You can help me with that. Call my office in the morning, and we can talk."

Mother had everyone's full attention.

"Okay, Mrs. Martin, we will, but for now, go get some rest and have a nice night."

Mother walked up the stairs and I followed close behind her. When she reached the second floor, she became confused about where her bedroom was and where she was. I took the lead, and she followed me into her bedroom.

She started taking off her clothes to put on her nightgown and said, "You may not be all that I wanted you to be, but you are a good daughter. You are going to have to be strong! Do you hear me? You are going to have to be strong. Nobody I know has ever said that life is easy; I always heard life was pretty hard."

A short time later, I returned with a bowl of sherbet. She was in bed, fumbling with some work folders. "Thank you, doll. I am going to pray for you, and you pray for me. You need to keep smiling and stop frowning so much. See? Smile, like this." She gave me a big smile and said, "Isn't that better? A smile is prettier than a frown, any day of the week."

I turned the television on to her favorite gospel show and sat in the chair next to her bed while she finished her sherbet and fell asleep. In the mirror on the wall, I watched myself and my mother behind me asleep. For so long, I had gone out of my way to make her happy and proud—but this time I could not figure out how to bring sunshine into her life. I wanted her to believe that I could be strong and would take care of her.

I looked at my reflection in the mirror and heard the TV pastor say, "God is in charge," and I remembered my grandmother always saying, "There but for the grace of God go I." I turned off the TV, gave Mother a kiss, went to bed, and struggled to get to sleep. I was scared beyond belief. I wanted her to know that everything I was doing was because of my love for her.

Floating in and out of sleep, I thought about how she had always lifted me up, given me faith, and stood by me through both good and bad times.

Ermestine and Gloria on Gloria's wedding day in 1974

Looking towards the horizon with plans for the future

GAME CHANGER 45

A BEAUTIFUL, PURPOSEFUL LIFE

Conservatorship required 24/7 working hours and caregiver hours. I enrolled Mother in weekly voice and piano lessons to get her mind off working. I put a portable piano in her bedroom, and she would practice playing and singing for hours. If she became agitated because she wanted to go to the office, mentioning her next music class would return her focus to practicing. I hired caregivers to assist Mother, which began a routine of women entering and leaving my house on a daily basis. I would retreat to my bedroom, which quickly became my home office, as I discovered the complexity of the job before me.

When Mother was determined to go to the office, a caregiver would take her. The challenge for the caregiver was to get her to leave the office, to be able to calm her down after interactions with tenants or employees. After a while, it was clear that office visits affected her mood and sparked her anger. I never knew if I would be greeted with open arms or be immersed in a clinical nightmare when she returned home.

While working in my bedroom, I could hear dialogue between the caregivers and Mother. On one occasion, the caregiver was a young lady, and Mother was her first assignment.

I heard Mother say, "Look, I can't babysit you. You need to go to your mama. When you going to pay your rent? Why do you think I can take care of you? Call your mama and let me talk to her."

The young caregiver was silent.

I heard Mother's voice again, "Hello, this is Mrs. Martin. Listen, I can't take care of your child. She is going to have to move in with you, unless you can pay her rent."

I walked into her bedroom, and Mother was sitting on the piano bench, consumed in conversation on the caregiver's cell phone. The caregiver moved close to me and motioned for me to follow her.

Standing outside Mother's view, she nervously said, "Your mom was going off on me and insisted on talking to my mother. Instead of calling my mom, I called my sister, hoping to calm her down. Sometimes I don't know what to do when your mom is upset at me."

Mother ended the telephone call with, "Okay, doll, and it was nice talking with you." She turned, placed the cell phone on the piano, and started playing. "Come on, doll, sing with me."

The caregiver picked up her cell phone, stood behind Mother, and we all sang songs until lunchtime.

Often, while Mother was in her room, playing the piano and singing, I would go into the kitchen and find the caregiver watching TV. Upon my entrance the caregiver would say, "Your mom told me to get out of her room and leave her alone. I'm giving her some space right now. I think we both need it."

When Mother was ready to reengage, I could hear her voice saying, "Hello, hello, this is Mrs. Martin speaking."

"Yes, Mrs. Martin," the caregiver responded. "I am downstairs, are you ready to eat?"

"Yes, doll, what are you cooking down there?"

"Come on down, Mrs. Martin, let's eat something."

• • •

Mother could never remember her caregivers' names. She would frequently accuse the caregivers and Al of not paying their rent or ask them, "Do you want to rent an apartment? How much money do you make? How much rent can you pay? How is your credit?"

Often when I walked into the room, Mother would say, "Who are you?"

If I said, "Hello, Mother," her response was "Hello, doll." She no longer addressed me as Glo. She would look at me and say, "Where is Glo?"

Her cognitive issues were becoming more pronounced. More often than not, she did not recognize family members or her surroundings, and her moods became volatile. She had several falls, and her physical condition was beginning to deteriorate. Within nine months, there was a significant decline in her mental condition. Mother had lucid moments, but they were becoming more infrequent. Every day, she made it known that she wanted to go to her home. Every day, she talked about going to her office.

As I dove deeper into her business, I discovered the declining population of Black tenants living in her properties. Most of Mother's properties were in Richmond's Iron Triangle, the boundary of racist housing policies Blacks faced when they migrated to the city.

Through day-to-day interactions at Mother's office, I appreciated more fully her personally supportive and caring relationships with her tenants. She wanted to see the neighborhoods thrive, and she embraced those who were working to get ahead. At the same time, she would never hesitate to tell you off if she felt you were not doing your part to better yourself, take care of her property, and respect your neighbors. Tenants would always ask, "How is Mrs. Martin?" Eagerly they would share a memorable experience they had with Mother, ending with, "She would tell me off, sing with me, and wish me well." Tenants frequently brought gifts for me to give Mother as expressions of love.

One tenant shared, "Mrs. Martin told me that we can always find fault in one another. She said, 'I'm trying to focus on the good I see in people. I see growth and improvement in you. I see a positive change in you. You just have to keep your hustle and stay strong.'" The tenant smiled and said, "Your mother had a significant influence on who I am today."

The last house Mother sold was my home in 2003. She was our broker and listed the house on the market. Our home, located in a mixed-race neighborhood, drew many potential home buyers. Every Sunday after church she would arrive, glamorous, professional, carrying her briefcase. My husband, children, and I would leave our house for the four hours of open house while Mother was left alone to greet potential buyers.

After being on the market for several months, consistently hosting open houses, we received two offers way below market value. Mother suggested, let's take down all our family pictures and Afrocentric art. You know, there are people in power who continue to drive down home values for Black families who live in racially mixed neighborhoods. People who carry the same attitudes and beliefs that restricted Blacks in the past. The following Sunday, two potential buyers submitted market-rate offers for our home, from which all signs of blackness had been removed.

By 2005, Mother had stopped engaging with clients as their real estate broker in property sale transactions. But she continued to advise and encourage tenants who expressed a desire to become homeowners, informing them about racial and economic inequity and the challenges they might experience in reaching their goal. All of her tenants had heard about the Forty Acres and a Mule property her mother had received, and the value of being a property owner, and the importance of knowing how to make the land work for you while treating the property with respect.

Discrimination came in so many forms. Mother had a specific message to women, and that was to always be ready to battle for equality. She lamented the lack of women represented in high-level positions in banks, lending agencies, and government. She was a storyteller, a motivator, and the biggest cheerleader of women exhibiting a desire to better their lives.

She would inspire women to be ambitious and to prepare carefully for any steps they might take. She believed Black women had to break down barriers and balance being a good mother and a career person. She had been the Black woman who fought for her rights for many years against White men in power, always forging ahead. All her life she viewed being Black and a woman as a double whammy as she tried to navigate her life, fighting battles of racial and gender inequity.

As long as she could, Mother continued going to her office, sharing her personal stories, encouraging, educating, and inspiring all who would listen. When she was still demanding to go to the office and encountered resistance, she said, "No obligation, No desire, No go. But I have both the obligation and desire to go to work. Let's go! I have work to do!"

She was so creative in making the office her gathering place for family, friends, and associates—until Alzheimer's stopped her physically and mentally.

• • •

In her lucid moments, before Alzheimer's prevented her from recognizing me as her daughter, she was always telling me, "You are going to have to be strong. This is hard work. I refuse to let you be collateral damage. I want my grandchildren to have more opportunity than I did."

One night, I thought about the Republican fundraiser at HS Lordships. That event was etched in my being, a rewind in my brain for all these years. I turned to Mother and asked, "You were a lifelong Democrat. What made you support and vote for the Republican Party?"

She didn't respond, but continued to put rollers in her wig. I stood watching her, handing her rollers, but no words were spoken. I accepted her silence as part of the Alzheimer's.

She started singing, continued working on her wig, and she and I talked about meaningless things. After a while she got into bed and looked at me in her sincere and loving way.

She said, "My mind is my own; no one can tell me what to think or how to act, and you must have that same attitude. Be an independent thinker and not a follower. Negative forces have victimized Blacks for years, so go about your days taking care of business. I refuse to let fear of anybody tie me down or keep me from what I need to do."

As Mother began to realize the truth in her doctor's diagnosis of Alzheimer's, she would say good night in messages of motivation, wisdom, and strength when she recognized me as her daughter.

Becoming my mother's conservator, representing her from a business standpoint, expanded my view of who she was. I heard so many stories of her beauty and glamour, her personality as a hard-hitter, determined and gutsy. The reminiscences of her employees, tenants, business associates, and contractors awakened my understanding of the lady my mother was. I admired her beautiful, purposeful life.

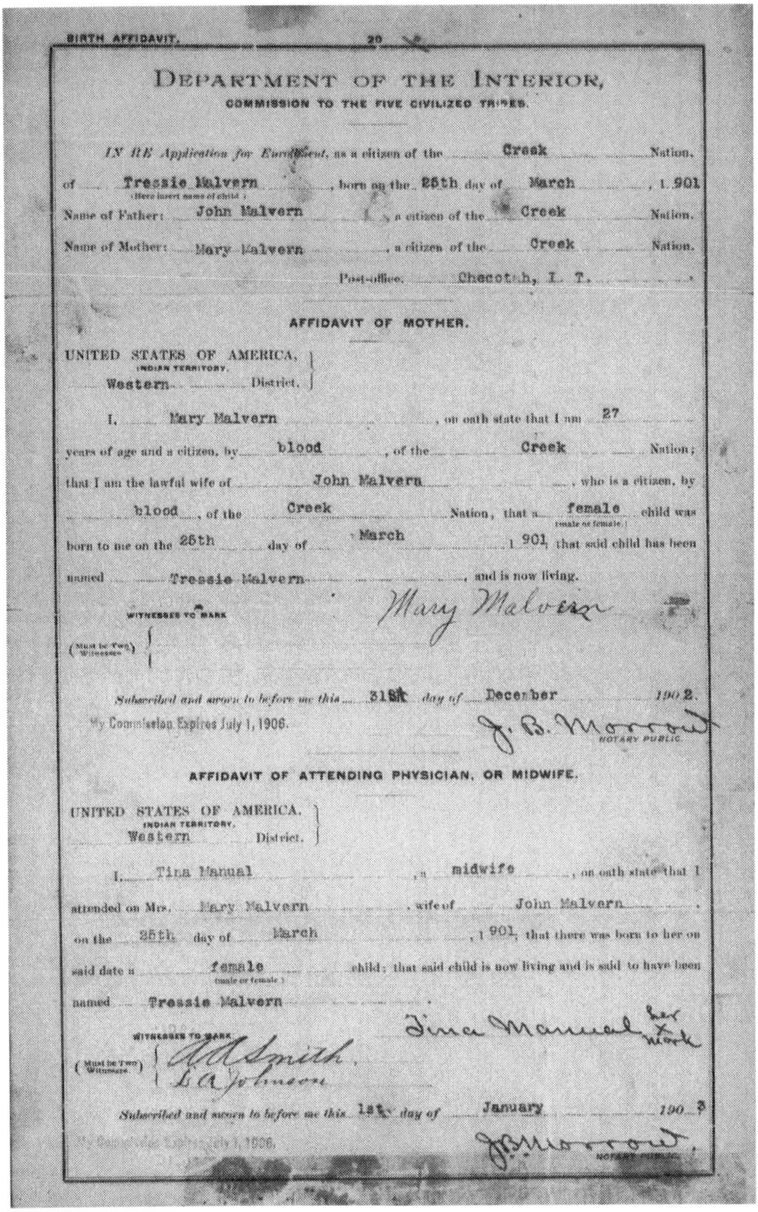

BIRTH AFFIDAVIT. 20

DEPARTMENT OF THE INTERIOR,
COMMISSION TO THE FIVE CIVILIZED TRIBES.

IN RE Application for Enrollment, as a citizen of the Creek Nation,
of Tressie Malvern (Here insert name of child.), born on the 25th day of March, 1901
Name of Father: John Malvern, a citizen of the Creek Nation.
Name of Mother: Mary Malvern, a citizen of the Creek Nation.
Post-office. Checotah, I. T.

AFFIDAVIT OF MOTHER.

UNITED STATES OF AMERICA,
INDIAN TERRITORY,
Western District.

I, Mary Malvern, on oath state that I am 27 years of age and a citizen, by blood, of the Creek Nation; that I am the lawful wife of John Malvern, who is a citizen, by blood, of the Creek Nation, that a female (male or female.) child was born to me on the 25th day of March, 1901, that said child has been named Tressie Malvern, and is now living.

Mary Malvern

WITNESSES TO MARK
(Must be Two Witnesses)

Subscribed and sworn to before me this 31st *day of* December 1902.
My Commission Expires July 1, 1906.

J. B. Morrow
NOTARY PUBLIC.

AFFIDAVIT OF ATTENDING PHYSICIAN, OR MIDWIFE.

UNITED STATES OF AMERICA,
INDIAN TERRITORY,
Western District.

I, Tina Manual, a midwife, on oath state that I attended on Mrs. Mary Malvern, wife of John Malvern, on the 25th day of March, 1901, that there was born to her on said date a female (male or female.) child; that said child is now living and is said to have been named Tressie Malvern.

Tina Manual her X mark

WITNESSES TO MARK.
(Must be Two Witnesses)
A. A. Smith
L. A. Johnson

Subscribed and sworn to before me this 1st *day of* January 1903
My Commission Expires July 1, 1906.

J. B. Morrow
NOTARY PUBLIC.

Grandmother Tressie's allotment of land,
the seed that created the family's journey

Ermestine with her first great-great grandson

GAME CHANGER 46

THE COMPLETE JOURNEY

The entire time Mother was residing with me, she repeatedly expressed her desire to return to her house. In 2017 she happily moved back to her home with 24/7 caregivers. She appeared far more comfortable in her own home and supervised her caregivers as employees. Her neighbors and friends became frequent visitors, and she seemed to enjoy their company. She entertained herself playing the piano and singing in the home environment she had created through the years. She spent time by herself in the prayer room, thinking, browsing through her belongings, or sitting quietly with eyes closed. She tried to resume life as she remembered it, but Mr. Bob and the office were no longer on her mind. Eventually life as she had known it slowly came to an end. She created her unique path and trail.

In August 2019 the house directly across from my mother's home was put on the market. One Sunday, while visiting Mother, I noticed an open house sign and walked across the street. Potential buyers were coming and going as I entered the house. The neighborhood is still predominantly White, and none of the potential buyers I observed were people of color.

The real estate agent, a White man who looked to be in his late sixties, greeted me at the door with a smile and handed me a flyer about the house. I noticed it was built in 1949, the year I was born. The house was a small two-bedroom, Spanish-inspired home with all of its original characteristics intact.

I had stepped into a time capsule from the 1940s era that provided a real sense of my mother's life and my history. The house was an undisturbed legacy of earlier generations.

Walking slowly through the rooms, I was in my own zone, traveling through time. The curtains were drawn in the living room, and through the window, from every angle, Mother's house was center stage. I could hear the agent and interested buyers chatting in low tones behind me. My eyes were focused on Mother's house, and my mind raced back to the first time she brought me to this street. She parked in front of a vacant lot and excitedly said, "Glo, we are going to build our home here!" I remember walking around the lot with her and being captivated by the exceptional panoramic views. On both sides were large, well-maintained houses, and directly across the street was the smaller house I was now standing in.

Every Sunday after church, my parents would take me by their lot to see the week's progress. As the interior became defined, I was astonished to discover all the upscale touches. A sauna room in the master bedroom. A deck that overlooked an incredible view of both the bay and the freeway. A master bathroom with the largest sunken bathtub I had ever seen, and a bidet, a fixture I never knew existed. Exceptionally large windows in each room provided natural light. The gorgeous, large crystal chandelier in the entryway glistened as the light reflected its beauty.

I remembered the battles my parents had fought to build their home on top of the hill, and I reminisced about my journey. In junior high school, I traveled alone, riding the bus to and from school. These were the houses we passed on that bus ride, houses I viewed as incredible mansions that were so very different from where I was living above the store. White children came out of their homes like clockwork every morning to catch the bus. The bus driver waited patiently at the bus stop for these kids to reach the open doors. But when I was late and he saw me running down Macdonald Avenue, waving my hands and hollering, "Wait!" so I, too, could catch the bus, he simply drove off.

I was the first student to board the bus in Downtown Richmond. A couple of older Black women and I got on at the same time. We always sat at the back of the bus. They sat in front of me, talking about their jobs as maids and their families in the Canal Projects. By the time the bus reached San Pablo and Barrett, the bus was practically full of Black women on their way to work in White people's homes in the hills.

Many of them recognized me as Mrs. Petgrave's daughter, having seen me working in the store. Some of their children were my friends, so they also knew me because I played in the neighborhood with their kids. They spoke to me or smiled at me as they got on or off the bus. The air was full of chatter and laughter as the women shared bits and pieces of their personal lives with one another. As the bus proceeded up the hill, the women would get off, and White children would get on, sitting up front. When the bus arrived in front of Portola Junior High school, it was full of White boy and girl students, and one Black girl student, me, sitting in the back. The White students never spoke to me or acknowledged me, and I was happy just to be left alone. The bus ride to Portola was eye-opening, my first real awareness of how some White children lived in their fancy communities.

Mother picked me up from school frequently, and she would say, "See, this is how White folks live," while we wandered around the neighborhoods looking at property, taking notes about vacant lots or houses for sale. She stopped and talked to contractors who were working in the area. As soon as we arrived home, she would go into her real estate office and follow up by calling realtors listed on properties for sale—asking questions and learning more about the housing market in El Cerrito.

While I was reminiscing, the real estate broker suddenly appeared again, gazed out the window, and observed, "That's a beautiful house, isn't it? And it will definitely enhance the selling of this one."

I smiled and said proudly, "That's my mother's house!" I shared that my mother began her career in real estate in the late 1940s in Richmond.

He looked at the house again and asked me, "How old is your mother?"

"She's ninety-three, and she retired four years ago because of medical issues."

He observed, "I've not seen that particular house design before. It's the nicest house in this whole neighborhood!"

The next words from his mouth shocked me. "I bet your mother dealt with some huge challenges in the 1950s as a real estate agent."

He had my total attention now, and I zeroed in on his face. He shared that he had started his real estate career in the 1970s and knew from talking to some old-timers in the business that times were difficult for Blacks then.

As he turned to welcome a couple walking in, I again focused on my mother's house, thinking of the memories, both happy and sad, and family events with loved ones no longer alive. The couple walked up beside me and looked out the window. The woman said, "That is really a beautiful house." They walked away and continued their tour of the house for sale.

But I was frozen in that very spot. I was thinking about what the real estate broker had just said, reflecting on the truth of his words.

* * *

Like a videotape, my mind rewound to a Sunday in 1978 shortly after Mother and Mr. Martin had moved into their new El Cerrito house. We were returning from church, and there was a birthday lunch celebration for my daughter, Kim.

Pop pulled into the driveway, and we all scrambled out of the car. Mother was ahead of Kim and me, searching for the door key in her purse while singing "Precious Lord." Pop was lagging behind, getting his briefcase and Bible out of the car. Kim was slowly walking behind me, carrying her favorite doll. From out of nowhere, a baseball whizzed by, hit the house, and bounced into the yard. An angry man's voice shouted harshly, "Keep your dirty ball out of my yard! Don't you dare start trashing up the neighborhood!"

Mother, who was on the porch, placed her purse down on the step. I grabbed my daughter's hand and continued walking toward the porch. My mother rushed past us, picked up the ball, and threw it back across the street as hard as she could.

"That's not *our* dirty ball," she yelled. "It was in *your* yard, so it must belong to you!"

In an effort to dodge the oncoming ball, the neighbor struggled to remain standing. By this time, Pop stood right next to Mother, glaring at him, both of my parents waiting for him to respond. He appeared to be about my parents' age; his facial expression and body language were unsettling.

Pop, in his Pandora hat, with his briefcase by his side and his Bible in his hand, spoke firmly. "Listen, partner. That ball doesn't belong to anyone over here in this house. So go on about your business, and leave us the hell alone."

The White man turned away, walking toward his front door, screaming, "You're not welcome here. We don't need trash in our neighborhood!"

My fear of the White man reared its ugly head at that moment. I imagine the emotions released in my soul were similar to Mother's when that cross was placed on the lawn of her first house. She had struggled all of her life to have a house in the El Cerrito hills, an address allowing her child to attend some of the best schools in the district. Her struggle was real, and she had achieved her goal. No wonder she was considered by many to be a shrewd businesswoman.

Pop opened the front door, and as we walked in, Kim said, "Grandma, why did he throw that ball at you?"

"Because he is a fool—a fool I don't want you to ever be around."

She put her purse down, took off her church hat, then started playing the piano and singing her favorite song, "Precious Lord."

Kim walked over next to her and said with a smile, "Grandma, I didn't know you knew how to play ball."

Mother smiled and responded, "There's a whole lot this old lady can do! Now, listen to me sing."

Pop took Rocky Road ice cream out of the fridge, put some bowls on the counter, and started serving everyone. Mother joined us at the dining room table. We sat quietly, eating ice cream while listening to their favorite religious radio broadcast: Pop was on the radio, KEST from San Francisco. Pop's sermon was inspiring, and Mother's voice was crystal clear as she introduced gospel songs and provided uplifting Scriptures.

Later on, as Kim and I left Mother's house, the image of the neighbor struggling to stay on his feet when that dirty ball whizzed by him made me chuckle, and it was an instant replay in my mind for a long time afterward. I drove down Arlington Boulevard as Kim played quietly with her doll. I was still reflecting on how crude and hateful the neighbor had been. Kim could be entertained for hours by her dolls, but she wasn't into balls. That ball in his yard had nothing to do with us.

Driving past the Mira Vista Golf and Country Club, I glanced to my right at houses I was very familiar with: five custom-built homes overlooking the golf course. Five Black families using the same driveway entrance, living side by side, with breathtaking views as far as the eye could see from their backyards—views of San Francisco, the San Francisco Bay, both the Golden Gate and Bay Bridge. In each of the houses had lived children around my age whom I'd met attending El Cerrito High school or at a Links Cotillion event.

Two of my best friends, Priscilla and Marie, lived next door to each other. Priscilla told me that her parents had bought the land and built their home in 1961. Her home was the last of the five constructed. Her parents were working hard to live in El Cerrito, and Priscilla enjoyed the beauty of the scenery and was proud of her new home.

At this point I realized something that had never come to mind while we were in high school and I spent time visiting Priscilla and Marie. Priscilla's front deck offered clear views of White men happily golfing. Priscilla's father would sit on the deck watching these men golf, knowing he could not step on the course. Like a bull's-eye, I homed in on the fact that in this one driveway on Arlington lived five Black families nestled in the El Cerrito hills, creating their private oasis and trying to give their children every opportunity to find their success. And yet they were still segregated, surrounded on all sides by barriers.

Several years later, there was an estate sale at the angry neighbor's house; people were leaving with furniture they had purchased. I asked Mother if she wanted to walk over there and take a look. But she had no interest. She observed, "Since the day he threw the ball at us, I left him alone, and he left me alone. That's the only way we got along. I don't want any of their stuff in my house!"

* * *

I leave the open house, step back into the present, and enter my mother's house across the street. My daughter, three granddaughters, and two great-grandsons are sitting near my mother. The caregiver, who is giving Mother a glass of water, greets me with a smile. There is chatter, laughter, and a warm, loving environment surrounding Mother.

My mother, who was diagnosed with Alzheimer's in 2015, is lying in her hospital bed, surrounded by windows overlooking a beautiful park-like backyard setting and dramatic views, hearing water flowing gently through the fountain outside. She opens her eyes less frequently, mainly when she is asked to do so.

Currently, Mother is always talking about the real estate business, engaging with people in her past. Thinking out loud about meetings she has scheduled for that day and projects she is working on. Ongoing conversations with tenants, employees, and contractors about one issue or another. She is still inquiring about property, thinking about possibilities, and often getting visually upset about the person's unspoken response.

Several years ago, there were clear indications that she no longer knew who I was. She would say, "Who are you?" and "Where is Gloria?" I never know when, and for sure, if she knows who I am. Mother often responds to my voice with, "Hello, doll," which is what she began calling me after Alzheimer's effects became quite noticeable. Most of the time, though, there appears to be little or no connection between her thoughts, but rather ramblings about things she needs to do and people she needs to see. Sometimes she is talking to her dad or mom, asking for their help to resolve a problem.

The girls are still chatting and passing around the one-month-old newest addition to our family. Mother has fallen asleep. I walk into her living room and look out the window. The real estate broker is removing the Open House sign. I stand there watching until his car disappears down the hill. Then I stare at the house I knew so well from the outside. Today, I discovered the inside, a time capsule of the memories shared by my mother, her parents, and her siblings.

* * *

Mother would often tell me, "Unless you have walked in my shoes, you can't understand what I'm saying or feeling. Just keep on living and remember my words, and one day you will figure it out."

My whole life I walked by her side, or a few steps behind her, or in front of her. I listened to and learned the paths she walked, and the detours she was forced to take, in order to accomplish her goals and aspirations.

The Forty Acres and a Mule in Oklahoma provided the foundation for her life, instilling strong work ethics and determination passed on from my grandparents. Forty Acres and a Mule resulted in higher levels of income, knowledge, and skills for her family. But she always stressed that hard work was what got them through the difficult times.

Her parents had taught their children how to work the land and acquire the skills they took with them to Richmond. My "Okie" Mother did the same with me, every step of the way, training me, teaching me, and making me aware of the world around us.

My mother gave me the gift of love and firsthand learning opportunities while I worked in the store and in her real estate office. This was the most valuable on-the-job training to prepare me for whatever was to come.

We all have choices in life, decisions to make, risks to take, and goals that inspire our very being. These are the attributes that determine who we are. Blacks who migrated to Richmond after World War II, however, didn't have many choices.

Systemic racial discrimination determined and defined who they were and how they lived. The social and legal structure of the Jim Crow era was still alive in Richmond during the 1940s and 1950s.

Throughout her real estate career, Mother had the self-determination and confidence to deal head-on with all the uncertainties and resistance she faced.

Forming a strong husband-and-wife team, my parents discovered innovative paths to change the status quo. Together, they adapted their business approaches to deal with individuals, organizations, or businesses they perceived as racist, unjust, discriminatory, illegal. Their creative tactics, bold ways of thinking, and strong style of attack disrupted business-as-usual in the real estate game, transforming the landscape.

Mother was a visionary, continually strategizing to create opportunities for Blacks to own and live in housing of their choice. She was a game changer, breaking down barriers, helping Blacks achieve economic growth and prosperity.

The experiences in my mother's life were game changers, passed on to me by the stories she shared—sometimes with laughter, sometimes with tears. The wisdom of the Creek Nation Tribe was mirrored and preserved in my grandfather's thinking and storytelling and then passed down to all of us, and from me to you in this story.

My gorgeous Mother is one of the lucky ones. She is unstoppable, fighting still, and still accomplishing what she wants to do. As she said throughout my childhood, "There is one secret to success—never give up!" And she never has.

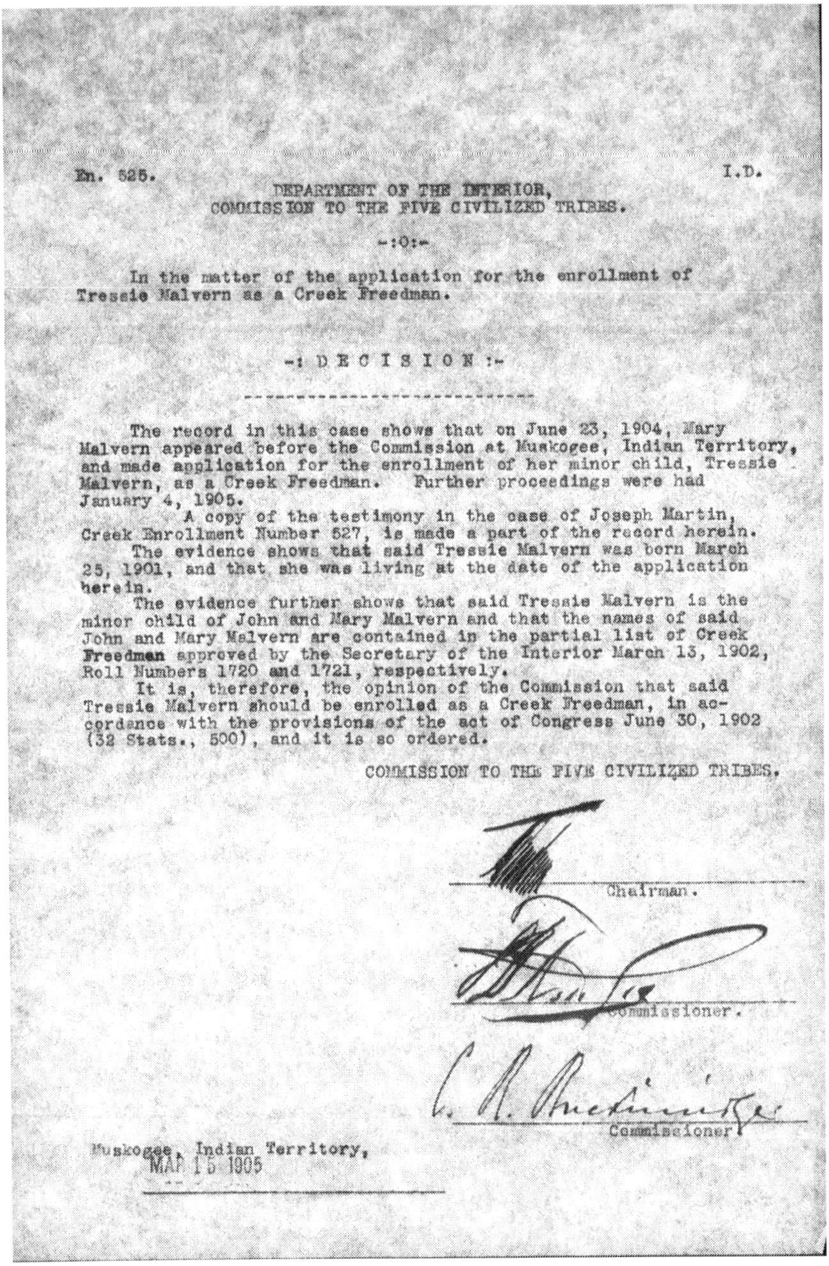

En. 525. I.D.

DEPARTMENT OF THE INTERIOR,
COMMISSION TO THE FIVE CIVILIZED TRIBES.

-:O:-

In the matter of the application for the enrollment of Tressie Malvern as a Creek Freedman.

-: D E C I S I O N :-

The record in this case shows that on June 23, 1904, Mary Malvern appeared before the Commission at Muskogee, Indian Territory, and made application for the enrollment of her minor child, Tressie Malvern, as a Creek Freedman. Further proceedings were had January 4, 1905.

A copy of the testimony in the case of Joseph Martin, Creek Enrollment Number 527, is made a part of the record herein.

The evidence shows that said Tressie Malvern was born March 25, 1901, and that she was living at the date of the application herein.

The evidence further shows that said Tressie Malvern is the minor child of John and Mary Malvern and that the names of said John and Mary Malvern are contained in the partial list of Creek Freedmen approved by the Secretary of the Interior March 13, 1902, Roll Numbers 1720 and 1721, respectively.

It is, therefore, the opinion of the Commission that said Tressie Malvern should be enrolled as a Creek Freedman, in accordance with the provisions of the act of Congress June 30, 1902 (32 Stats., 500), and it is so ordered.

COMMISSION TO THE FIVE CIVILIZED TRIBES.

Chairman.

Commissioner.

C. R. Breckinridge
Commissioner.

Muskogee, Indian Territory,
MAR 15 1905

Even in the darkest days, hope is alive and well.

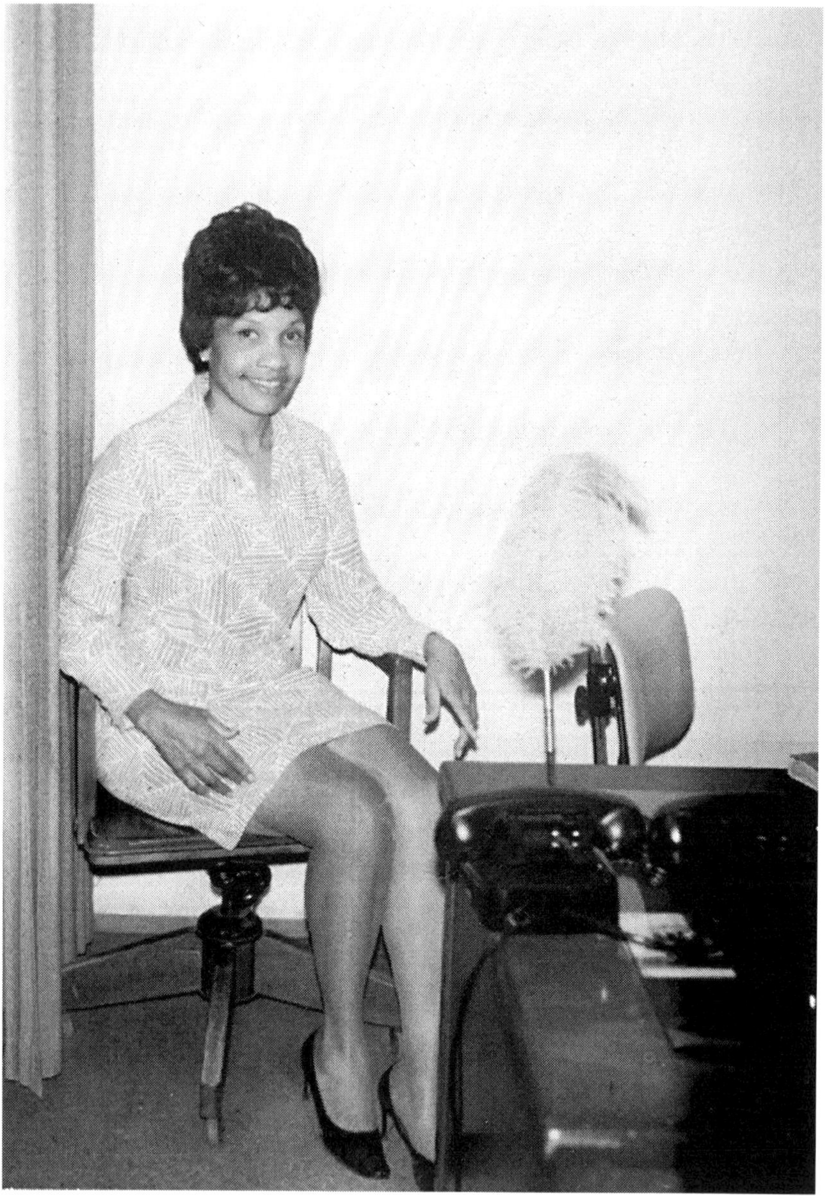

Ermestine, mastering her craft, by improving skills and expanding knowledge, every step of her journey to right a wrong

AFTERWORD

ACQUIRING PROPERTY WEALTH

Throughout Mother's journey, people often asked, "How did you acquire property wealth?"

Her response was always, "Hard work, faith, determination, and fighting for every opportunity to achieve my goals, regardless of the opinions of others."

Refusing to be intimidated by racial injustice, possessing a deep desire to overcome challenges and disappointments, she designed her own paths to success.

She sought knowledge and educational opportunities to overcome the stereotypes that engulfed her experiences of being a Black woman from Oklahoma. Politically savvy, Mother attacked policies she believed hindered financial success for Blacks.

She never subscribed to the victim mentality but rather created and shared a clearly defined plan for obtaining personal goals. She aggressively pursued individual rights to property wealth. Her true character emerged in the toughest of times, fighting battles to secure the same financing opportunities available to Whites.

Mother never gave up on her conviction that Blacks should be able to purchase homes in locations that afforded Black children quality educational opportunities. But properties available to a Black businesswoman were in less desirable locations and required lots of repair work to make them ready for market rentals. For the most part, the properties she acquired didn't have an immediate positive cash flow. In most of her real estate deals the monthly rental incomes were not equal to or greater than her initial investment in the property. It took time and unthinkable amounts of work for her to build up her personal wealth.

Today, my mother holds the keys to more than 150 units in apartment buildings, single-family homes, and commercial buildings, as well as vacant lots.

How did she do it? First, she did due diligence on all aspects of every deal. She was good at asking questions. She enrolled in college classes, gained experience, and was consistently researching and analyzing real estate deals.

She was also forceful and to the point with negotiation strategies and did not back down. She didn't make an offer and walk away if it wasn't accepted, unless she knew for sure that discriminatory practices weren't guiding the deal. If the transaction costs were high, or the contract didn't make sense, she demanded fair and equitable treatment.

Mother stayed focused on and excited about her goals, and she celebrated each accomplishment by doing or buying something special for herself. But she reaped the fruits of her labor with the basic premise of frugality, consuming only a small percentage of her total earnings. A credit card would never be found in her wallet; she always paid with cash.

She struggled to maintain good credit and keep her debt-to-income ratio aligned with lenders' requirements. She learned these values from my grandmother, whose joy was shopping for hours in Goodwill stores with her daughters and grandchildren. The tradition was passed on to her daughters, and they both expressed pride in the treasures and clothes they purchased from secondhand stores.

Mother's to-do list was always chock-full—except for on Sundays. In the family tradition, she dedicated Sundays to building her relationship with God, nurturing a faith that provided inner strength and inspiration. This faith helped keep her eyes focused on her goals and her vision. Through sheer tenacity and an ever-present faith in God, she found a way to balance and enjoy her life.

Grandmother's Forty Acres and a Mule in Checotah planted the seed idea in Mother's heart to invest in real estate to build wealth. Acres of land remain today as property in my grandmother's estate and our family's legacy.

In a 2021 article, Snoop Dogg explains how his legacy would exist well after he himself is long gone, merging the two worlds of personal and professional.

"That's our problem as Black men sometimes. We get so caught up in our business that we forget to let our spouse in the business. Then when something happened to us, in comes some man or some company taking it from this lady who has no understanding of business and how to hold on.

"But in the other world, they teach their whole family. Everybody knows the business, in case something happens to one member of the family. I'm teaching my sons, my daughter, and my wife the business."[12]

Snoop Dogg's net worth is estimated to be $150 million and he is one of the richest rappers in the world.

Right on, Snoop Dogg, keep generational wealth flowing to and for future generations. Teach them well!

Few Blacks fit into Snoop Dogg's tax bracket, but Blacks have acquired generational wealth that needs to be protected for our descendants. We need to focus on acquiring generational wealth in multiple ways. We need to make sure family members are prepared with knowledge to move forward long after we are no longer on this earth.

NOTES

Game Changer 1: Forty Acres and a Mule

1. Since 1979, membership in the tribe has been based on documented lineal descent from persons listed as Creek "Indians by blood" on the Dawes Rolls. Creek Freedmen continue to fight this disenfranchisement.

2. There is some question about when Luanna died. The commission transcript suggests that she died as a young child, as per testimony by both John and Robert Malvern, but a headstone in Paradise Cemetery has her death at age nineteen.

Game Changer 2: Keeping the Land

3. Booker T. Washington, "Boley, a Negro Town in the West, 1908," *Outlook* (4 January 1908): 28–31.

4. In 1975, sections of Boley were identified as the Boley Historic District. The downtown business district was listed in the National Register of Historic Places and designated a National Historic Landmark by the National Park Service.

Game Changer 16: The Paper Shack

5. Eli Moore, Nicole Montojo, and Nicole Mauri, "Roots, Race, & Place: A History of Racially Exclusionary Housing in the San Francisco Bay Area" (Berkeley: Haas Institute, 2019), 45–48.

Game Changer 23: Black Panthers and Cowboys

6. Brandon Kooi, *Seven Highly Effective Police Leaders: 1895–Modern Times* (New York and London: Routledge, Taylor & Francis Group), 384.

Game Changer 26: Guardians of Justice

7. "A CBS-TV '60 Minutes' Segment on Civil Rights Problems," UPI, originally published February 27, 1984, accessed October 29, 2021, www.upi.com/Archives/1984/02/27/A-CBS-TV-60-Minutes-segment-on-civil-rights-problems/1427446706000/.

8. Henry Ramsey Jr., *The Life Story of Henry Ramsey Jr.: An Autobiography* (Walnut Creek, CA: Hardscratch Press, 2008), 441–58.

Game Changer 34: New and Expanding Horizons

9. Gary Orfield and Jongyeon Ee, "Segregating CalIfornia's Future: Inequality and Its Alternative, 60 Years after Brown v. Board of Education" (Los Angeles: The Civil Rights Project / Proyecto Derechos Civiles, May 2014), 3–4.

10. Stephen Menendian and Samir Gambhir, "Racial Segregation in the San Francisco Bay Area, Part 1," Othering & Belonging Institute, originally published October 30, 2018, accessed December 6, 2021, https://belonging.berkeley.edu/racial-segregation-san-francisco-bay-area-part-1.

Game Changer 35: Sisterhood

11. "TWENTY PEARLS Documentary Film about First Black-Greek Letter Organization Now Available Nationwide," Alpha Kappa Alpha Sorority, Inc., March 31, 2021, https://aka1908.com/news-events/online-pressroom/twenty-pearls-documentary-film-about-first-black-greek-letter-organization-now-available-nationwide.

Afterword

12. Angelina Velazquez, " 'I've Put Her through So Much': Snoop Dogg Explains Why His Wife Is the Perfect Steward of His Career and Legacy," *Atlanta Black Star,* December 11, 2021.

MORE MEMORIES FROM THE FAMILY SCRAPBOOK

Roy Williams, World War I

1940s – Williams family cows and barn

Back view of Williams Checotah house – circa 1940s, pets in view

Side view of Williams Checotah family home – circa 1940s

Ermestine, 1940s

Ermestine, leaving Choctoh to attend Langstonn University, circa 1940s

Ermestine, 1940s

A family excursion to San Francisco,
planned by Ermestine, Tressie, and Baldie, circa 1940s

Teenage Baldie, enjoying life in Checotah, circa 1940s

Baldie, viewing the land in Checotoh
with memories of farm life, circa 1970s

Mother and daughter time at Grandmother's house
Ermestine, Tressie, Gloria, and Kim – 1977

Priscilla and son sitting on the curb at the driveway entrance for five Black families on Arlington Boulevard, with the golf course in the background, circa 1980s

Tressie visiting Oral Roberts University, one of the largest Christian universities in the world. Tulsa, Oklahoma, circa 1970s

Ermestine visiting Valley View School, circa 2000
Ermestine, parent, student, Gloria

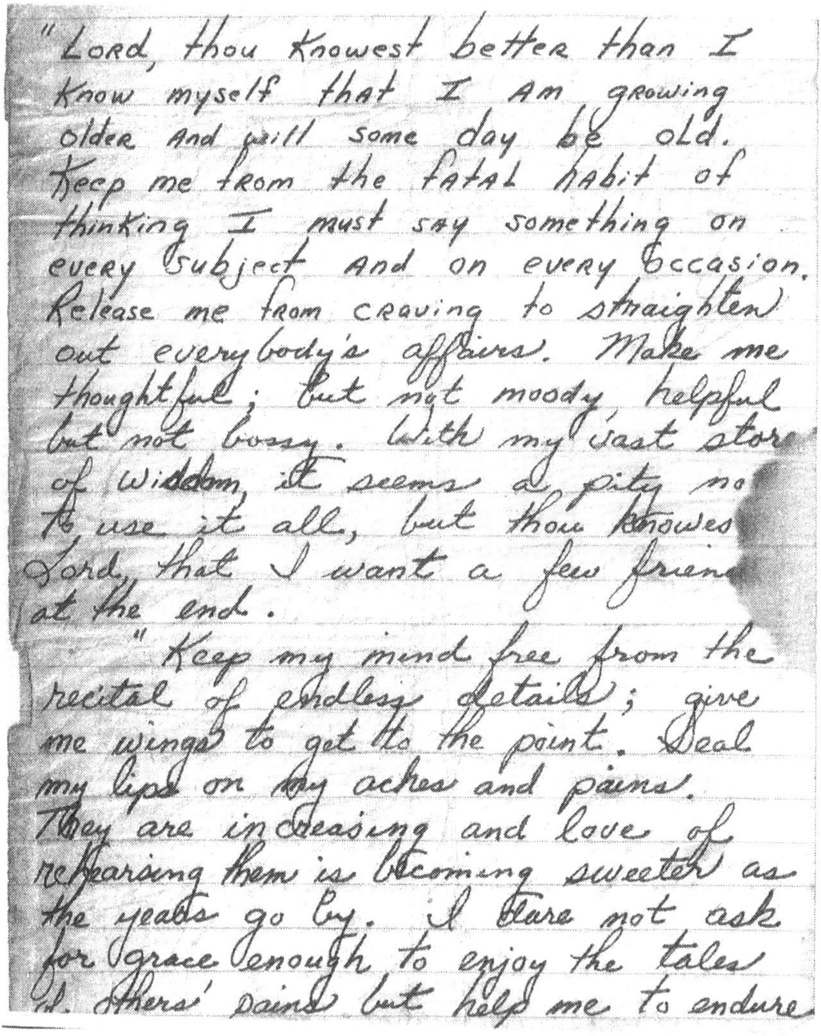

"Lord, thou knowest better than I
know myself that I am growing
older and will some day be old.
Keep me from the fatal habit of
thinking I must say something on
every subject and on every occasion.
Release me from craving to straighten
out everybody's affairs. Make me
thoughtful; but not moody, helpful
but not bossy. With my vast stor
of wisdom, it seems a pity no
to use it all, but thou knowes
Lord, that I want a few frien
at the end.
"Keep my mind free from the
recital of endless details; give
me wings to get to the point. Seal
my lips on my aches and pains.
They are increasing and love of
rehearsing them is becoming sweeter as
the years go by. I dare not ask
for grace enough to enjoy the tales
of others' pains but help me to endure

*Tressie kept this handwritten prayer with her keepsakes,
its message written by a dear friend.*

them with patience.

"I dare not ask for improved memory but for a growing humility and a lessening cocksureness when my memory seems to clash with the memories of others. Teach me the glorious lesson that occasionally I may be mistaken.

"Keep me reasonably sweet; I do not want to be a Saint—some of them are so hard to live with—but a sour old person is one of the crowning works of the devil. Give me the ability to see good things in unexpected places and talents in unexpected people. And give me, Lord the grace to tell them so. Amen."

INDEX

Dates

A

B

J

K

L

M

N

O

P

R

U

V

W

ABOUT THE AUTHOR

Gloria Petgrave Scoggins, daughter of Ermestine Martin, is a native of Richmond, California, and active in the field of education for 43 years, with two master's degrees: one in Elementary Education from the University of San Francisco and a master's degree in Education from Mills College. Gloria has worked in Oakland Unified, Stockton Unified, and West Contra Costa Unified school districts in a variety of teaching and administrative positions, including teacher, principal, and coordinator.

In addition to these duties, she has consistently held leadership positions in many Contra Costa County-based community programs focused on education. Serving as President of The Blackboard of West Contra Costa, Gloria worked in collaboration with other community-based organizations to eliminate the opportunity gaps of targeted populations.

She also sat on the Richmond's Girls Inc. Board of Directors for several years, focusing on implementing the College Bound Girls Program. In addition, from 2012-2014, Gloria was a co-chair of the Alpha Nu Omega's Emerging Young Leaders Program for middle school girls (ANO is a chapter of the Alpha Kappa Alpha Sorority).

After retiring from West Contra Costa Unified, Gloria worked as a Field Instructor at Loyola Marymount University and as a University Supervisor at California State University, East Bay for ten years before becoming conservator of her family's real estate and business holdings.

Made in the USA
Las Vegas, NV
17 October 2022

57530164R00289